THE EXPERTS' WAR ON POVERTY

A Volume in the Series

AMERICAN INSTITUTIONS AND SOCIETY

Edited by Brian Balogh and Jonathan Zimmerman

A list of titles in this series is available at cornellpress.cornell.edu.

THE EXPERTS' WAR ON POVERTY

Social Research and the Welfare Agenda in Postwar America

ROMAIN D. HURET

TRANSLATED BY JOHN ANGELL

CORNELL UNIVERSITY PRESS
ITHACA AND LONDON

Originally published as La Fin de la Pauvreté? Les experts sociaux en guerre contre la pauvreté aux Etats-Unis (1945–1974) (Éditions de l'EHESS, 2008).

First published 2018 by Cornell University Press

Printed in the United States of America

Library of Congress Cataloging-in-Publication Data

Names: Huret, Romain, author. | Angell, John (Translator), translator.
Title: The experts' war on poverty : social research and the welfare
    agenda in postwar America / Romain D. Huret ; translated by
    John Angell.
Other titles: Fin de la pauvreté?. English
Description: Ithaca [New York] : Cornell University Press, 2018. | Series:
    American institutions and society | Includes bibliographical references
    and index.
Identifiers: LCCN 2018007694 (print) | LCCN 2018021283 (ebook) |
    ISBN 9781501709531 (pdf) | ISBN 9781501712173 (epub/mobi) |
    ISBN 9780801450488 (cloth : alk. paper)
Subjects: LCSH: Poverty—United States—History—20th century. |
    Poor—United States—History—20th century. | Economic assistance,
    Domestic—United States—History—20th century.
Classification: LCC HC110.P6 (ebook) | LCC HC110.P6 H5913 2018
    (print) | DDC 362.5/560973—dc23
LC record available at https://lccn.loc.gov/2018007694

To my dream team—Ariane, Emilien, Melvil, and Raphaël

CONTENTS

THE EXPERTS' WAR ON POVERTY

INTRODUCTION

In 1983, at the same time that the conservative president Ronald Reagan was lamenting the presence of "welfare queens" on inner-city streets and of "poverty traps" inherited from idealistic 1960s reformers, the Wisconsin economist Robert Lampman was recalling the heady days in 1964 when President Lyndon Baines Johnson launched the War on Poverty. Persistent, grinding poverty in such a prosperous country came as a surprise to many Americans, who believed that such a plight had disappeared amid the postwar economic boom. Lampman candidly acknowledged that even economists had been blinded by the feverish economic growth and seemingly unlimited abundance of the 1950s: "We never used the word 'poverty.' We used other words. And so it was something of a shock to an economist to have the word poverty suddenly remerge. It had been consigned to the dustbin. Other words like . . . Low-income population is one phrase for the poor. So it wasn't fashionable to talk about the poor or talk about the poverty problem."[1]

Prosperity had caused an overall increase in wealth, relegating poverty to the background and, in people's minds, to the distant prewar past. Advertising and television reinforced the image of an America abandoning itself to "fables of abundance," in the historian T. Jackson Lears's eloquent words. In the early days of the Cold War, material comfort defined the daily lives of most Americans. Amid rising anti-Communism and McCarthyism, anyone who dared to suggest that misery and suffering were present on American soil or questioned prevailing patterns of income distribution was immediately suspected of being at best unpatriotic.[2]

Lampman, however, along with a team of like-minded men and women, eventually managed to make it "fashionable" to talk about poverty, and they nudged their fellow citizens into waging war on it. As an adviser to Johnson in the mid-1960s, Lampman proclaimed that by the year 1976, poverty would be a relic; two hundred years after the Declaration of Independence, the pursuit of happiness, at least on a material level, would represent something besides mere words for legions of urban and rural poor citizens.

A book by Michael Harrington, *The Other America* (1962), is often cited as an important turning point in popular histories. Harrington's sensitive portrayal of the poor, as well as the review of the book by Dwight McDonald in the *New Yorker*, ignited a political reaction that eventually culminated in the War on Poverty. But the individuals who did the hard work that eventually brought the problem of poverty into the national limelight have been largely unrecognized; they include Robert Lampman, Mollie Orshansky, Ida Craven Merriam, Herman Miller, Dorothy Brady, Helen Lamale, Selma Fine Goldsmith, Alvin Schorr, and many lesser-known bureaucrats and academics. The stories of these middle-class Americans—economists, home economists, social workers, and statisticians—have remained in the background despite the fact that they were the driving force behind a vast postwar reform project to eradicate American poverty.[3]

The rise of such a nationwide effort involved a conjunction of two elements: first, scientific evidence that, even in affluent, postwar America, rampant poverty persisted and, second, a functioning federal system capable of aspiring to eliminate this social and economic blight from the national landscape. In the postwar United States, achieving this conjunction was far from easy, both because prosperity was so pervasive and because there was powerful, widespread opposition to federal intervention in the social arena in the 1950s. In other words, the War on Poverty was not created out of thin air; nor was it a product of the zeitgeist. Instead, it was the result of an extended scientific, bureaucratic, and social process that drove a generation of middle-class bureaucrats and academics to extend and expand upon the idealistic, reformist zeal of the New Deal.

This book conjures these key figures back into existence. All of them were professionals with similar personal and professional backgrounds, and many had experienced poverty first-hand as children. They were all educated in American universities in the 1930s and 1940s and were influenced by intellectuals and philosophers for whom social justice was a moral, and often religious, imperative, among them Richard Tawney, Max Otto, William James, and Elizabeth Brandeis Raushenbush, to name just a few. They all supported Franklin Delano Roosevelt's New Deal programs and were impressed by the massive growth of the federal government, especially during World War II. To some extent, though, historical scholarship has demonstrated that these same reformers are part of a lost generation who struggled to make themselves heard between the New Dealers of the 1930s and the New Leftists of the 1960s. They constitute a cohort of scholars and officials who belong to the shadowy 1950s that has so often been taken for granted by historians.[4]

Our understanding of this community of poverty experts is obscured in part by the common portrayals of the decade as a period of consensus and complacency under the influence of McCarthyism, the Cold War, and domestic conservatism. The idea of a consensus, however, needs to be challenged. Postwar liberalism was defined by conflicting views and a growing awareness of the social and economic costs of the nation's stark inequalities in the midst of rapid economic growth and rapidly rising mass consumption.

While liberals shared many white middle-class values, believing in the primacy of a male breadwinner, the importance of a classless society. and the assimilation of minorities, they disagreed about the ultimate shape that reforms should take as well as the means of achieving those ends. Some continued to believe that the reformist impulse of the 1930s had not ended with World War II, particularly at a time when conservative thought and activism were on the rise. As they questioned the postwar affluent society, poverty experts looked closely at the flaws of the welfare state created in the 1930s and 1940s.[5]

When he signed the Social Security Act in 1935, President Franklin Roosevelt made a clear distinction between insurance and welfare programs, reinforcing to some extent a timeworn distinction between the "deserving" poor—orphans, single women, and the elderly—and the "undeserving" poor, mostly able-bodied men of working age. After World War II, this two-track system led to a crisis of legitimacy in the welfare system, which was sometimes labeled a "welfare mess." One problem was the poverty paradox of the 1950s: the persistent presence of so many poor people in spite of widespread mass consumption and steady economic growth. Although conservatives interpreted this paradox as evidence of fraud and laziness, poverty experts offered a compelling, different narrative, according to which economic growth failed to eliminate poverty. The welfare state needed to be redesigned to reduce ingrained inequalities and cope with the new faces of American poor.[6]

As liberals very well knew, New Deal policies situated security at the center of American political and economic life. But this did not imply a welfare state that paid for social benefits by using the tax system to redistribute resources, because economic security would be exchanged for full-time employment. Both pensions and unemployment compensation were therefore to be paid for by employer and worker contributions. This also meant that New Dealers never regarded the benefits of means-tested programs as a basic right but saw them as a temporary form of charity for women and children living outside traditional breadwinner families. New Deal social policies—whether they doled out relief or conferred new social rights—targeted accidental poverty and were not implemented without heated debate. Historians have noted that a number of far-reaching ideas, from health care reform and equitable tax plans to full employment, were discussed beginning in the 1930s. FDR's famous Economic Bill of Rights speech captured this reforming spirit, but his ideas and policies had a hard time gaining political traction.[7]

After the war, a generation of experts tried to transfer the security promised by prevailing politics to welfare programs after their research revealed a growing atmosphere of insecurity around the country. A citizen's basic right to welfare lay at the heart of their scientific and political agendas. By promoting universal entitlement to government assistance, they were following in the footsteps of welfare officials who were committed to honoring FDR's promise that freedom from want was the right of every citizen. Policy change on this scale would mean reforming the entire federal welfare apparatus, which was widely criticized in the 1950s. Poverty experts believed that the responsibility of welfare programs was not to moralize assistance, but to help the poor meet their basic needs. Many of these experts were white male veterans who benefited from specific postwar provisions through the GI Bill—guarantees of health care, education, tax breaks, and home loans, to name just a few. It came as no surprise that they sought to include low-income families in a comprehensive welfare state.[8]

There was consensus among them that the federal government possessed the necessary tools to solve the poverty dilemma. In the years immediately following the war against Germany and Japan, a victorious afterglow elevated the status of public experts, who became central figures in American public life. Their knowledge had played such a decisive role in winning the war—one significant example being the Manhattan Project—that it seemed reasonable to believe that they could help defeat social inequalities. Within the context of the Cold War, the country was fertile ground for this modernist faith in applied expertise, as the expanding federal bureaucracy gave rise to a "prominstrative government," a term used by historian Brian Balogh to describe the postwar alliance of academics and administrators. Once they concluded that their research provided the foundation for progressive policies and programs, poverty researchers who were invisible in the 1950s were catapulted into the role of public experts. "Ending poverty" was no longer a mere slogan; the concept had been transformed into a political proposal that, pending government support, could offer meaningful ways to implement experts' dreams of eradicating poverty.[9]

Poverty researchers tended to see the poverty paradox primarily in terms of income distribution. Their objectives were to locate the mechanisms causing poverty and establish a poverty threshold to distinguish the poor from the rest of the population. The findings of this growing body of groundbreaking social science research gradually filtered into the public sphere from the confines of government offices and universities. In January 1964, after President Johnson launched the War on Poverty in that year's State of the Union address, previously unknown researchers were suddenly asked to develop practical solutions to the poverty paradox, occasionally thrusting them into public view. Although the poverty community later became divided internally over specific approaches, with some backing a negative income tax and others preferring a system based on family allowances or reforming the existing welfare system, they concurred that an effective antipoverty program would mean some form of income redistribution.[10]

Persuading the public and the federal government to support the idea that such income transfer was inevitable for curing poverty entailed facing a huge obstacle: the predominant belief that individual behaviors and culture were the basic explanations for poverty. Amid the prosperity of the times, this behaviorist vision, combined with a venerable and deeply held distinction between "deserving" and "undeserving" populations of poor Americans, fueled suspicion about low-income segments of society. These views supported explanations for the poverty paradox that blamed personal pathologies and that tended to focus on African Americans, particularly in the context of the civil rights movement. Philanthropic organizations supported a behavioral paradigm that blamed social problems on a lack of opportunity, coupled with psychological impediments to motivation that disproportionately afflicted certain social groups. The idea of a "culture of poverty" gained momentum in the early 1960s, further undergirding behavioral views among President Johnson's staff holding that that low-income people needed to be empowered rather than enriched. Poverty experts were forced to take it upon themselves to broaden these key players' narrow understandings in the name of reform.[11]

Unsurprisingly, interactions between experts and policymakers quickly became complicated. President Johnson adamantly refused to consider any proposal to directly redistribute income. He eventually backed a plan to establish a network of Community Action Programs (CAPs) in poor areas to provide targeted social services on a local level. This empowerment strategy sidelined experts at a crucial moment during the War on Poverty, unleashing a quiet, internal struggle in the poverty community to keep promoting income transfer. This struggle eventually took public shape as a proposal for a universal guaranteed minimum income.[12]

This book is intended to correct the negative image of unelected social policy experts by telling their story. It is a story of the failure of grounded professional expertise that resulted from a large body of social science research and the efforts of numerous committed public officials to shape public policy at a critical historical moment. The scholarly gaze of experts has long been directed toward "authority" and power. According to one view, an expert is responsible for offering an empirical foundation for policies that serve his or her own social and professional interests, albeit cloaked in universal rhetoric. This book focuses instead on the failure of experts to influence the political process of helping the poor at a major moment in postwar American history.[13]

After the war, the professionalization of the reform movement and the rise of powerful federal agencies paradoxically widened the gap between experts and society at large. This meant that experts' strengths ultimately became their main weaknesses. Unlike what had happened in terms of social policy in the 1930s and 1940s, the idea of a direct link between citizens and the federal government through income distribution prevailed over a system of matching funds with the individual states. This tendency of the federal government to become isolated increased tensions. After the mid-1960s, this trend aggravated growing mistrust between citizens and institutions. In other words, this book also tells the story of the failure of governance that grew out of a division between professionals and citizens.[14]

In fact, the experts were unable to form a strong enough coalition to support income redistribution. Their inability illustrates how conflicting strands of postwar liberalism became particularly strong in the 1960s, ironically resulting in strengths being transformed once again into handicaps. Experts were to some extent prisoners of their own views of society, family, and minorities, that had evolved in the span of twenty years. While strongly advocating for broader access to welfare benefits, experts found it difficult to create an alliance with the welfare rights movement that developed later in the decade. The Poor People's March in the spring of 1968, led by civil rights groups, demonstrated their failure to effectively communicate with the very people whom their research and policies were supposed to help. The crisis of "racial liberalism" exacerbated race- and gender-based tensions among liberals. George McGovern's proposal in 1972 for a universal guaranteed minimum income, a proposal inspired by the poverty community, epitomized the experts' incapacity to persuade Americans to back the experts' empirically solid and well-conceived program. Simply put, the War on Poverty was ultimately a Pyrrhic victory.[15]

The defeat of McGovern's initiative is an example of the "path dependency" process used by political scientists to explain institutional limitations on the best-laid plans of policymakers. For the poverty community, the dependency phenomenon was twofold. First, they overestimated the central authority of the federal government, and second, they shared traditional views of the family and minorities that led them to frame issues in an involuntarily contradictory way. These two worldviews collapsed in the 1960s, contributing to insufficient support for the experts' innovative proposals. While questioning the liberal consensus and enriching our understanding of postwar liberalism, this book also underscores the conflicting and even contradictory views that prevailed—and continue to prevail—among liberals.[16]

In examining the agency of key players in the poverty community, I have tried to address a methodological problem by situating individuals at the core of my narrative. Their publications, initiatives, and even names appear only as footnotes in the literature. Because they were relegated to the background during key moments in twentieth-century American history, the influence of these dedicated bureaucrats and scholars has been greatly underestimated. Many experts were successful in promoting activism and concerted action despite being small cogs in large, anonymous institutions. From a functional point of view, the federal government is too often characterized as a vast, cold, inhuman behemoth, particularly in the area of social policy. Scholarship on the Social Security system is an excellent example of this tendency. With some notable exceptions, most historians have tended to focus on institutions and congressional debates, neglecting the actual men and women who built up the Social Security program.[17]

One purpose of this book is to enliven the often-dry history of social expertise and policymaking. The men and women portrayed here were members of what the French sociologist Christian Topalov calls a "nebula"—an informal and often invisible community of reformers who were briefly able to attract policymakers' attention. I have used a synchronic rather than a diachronic approach to describe the contours of such a community, particularly in the book's early chapters. This is partly related to the fact that federal agencies, philanthropic foundations, and universities, and the researchers and experts themselves, were sometimes working toward a common purpose but in the absence of any formal connections, especially in the 1950s.[18]

To ensure that agencies and institutions did not overshadow the story's true protagonists, the early chapters begin with detailed portraits of key figures from the expert community. This approach has allowed me to situate each of them within his or her social and professional context and, in turn, to give life to these forgotten players or "indecisive shadows," as French historian George Duby has called women in the Middle Ages. Ironically, maintaining their institutional roles and low profiles enabled the experts, and their ambitious social engineering projects, to remain relatively independent. The book's first section, "A Science of Poverty (1945–1963)," illustrates how the poverty "black box" successfully emerged despite low-level postwar distrust of the social sciences among politicians and the public. Poverty researchers focused on defining and quantifying the paradoxical persistence of grinding poverty during a period of unparalleled American prosperity in an effort to solve one of the country's greatest social difficulties.

The book's second section, "From Science to War (1963–1974)," takes a more traditional narrative approach to describe how the president's advisers appropriated the question of poverty and how experts' proposals for eliminating poverty failed to survive the resulting public and ideological challenges. In the end, the experts, as well as their monumental, progressive, and well-conceived proposals, were blindsided by a public debate that they were able to avoid as long as they operated inside their respective institutional shadows. The second section also shows how experts proposed viable alternative plans for eliminating poverty when their initial proposals were blocked. After poverty took center stage in the explosive public debates that followed, experts scurried to create workable alternative solutions that would have a better chance of surviving the firestorm. Unfortunately, this second wave of frantic activity within the poverty community eventually produced internal divisions that became public.[19]

Poverty experts pushed their ideas for definitively eliminating poverty to their political and institutional limits. Although their efforts proved to be almost entirely futile, the poverty community nevertheless represents a singular achievement that deserves to be better understood. The historical record of mid-twentieth-century America was made brighter by this doomed but singularly well-intended proposal within an affluent society. This book contributes to our understanding of this period by tracing the unprecedented efforts of men and women who paved the way to the War on Poverty.

Part I

A Science of Poverty (1945–1963)

1

THE POVERTY PARADOX

The economist Dorothy Brady, in December 1949, was the first to point out the poverty paradox in postwar America. After earning a PhD in mathematics from Berkeley in 1933, she turned to economics, with a focus on income distribution. To members of congress who questioned her expertise, she inverted the question about the elimination of poverty *as a result of* economic prosperity, asking why poverty persisted *in spite of* increased general wealth: "Social scientists have an obligation to resolve the paradox of an apparently invariable proportion of inadequate income throughout a long period which has seen spectacular gains in the general standard of living and improving social legislation." This notion of a "poverty paradox," based on the principle of relative poverty, supplanted the idea of absolute poverty, a notion that had prevailed earlier in the century, particularly after the Great Depression. Brady's paradox and her appeal for a solution became a central concern for the small community of researchers studying low-income populations after World War II.[1]

The rapid expansion of a middle-class lifestyle was a striking feature of the postwar years. Little space was devoted to poverty in the new economic context and among politicians promoting economic growth. The rise of mass consumption in the country's expanding suburbs transformed the very definition of poverty. The Cold War, and the identity questions that it awoke in the nation, confirmed consumerist norms as an integral feature of what it meant to be an average American. The poor remained outside these norms and thus outside of the "American Way"—an anomaly that would soon disappear.[2]

Research conducted by federal agencies revealed that poverty was a persistent problem in the newly affluent nation, however. Understanding this paradox became a major purpose for researchers, among them Ida Craven Merriam, who employed the research resources of the Social Security Administration (SSA) to measure, analyze, and question the prevalence of low-income families in affluent America. With new statistics and figures, she helped to construct a scientific approach to an issue that often incited indignation in public discourse. Cloaked in the anonymity of their agencies, the small group of researchers around her endeavored to make sense of such blatant paradox in postwar American society.[3]

Ida Craven Merriam

In May 1946, while Congress was debating the universal health care proposal promoted by the SSA, a staff member in the agency's Bureau of Research and Statistics named Ida Craven Merriam drafted an internal report to Isidore Falk, the bureau director. Prior to joining the federal government, Falk had taught at the University of Chicago and was an instructor in public health at Yale University. He joined the Social Security Board in December 1936, initially as an economist. Later, he was asked to direct the agency's research unit. The report that Merriam submitted to him addressed the insincerity of Congress members who complained about even having to read the proposed legislation. "Health insurance," she lamented, "is now added to the list of so-called 'communistic' and 'socialistic' proposals." However, she optimistically maintained that a "historical perspective is comforting to those who introduce social legislation." Her progressive position on trends in American history expressed less a historical truth than the growing unease among a generation of postwar liberals forced to face the resurgence of conservative policymakers after the high hopes that came out of the war and President Franklin Delano Roosevelt's promise to ensure "freedom from want."[4]

Ida Craven Merriam was born in Philadelphia in 1904, the second child of an upper-middle-class family. Her father was a prosperous businessman, an archetypal Teddy Roosevelt Republican, who transmitted his Presbyterian faith and the ethical values and moral rigor typical of the Progressive Era to his daughter. Years later, Merriam recalled her amazement that even Democrats could be respectable. As an adult, she attempted to distance herself from her strict Christian upbringing, and like many young people of her social level at the time, she experienced a moral and spiritual crisis that prompted an effort to reconcile her Christian faith with the brutal nature of industrialized society. Years of university education helped her come to terms with the contemporary world's contradictions and with her anguish, as she described it, about the profound social changes caused by economic modernization.[5]

Merriam enrolled at Wellesley College in the early 1920s. The university environment marked a clear break with her past, and under the influence of a friend, she became interested in Christian socialist thought, particularly in the writings of the British economist Richard Tawney (1880–1962). Tawney's book *The Acquisitive Society* (1920) denounced the corruption of the capitalist world, which he described as rotting from within because it lacked a religious or moral foundation. An advocate for socialism with a human face and a follower of Max Weber, Tawney argued for the reconciliation of capitalism and Protestantism, arguments that heightened Merriam's interest in economic and sociopolitical issues. Although she graduated with a double major in English and history, she followed in the footsteps of numerous Wellesley students by pursuing graduate studies in economics at the University of Chicago. In the city, she also encountered the feminist movement and its social implications through the influence of her residence hall director, the feminist Sophonisba Breckinridge. Under Breckinridge's guidance, Merriam's interest in social issues continued to develop. Chicago initiated the largest pension program for mothers in the United States in 1911. Evolving alongside movements for industrial justice and women's suffrage, the mothers' pension movement sought to provide "justice for mothers" and protection from insecurity. On the advice of the well-known political scientist Charles Merriam, whose course she took at Chicago and with whom she worked on the city council for a few weeks in 1923, Merriam decided to enroll in a new doctoral program at the Brookings Institution in Washington, DC.[6]

The Brookings Graduate School was founded in 1923 to train experts in public policy to staff organizations and agencies in Washington. The multidisciplinary curriculum spanned a wide range of social sciences, greatly enhancing Merriam's knowledge of economics and statistics, a rarity among women of her generation because of powerful academic segregation that reserved economics departments for men, channeling women toward home economics. This stark academic division along gender lines was mirrored in research topics, with women scholars tending toward subjects related to social work rather than social policy.[7]

Merriam's dissertation explored the nineteenth-century French railway system as well as the water-borne transportation system in New England during the same period. When she completed her doctorate in 1928, job offers flooded in, and she was hired as an editorial assistant for an encyclopedia of the social sciences edited by tax scholar Edwin Seligman and economist Alvin Johnson. Funded by a consortium of scholarly organizations, the encyclopedia project was designed to provide a complete portrait of the social sciences in the late 1920s. Merriam created the list of the principal themes to be explored in each entry and authored six of the encyclopedia articles. She also maintained a cross-indexed reference list that traced the projected links among entries.[8]

This editorial position provided Merriam with an understanding of the academic organization of the social sciences while also cultivating her talent for what she called "classification." During the 1929 crisis and after her editorial work, Merriam drifted professionally for a number of years, finding her job search frustrated by academic gender segregation. It was difficult for women scholars to join social science departments, and they tended to be concentrated in research positions in philanthropic foundations, the federal government, or the private sector. Merriam was forced to settle for temporary positions at universities such as the Connecticut College for Women or socially progressive institutions such as the Bryn Mawr Industrial Summer School, which offered education to immigrant and working-class women.[9]

This period of relative inactivity provided ample opportunity for her to analyze the causes of the Great Depression and reflect on possible solutions. The collapse of the capitalist system demonstrated the deficiencies of President Herbert Hoover's regulatory model, which limited the role of the federal government to cooperation with businesses and minimal direct intervention. The economic doldrums reinforced Merriam's convictions about the inhumanity of the contemporary world. As a product of the reformist branch of liberal Protestantism concerned with primarily social justice, she symbolized the "surrogate socialists" of the interwar period who, according to Gary Gerstle, constitute one strand of American liberalism.[10]

These liberals believed that only the efficiency of science could defeat poverty. Within the internal debate in the social sciences in the 1930s that focused on how to apply knowledge and the role of researchers in the process, Merriam sided with "purposive thinkers" for whom social science should serve a commitment to personal authenticity and social justice. This perspective on the crash of 1929 led her to support the New Deal as the only credible solution to the country's economic, moral, and spiritual crisis. Roosevelt's political project also offered her a professional boost, and at the invitation of the director of the Brookings Graduate School, she returned to Washington and joined the Bureau of Research and Statistics (BRS), the new research division of the SSA.[11]

The research unit was created in 1935 in response to a congressional mandate for predictive studies that would forecast the viability of the Social Security system. Merriam joined the bureau in 1936, eventually scaling the bureaucratic ladder to become director of the division that coordinated these studies in 1942. At the BRS, she befriended Isidore Falk. Inspired by President Roosevelt's famous Four Freedoms speech, Merriam and Falk funneled their energies into a universal health care proposal based on a 1942 report by the British economist William Beveridge. Falk was responsible for the scientific portion of the report, and Merriam compiled notes and collected data.[12]

After the war, Merriam and Falk published two reports that served as the basis for congressional debates regarding an updated version of the health care proposal known as the Wagner-Murray-Dingell Bill. They were closely involved in stormy debates in Congress in which Merriam

tried to allay fears of universal medical coverage and her alleged communist affiliation. Unfortunately, however, they failed to predict the strength
of Republican opposition, and the BRS paid a heavy price for its public
support of the program.[13]

Merriam was criticized with particular vehemence by Congress members for using research for partisan purposes. The annual budget of the
BRS was reduced by 30 percent in 1947 and by 80 percent in 1948, leading to savage staff reductions from 160 in 1946 to a mere 30 in 1948.
In this hostile environment, the powerful lobbying arm of the American
Medical Association arranged for Falk to be removed as director, and
a blacklist that circulated within the SSA caused the internal cohesion
of the staff to collapse. While Merriam was not blacklisted, she accused
the director, Arthur Altmeyer, of failing to support staff members whose
names appeared on the list and of sacrificing some of them to ensure the
institution's survival.[14]

This episode was a powerful lesson. Merriam lucidly attributed the
bill's failure to the lack of preparation and political naïveté of the BRS
staff. At one point in the congressional hearings, she had replied candidly to a senator that further study was needed to assess the effect of a
proposed quantitative change on overall costs. Robert Myers, an actuary
with the administration who testified with her, later lectured her on the
disastrous effects of her answer, and she acknowledged that it would be
critical in the future to consider the full political context. Once again,
Merriam's hopes, born of the war, collided with institutional complexi-
ties. The anti-intellectual atmosphere of the early 1950s, fueled by Mc-
Carthyism and the Cold War, was not propitious for the emergence of
innovative social programs. It was possible, however, to continue to focus
on social issues by coordinating statistical research in the Census Bureau,
the Department of Labor, and the Department of Agriculture, but only
with discretion.

Measuring Income Distribution in the Census Bureau

In February 1946, a demobilized soldier named Herman Miller answered
an advertisement for a statistician position with the Census Bureau. Born
in February 1921 in New York, Miller was the son of German emigrants

and a prime candidate for the job. A brilliant student, he studied economics and statistics at the City College of New York, whose student population was composed of primarily the children of immigrants. During the 1930s, both students and faculty enthusiastically supported the New Deal. On graduating in 1942, Miller was drafted and sent to the Pacific front. After the war and a period of professional uncertainty, he was considering resuming his studies to take advantage of the 1944 GI Bill when the Census Bureau ad caught his eye. The position appealed to him partly because it would allow him to pursue a doctorate while also working for the agency.[15]

At the time of Miller's hiring, the Census Bureau was in the process of updating its data collection and management methods. Between 1930 and 1960, new survey methodology and improved national record keeping, eventually aided by the first computer, Universal Automatic Computer (UNIVAC). Designed by the Remington Rand Company, it was the first computer able to handle both alphabetical and numerical information easily. It greatly enhanced the agency's statistical capabilities. A new generation of academically trained statisticians was replacing turn-of-the-century pioneers, prompting a scientific shift as training and the economic crisis compelled this new generation to value economic data over traditional demographic information. An economist and statistician by training, Miller was perfectly suited for this transition. His academic orientation in the field of income distribution reinforced the porous relationship between academics and the federal administration at the time.[16]

In 1950, Miller enrolled in the doctoral program at the George Washington University, later transferring to the American University to specialize in income measurement. His doctoral research complemented his work in the housing and population division of the Census Bureau, where he focused on improving census takers' techniques for collecting income data. Beginning in 1940, data on individual and family incomes had been collected by census takers, partly in response to the economic crisis. When they called on residents, households were asked to indicate their previous year's earned income, as well as income from other sources for the current fiscal year. To avoid popular protest, agents phrased their questions carefully, asking simply whether household income was above or below five thousand dollars and providing confidential answer sheets. The resulting statistical study drew a fierce response from a number of politicians, and

Figure 1.1. Census Bureau agent with an American family (1950). Courtesy of United States Census Bureau.

New Hampshire senator Charles Tobey broadcast a nationwide warning on the radio that these questions represented a violation of citizens' constitutional rights.[17]

Because of the controversial nature of this aspect of the census, only a handful of income studies were completed during the war. The 1950 census, however, marked significant advances in measuring income. The Social Science Research Council and the Russell Sage Foundation formed a committee to summarize the census findings. Chaired by the foundation's director of the Department of Statistics, Ralph G. Hurlin, the committee received additional financial support from several universities, including Princeton,

Columbia, Cornell, and Chicago, as well as the philanthropic foundation the Twentieth-Century Fund. The report was the first large-scale study of American incomes since the National Resources Committee had published "Consumer Income in the United States, 1935–1936" in the wake of the 1929 crash. Conservatives fiercely opposed this renewed interest in quantifying income. Clarence Brown, an Ohio congressman, described income research as a prime example of socialism in action that would require citizens to "tell Washington everything." Despite repeated attacks, the Census Bureau persisted and asked Philip Houser, a University of Chicago demographer, to synthesize the study's findings.[18]

Modifications were made to the 1940 questionnaire, and it was decided that a 20 percent sample would be questioned about earned income, although significant gaps in the data remained. According to Miller, 6 percent of those polled about their incomes declined to respond, and the majority of those who did respond did so from memory instead of providing documentation. The collection method amplified inaccuracies because reported income levels reflected a particular moment in the year, further limiting generalization to the entire country. Miller was determined to reduce the margin of error, and he pushed for verification of the 1950 data by comparing them to data collected by the Commerce Department national incomes division, which was directed by Selma Fine Goldsmith.[19]

After graduation from Cornell and a PhD from Harvard University, Goldsmith worked for the Department of Agriculture before entering the Commerce Department, where she tracked income distribution since World War II. She paid close attention to personal income, which included both earned and unearned income. The Census Bureau, on the other hand, recorded only total earned income. The divergences between these methodological variations meant that the 1950 census estimate represented only 91 percent of the Commerce Department estimate.[20]

Miller validated the data by cross-referencing them with the "Current Population Survey" (periodic studies drawing on census data). Comparing the 1949 findings and the 1950 census showed that the family income estimates of the two agencies were similar but that the Census Bureau study was less accurate for individual incomes. Internal Revenue Service data helped validate the census findings, and representative sampling confirmed the overall quality of the resulting data.

TABLE 1.1. Americans' incomes in 1950

Family income	Percentages: Census Bureau	Percentages: Internal Revenue Service
No income	1.5	—
Income loss	0.1	0.4
$1–$499	1.6	1.1
$500–$999	2.1	3.7
$1,000–$1,499	4.1	4.7
$1,500–$1,999	5.7	6.7
$2,000–$2,499	8.9	8.2
$2,500–$2,999	10.7	10.1
$3,000–$3,499	14.4	13.3
$3,500–$3,999	12.4	10.4
$4,000–$4,499	8.3	7.7
$4,500–$4,999	5.1	7
$5,000–$5,999	9.6	10.9
$6,000–$6,999	6	6.7
$7,000–$9,999	5.6	5.5
Above $100,000	3.8	3.7
Mean Income	$3,534	$3,591

Note: Comparison of estimates by the Census Bureau and the Internal Revenue Service.
Source: Herman Miller and Leon Paley, "Income Reported in the 1950 Census and on Income Tax Returns," in *An Appraisal of the 1950 Census*, by the Conference on Research in Income and Wealth (Princeton, NJ: Princeton University Press, 1958), 179–200.

Miller became increasingly aware of the effects of differences in computation methods among government agencies. For example, according to Census Bureau estimates that took all income into account, 19 percent of the population was considered to be low income, whereas according to the Commerce Department, the estimate was 13 percent. Miller argued that such variations between agencies were unacceptable for generalizability and made it impossible to know the characteristics of families with insufficient income with any accuracy. New studies were needed to correlate the income curve with variables related to family and profession.[21]

Miller's dissatisfaction led him to focus closely on the level and duration of income inequality. He also reviewed academic research on the subject in order to understand how income distribution had changed since the Great Depression. In a study for the National Bureau of Economic Research, the economist Horst Mendershausen had noted a significant shift in income distribution patterns at the end of the war, and by applying the Lorenz Curve—a graphic representation of income distribution designed in 1905 by Max O. Lorenz—to national incomes, he found that income inequality had become less pronounced between the 1930s and the postwar period in the United States. In Miller's view, these changes were linked to changes in the labor market such as the return to full employment, but Miller also contended that increased participation of women in the workforce was an important factor.[22]

The increasing contribution of working women to family incomes was indeed significant. Between 1940 and 1948, the working population grew from 46.6 million to 58.3 million, and because this rate of growth outstripped the increase in the number of new families, much of the increase in the number of incomes occurred within existing family units. Growth was particularly noticeable in working- and middle-class families, who benefited greatly from the additional income. While World War II reinforced these changes, the curve reflects the fact that the abatement in income inequality began to slow, a finding that induced Miller to focus on the segment of the population whose incomes had not increased. Statistically, this was a complex data set to isolate, because the official census did not include the category "low-income family." To target the poorest citizens, Miller improvised an approach based on a two-thousand-dollar-threshold income level, the same level that the Census Bureau had used since the postwar period. Using 1950 census data, he broke down the nation's income distribution, classifying families and individuals according to income levels

The condition of poverty was of particular concern for individuals who lived alone and was especially acute among the elderly. According to Miller, elderly people were unable to supplement their incomes and experienced a sharp drop in purchasing power during periods of high inflation. His calculation method tended to underestimate the income of this category of household, whereas the Commerce Department evaluated it accurately because it did include certain sources of unearned income. Despite statistical biases in the findings, Miller insisted that income had not increased among the 20% of the population with the lowest incomes.

TABLE 1.2. Income distribution among families and individuals in 1950

Total earned income	Number of families (millions)	Number of individuals living alone (millions)
Below $2,000	10.6	4.3
$2,000–$2,999	8.1	1.1
$3,000–$3,999	7.8	0.3
$4,000–$4,999	4.7	3.4
$5,000–$5,999	3.1	1.6
$6,000–$6,999	1.9	1.5
$7,000–$7,999	2.0	0.7
Above $10,000	1.0	0.7
Total	39.2	13.6

Note: According to total earned income (1950 census).
Source: Herman Miller, *Income Distribution in the United States* (Washington, DC: U.S. Government Printing Office, 1955), 218.

While completing his doctoral thesis from 1950 and 1955, he refined his statistical understanding of this poverty paradox.[23]

In April 1952, the US population was estimated at 151.5 million, of which 80 million earned no income. This nonworking population consisted of 42 million children under fourteen years of age, 8 million adolescents between fourteen and nineteen, 26 million nonworking wives, and 4 million elderly individuals. Among the 71 million income-earning inhabitants, one-fourth earned less than two thousand dollars. Although the size of this group had reached prewar levels at the end of the 1940s, it did not enjoy the same increase in income that other social categories had enjoyed.

It is typical of the twentieth-century division of labor between science and politics that Miller voiced only scientific interest in the issue of poverty and did not claim to be seeking solutions to problems related to income inequality. As a government statistician, he positioned himself only as addressing a new set of questions by refining how the number of poor was calculated, an approach to a charged issue that was designed to gain support within the federal government. In the context of McCarthyism, Miller used it as a self-conscious strategy to navigate a fraught political and bureaucratic situation. Over the years, people at the Census Bureau have developed methodological detours around provocative approaches, especially on racial matters. However, despite his caution, Miller became a key player in the community who provided crucial statistical knowledge about poor people to other members of the administration, notably in the Department of Labor and the Department of Agriculture.

Updating Working-Class and Rural Budgets

Ever since the end of the nineteenth century, these two departments have played a major role in the field of statistics and research. Under the statistician Carroll Wright, the Bureau of Labor Statistics (BLS) started publishing regular research reports on working-class-family budgets in different industrial regions. At the same time, the Department of Agriculture had made research a major priority and urged the department to work closely with the agricultural community to collect data. The crash of 1929 strongly increased the demand for statistics, leading to an expansion of the department's staff and to the creation of the Bureau of Home Economics and Human Nutrition. By gathering data on budgets of workers and people living in rural areas, their research unit contributed to the fledgling science of poverty, facing the same poverty paradox.[24]

Immediately after World War II, a new generation of BLS staff and scientists—over one thousand people in 1945—initiated substantial revision of the statistical instruments used by the agency. The following year, Ewan Clague was appointed to direct the agency. A statistician from the University of Wisconsin, he began his career as an analyst for the Metropolitan Life Insurance Company before joining the Institute of Human Resources at Yale University. When he took office, he faced a growing opposition from Congress members who regularly scrutinized economic indicators. In 1948, the agreement between General Motors and the United Auto Workers to use the consumer price index for adjusting wages reinforced the importance of the BLS's statistics.[25]

As a consequence, it was necessary to maintain public confidence by producing trustworthy statistics. To do so, Clague pursued a twofold objective: first, he wanted to enhance agency support of social scientists' efforts to come out of the "dark ages," as he phrased it, in the field of statistics; and second, he intended to improve the agency's outside contacts.

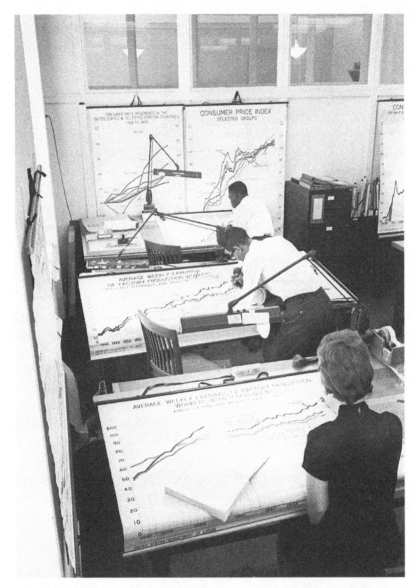

Figure 1.2. The Bureau of Labor Statistics (1960). Courtesy of Library of Congress, U.S. News & World Report Magazine Photograph Collection, LC-U9-8142-4.

Clague established partnerships with Columbia University and the University of Michigan, became president of the National Conference of Social Work, and promoted increased collaboration between the BLS and social workers. The final element of his strategy was supporting efforts to reform how budget studies were conducted, which led him to appeal to the economist Dorothy Brady for assistance. Brady soon became a major force in the community through her innovative work on family budgets and income distribution.[26]

Like many women of her generation who were excluded from academia because of their gender, Brady began her career during the New Deal at the Department of Agriculture, where she helped analyze and report the findings of a vast, two-year study to measure the effects of the crash on rural populations. Brady joined the BLS during the war and remained for five years, leaving in 1948. A civil servant with strong ties with academia, particularly the University of Pennsylvania, Brady also frequently collaborated with the National Bureau of Economic Research, which was directed by the prominent economist Simon Kuznets. She was acutely aware of the difficulty of defining a basic living standard, and she worked to develop an instrument that could assess the living conditions of working-class individuals and families. She modeled her efforts on methods first developed by the German statistician Ernst Engel in the nineteenth century. In a long career as a statistician and director of the Prussian Bureau of Statistics, Engel had focused on family budgets, particularly among low-income families. Significantly, his calculations led him to an important insight concerning the elasticity of food expenses as a function of family income level: the poorer the family, the larger the proportion of their income they spent on food. The objective of this kind of budget study was to reconstruct the basic consumption of a family to determine a sufficient income threshold to ensure their standard of living.[27]

In February 1948, Brady and Lester Kellog published a study of thirty-four cities that employed Engel's approach. The studies, conducted in March 1946 and June 1947, analyzed the composition of the "average" household budget that was demonstrated neither opulence nor poverty. A matched sample of families was selected for each city using highly specific model family criterion. Selected families lived in rented housing consisting of five rooms (including a kitchen and a bathroom), contained four members (two children and two parents, with the woman working at home and the father the wage earner), and lived in a residence containing a minimum number of modern convenience, including a "gas or electric stove, a refrigerator and a washing machine.[28]

Brady and Kellog attempted to accommodate criticisms of the agency that accused the BLS of including too many luxury items. They developed a methodology focused primarily on actual household expenses. In terms of nutrition, the caloric values of food items were integrated based on the assumption that meat was consumed several times a week. The researchers also assumed that a small fraction of the food budget was spent on food consumed outside the home. In terms of clothing, it was specified that the woman bought a winter coat once every four years and that each member of the household bought three pairs of shoes a year. These specifications illustrated the researchers' efforts to incorporate new, postwar patterns of consumption into the study design, but they also revealed the difficulty of objectifying an average family's existence in minute detail.

Brady's sampling method was influenced by Engel's law, yielding an elevated norm of what constituted an "adequate" living standard, a social index that would continue to influence BLS studies throughout the 1950s despite Brady's initial absence and eventual departure. Clague assigned the economist Helen Lamale to continue Brady's work. In 1960, Lamale published an extensive update of the 1948 survey that showed a general rise in the living standard of the American working class against the backdrop of strong economic growth. The expenditures of a young working-class family were found to average $5,390 a year, the equivalent of 91 percent of after-tax income, with the remainder devoted to savings and insurance policies.[29]

This increased living standard was matched by a corresponding decrease in the share of family income spent on food, housing, and clothing, which represented only 53 percent of family incomes, compared with 57 percent a decade earlier. To isolate results for low-income working-class populations, Lamale's study arbitrarily selected a poverty threshold of four thousand dollars for a family of four. The BLS adopted a higher threshold that placed a significant number of families—as much as 36 percent of the American population—below the "adequate" income level. Improvement in the living standard of the population was thus revealed to be a relative matter, and a large number of American families continued to spend an average of more than 59 percent of their income on food, clothing, and housing. For researchers, this confirmed Engel's law by showing that expenses were "elastic," especially during periods of economic prosperity. The notion that poverty was relative gradually took hold in the context of these attempts to transcend the basic measurement of working-class budgets, a change that unarguably enabled better understanding of the poverty paradox that Brady had first brought to the attention of Congress members.

The Department of Agriculture research unit, the Bureau of Home Economics and Human Nutrition, faced the same difficulty. After World War II, the staff was still composed of primarily women because of the prevalence of home economics graduates. The scientific heart of this highly dynamic discipline in the first half of the twentieth century was the American Association of Home Economics, established in 1908. Home economics differed from mainstream economics in focusing on microeconomic issues related to the economy of households that were entirely neglected by mainstream economists. Because of gender-based academic segregation, the federal government was the principal employer of home economics majors between the two wars. The continuing economic fallout of the crash guaranteed that the ensuing years were a period of intense activity for the Department of Agriculture. The Roosevelt administration wanted information about how Americans were feeding themselves during the crisis, and it soon became obvious that precise data would be needed to support the implementation of New Deal programs. The Agriculture Department director of research, Hildegarde Kneeland, was searching for ways to address this complex problem. Unlike much of her staff, she held a doctorate in economics, which she received from the Brookings Institution, where she had studied with Ida Merriam.[30]

Under Kneeland's leadership, four nutritional levels were used: a restricted diet for emergency use, an adequate diet at minimum cost, an adequate diet at moderate cost, and a liberal diet. As with the BLS budget studies, nutritional levels had to be updated regularly to keep pace with inflation and changes in nutritional practices, but they remained applicable throughout the 1930s because of the unusual conditions of the Great Depression. After World War II, when Hazel Stiebeling took office at the helm of the department's research division, the approach to studying rural nutrition was revised. Born in 1896 in Haskins, Ohio, Stiebeling grew up on a farm, where she developed an interest in food and nutrition. After

Figure 1.3. Hazel K. Stiebeling in 1959 receiving the President's Award for Distinguished Federal Civilian Service. Photographer: Unknown. Special Collections, USDA National Agricultural Library.

graduating from Skidmore, she entered Teachers College at Columbia University. In 1924, she completed her masters in nutrition and became a research fellow in chemistry. After passing the civil service examination, she started her career in the Department of Agriculture.[31]

When she became bureau chief in 1944, Stiebeling asked her research staff to integrate qualitative data into budget measurements in order to better understand the nation's food habits and food-related expenditures. These changes led to an increase in the baseline expenses that were used to compute rural budgets, as illustrated by the December 1948 updates. At Stiebeling's suggestion, "adequate" and "emergency" levels were given priority, and the highest-level plan was abandoned. Several years later, Stiebeling initiated a vast nationwide study to reassess nutritional data in light of the recent surge in prosperity. The study stressed the fact that despite increased prosperity, the nutritional behaviors of families at the bottom of the income ladder remained remarkably persistent, with one-third of their income continuing to be directed toward nutritional expenses.[32]

This troublingly stable pattern among the nation's poor led Stiebeling to reorient the agency's research around the consumption of the poorest families, and the resulting efforts to define an emergency budget level occupied much of the research team's energy. Depending on geographical location, it was established that at the low-cost level, annual food expenditures for four persons ranged from $760 to $1,630. Because similar revisions to reflect more prosperous times were undertaken by researchers at the BLS and the Bureau of Home Economics and Human Nutrition, the data collected showed a reasonable degree of consistency.[33]

Such similarity revealed statisticians' efforts to accurately define rural and working-class budgets in the 1950s, a decade of relative economic prosperity and steady increases in the general living standard. Significantly,

TABLE 1.3. Family nutritional budgets in 1955

Household size	Nutritional expenditures in low-income families (Bureau of Labor and Statistics)	Nutritional expenditures at the low-income level (Bureau of Home Economics)
1 individual	$449	$305–450
2 individuals	$737	$450–865
3 individuals	$941	$615–1,260
4 individuals	$1,140	$760–1,630
5 individuals	$1,393	$885–1,960
More than 6 individuals	$1,733	$995–2,240

Note: Comparison between the Bureau of Home Economics and Human Nutrition and the Bureau of Labor and Statistics (1955).
Source: Helen Lamale, "How the Poor Spend Their Money," speech before a faculty seminar on poverty at the University of California, in Margaret Gordon, ed., *Poverty in America* (Berkeley: University of California Press, 1965), 157.

both agencies incorporated nutritional and qualitative parameters into their updated studies in an effort to obtain stronger, more accurate data. For instance, when they worked on their budgets, the kind of meat poor people ate—if any—had to be taken into account. The same qualitative analysis had to be made for the clothes and the house if researchers wanted to measure the singularity of poverty in the land of plenty. The Social Security Administration (SSA) also paid attention to low-income families, with Ida Merriam at the head of its research capacity. By then, Merriam had free reins to implement with discretion her scientific agenda.

The Social Security Administration and Low-Income Families

Following the failure of efforts to reform health care under the Truman administration, the SSA decided to avoid broad reform movements and focus instead on specific categories of the population. This more gradualist and consensual strategy seemed to be the only means of ensuring the future of the agency, and it led to a focus on such groups as the working class, the unemployed, the elderly, children, the disabled, and widows. All these categories were used as the basis for assistance or social insurance, and it was in the context of this category-driven approach that the BRS began to show increasing interest in low-income families.

After Congress took retaliatory measures in the wake of the health care reform debacle, the research unit adopted a more cautious approach in an effort to regain confidence in the institution. It employed approximately twenty full-time researchers, with an annual operating budget of seven hundred thousand dollars (of a total research budget of four million dollars for the entire SSA). Following the departure of Isidore Falk, Merriam was named BRS director. While Merriam enjoyed the support of a very important member of the agency, Robert Ball, who became social security commissioner in 1962 and paid close attention to the scientific work, she was the only woman to hold a top-level position in the agency.[34]

The directorship offered Merriam a perfect setting in which to apply her zeal for classification, which, in keeping with the objectivist tradition of the 1920s, she expressed as "balanced and neutral, as it should be." Under her leadership, the bureau expanded its statistical study of social

Figure 1.4. Ida Merriam in her office at the Bureau of Research and Statistics. Courtesy of the Social Security Administration Historian's Office.

expenditures, through the Social Welfare Expenditure Series, occasional reports published since 1929. The series initially contained only information directly related to the Social Security program, but Merriam extended its reach by incorporating all available data relating to social expenditures in their broadest sense, including housing, education, and retirement pensions. Beginning in 1960, reports were published annually.[35]

In tandem with these initiatives, Merriam centralized the bureau's scientific activities. As director of the research coordination committee during the war, she had become convinced that the directors of different divisions were too busy with administrative tasks to effectively supervise research, and she made plans to reorganize the fragmented system of agency reports, which were regularly published in two distinct forms: the Bureau Memorandum and the Bureau Report. The purpose of these publications was to address technical questions related to how the Social Security program was applied. In the spirit of centralization, Merriam decided to make the funding of national studies a priority by using computing resources, even though her own agency lacked the necessary hardware; her solution to this lack of resources was to cooperate with the Census Bureau, which produced such statistical data.

In addition to such centralizing moves, Merriam turned her attention to recruiting outside researchers. The legal provisions of Section 702 allowed Merriam to hire legal experts and consultants without recourse to the Civil Service Commission, the traditional federal recruitment system. To obtain funding for external hires, she asked Congress to allocate half of the funds needed to hire them. A steering committee was created to establish research priorities that included five universities, two businessmen, and a union representative. This restructuring allowed a clearer definition of the bureau's scientific mission, and in the early 1960s, Merriam initiated an annual research planning process that presented the broad outlines of the coming year's research.[36]

In 1962, the research plan contained sixteen sections, two of which focused on two specific categories of the poor—the elderly and children. The social consequences of an aging population in the political landscape of the 1950s were cited to justify studies of the elderly. Merriam hoped that this strand of research would help the agency regain Congressional approval by proving that the BRS could produce neutral and impartial analyses of a social issue. Between 1951 and 1957, a number of studies on the health and medical coverage of the elderly were published. Data collection was complicated by such factors as the difficulty of identifying the number of insurance policy holders among elderly persons over 65. In the context of discussions about the proposed Forand Bill, which would have enabled the federal government to pay medical and surgical benefits and up to 120 days' combined hospitalization and nursing-home care per year for eligible seniors, the House Ways and Means Committee asked her to provide estimates on a range of options for hospitalization and home-care insurance for the elderly, widows, and the handicapped.[37]

Merriam composed the report, which described the elderly population, rates of medical coverage, and the costs involved in extending their health insurance coverage. The data were incomplete, however, and when Arthur Fleming, the Secretary of Health, Education, and Welfare, was questioned during a Senate hearing about retirees' living standard, he was not able to answer specifically. Fleming asked the bureau for a more thorough study, which was quickly completed under the title "Income Needs of the Aged." Conscious of the advantages of studies of the elderly for the agency and the bureau, Merriam began a vast national survey of elderly incomes, asking her assistant, Lenore Bixby, to coordinate the project. Bixby selected a representative sample of eighty-five hundred cases that was generalizable to the nation's elderly population. Published in 1963, the study provided a portrait of the very specific problem of poverty among the elderly.[38]

Merriam was also quick to perceive the strategic advantages of investigations of low-income issues. The BRS had consistently shown interest in social assistance, and Merriam had participated in many studies and articles on the subject, in particular a study ordered by the Congress on low-income families in 1949 as well as the working group on low-income families of the Council of Economic Advisers in 1954. In October 1962, Merriam conceived of expanding the project and asked Robert Ball to fund a study of low-income families who "do not receive assistance from public agencies." With Ball's approval, she followed the research plan adopted for the year 1962 and asked researchers to study the effects of poverty on children as well as an analysis of European family assistance payments. This sensitive research topic was a perfect match for the solid methodological foundation that she had established in the SSA's research center, bringing more evidence of the postwar poverty paradox.[39]

The Origins of the Poverty Community

Throughout the 1950s, a significant degree of cohesion developed among federal government researchers. Although men such as Herman Miller were regularly in attendance, women played a major role. Their preponderance was the result of generational trends in specialization and academic segregation, especially in departments of home economics, but also of the consequences of the 1929 crash. By the end of the 1950s, the shift toward accounting techniques based on statistics and economics in the administration led to an increase in the number of men, who tended to have training in these fields. Sexual identity, however, rarely entered into discussions of the community. Although women did refer to their singular status, they tried not to allow gender issues to infringe on the objectivity that was the basis of the community's internal cohesion. In the McCarthy era however, as Alvin Schorr, a member of the BRS, recalled, "it was no time for adventure; the rule was to avoid catching attention."[40]

In spite of their trust in numbers and statistics, knowledge about poverty remained unstable. Improving data collection and statistical tools became a major emphasis. Economist Selma Goldsmith frequently lamented the disparities between methods of measuring income. Comparing studies by the different research teams, she expressed particular dismay about differences in estimates of earned income. Estimates of the number of low-income families and individuals did vary widely, as mentioned earlier, with numbers ranging from 13 percent of the total population at the Commerce Department to 36 percent at the Bureau of Labor Statistics, and the Census Bureau and the Social Security Administration estimating an average of 19 percent. It is not a coincidence that all members of the poverty community were members of the Washington Statistical Society, which sought to improve collection of statistics in the federal machinery.[41]

By questioning and measuring the poverty paradox, researchers implicitly blurred the ancient distinction between the "deserving" poor—primarily orphans, single women, and the elderly—and the "undeserving" poor, mostly able-bodied men of working age. It was also a delicate matter as the idea of a specific culture of poverty loomed large in the nation. Contrary to what federal researchers expressed, it was still seen as the resulted of specific behavior and individual choices.

2

THE POVERTY CULTURE

In the 1950s, federal research investigating the low-income and disadvantaged segments of society remained invisible. A cultural and psychological view of poverty, however, tended to dominate public discourse. The poverty paradox was explained by individual choices and specific behaviors. Why so many communities, populated largely by racial and ethnic minorities, remained so poor in the midst of increasing wealth became the subject of intense debate. Poverty was still largely considered to be the result of individual shortcomings as opposed to structural or monetary factors. Racial bias strongly reinforced such a vision, which alleged that there was no paradox at all, just the sum of individual decisions.[1]

Such preconceptions were consistent with the old distinction made between the "deserving" and the "undeserving" poor. Furthermore, the process of modernization had increasingly marginalized the poor, who were accused of being incapable of participating in the affluent society. This view was reinforced by the ascendancy of behaviorist views among American elites after World War II. Both philanthropic foundations and the

National Science Foundation funded research that looked at the pathologies afflicting poor people, in particular African Americans. For homeless
people on the streets of New York or traditional populations in newly
independent nations, psychology was used as a way to cure pathologies
and to modernize backward societies.[2]

In the 1950s, as white middle-class families moved from cities to suburbs and the civil rights movement gained momentum, inner-city areas in
Harlem, Syracuse, and Detroit were home to increasing numbers of people whose cultural and familial patterns were seen as contributing to deviant behaviors. To make matters worse, according to the data and statistics
produced by research centers and foundations, these behavioral problems
were transmitted from one generation to the next through a distinct culture of poverty. Among these anxious observers was Paul Ylvisaker, who
concurred with this diagnosis and worked closely with charitable foundations to find out what was causing these new urban pathologies.

Paul Ylvisaker and Urban Pathologies

In 1956, Professor Paul Ylvisaker gave a talk to a group of young students
at Swarthmore High School that called attention to profound changes that
had occurred in the nation since the turn of the century. He noted, "In
our day, we have seen the explosive growth and acceptance of the idea of
change itself. This idea has been a governing ideal for the U.S. and a fact
of its history; it is now the aspiration—for better or for worse—of most
of the rest of the world, certainly for the majority of the world's population. The idea of change, and of change being synonymous with improvement, is one whose novelty is difficult for Americans to appreciate having
lived with it so long." This conception of modernization shaped Ylvisaker's thinking throughout a long career questioning the postwar urban crisis in the United States.[3]

Ylvisaker was born into a deeply religious family of Scandinavian origin in November 1921. His father, Sigurd Christian Ylvisaker, was from
a long line of Norwegian ministers and served as president of the Bethany
Lutheran Junior College. It seemed foreordained that his son, Paul, would
follow in his footsteps, and even as Paul distanced himself from his family's religious beliefs, this pious home environment exerted a powerful

influence on Ylvisaker. He claimed, "It's the nature of this complex life the Lord has put us into that there are no single or simple answers. I have seen both the virtues and the problematics of religious education and of public education. . . . I know I needed to be 'released' at one time from the prejudices and parochialism of Lutheran dogma, and to come to respect through wider association the myriads of truths and perceptions of truth that creation has given us." Despite second thoughts, Ylvisaker retained his father's faith that society's economic resources should be used to promote a more just and equitable world.[4]

He enrolled at the University of Minnesota at Mankato, later transferring to the main campus in Saint Paul. He was an excellent student, and he won a scholarship to continue at Harvard University, where he majored in public administration and ultimately completed a PhD in political economy and government in 1948. He accepted a teaching job at Swarthmore High School, a position that he held for many years—except for a single year, 1951, when he participated in a Fulbright exchange that took him to England. This opportunity allowed him to study sociology and political science there, and he developed a keen appreciation of Emanuel Kant's philosophy and of the moral imperatives behind it and their practical implications. He returned to Swarthmore the following year more aware of the singularity of the American experience but also that the high level of development in the Western world ought to allow society to be managed in more rational ways.

The New Deal provided the bare bones of precisely what he had in mind, although he saw room for improvement. Ylvisaker referred almost lyrically to the "visionary" planners who were are "now vice-presidents in charge of future operations in the best of our industries." He was eager to put the era's new ideas into practice, which led him to enter local politics. During a stint as the local Democratic Party leader, he met Philadelphia mayor Joseph Clark at a lecture by the celebrated urban planner Robert Moses. Ylvisaker was responsible for introducing Moses to the gathering, and he emphasized the planner's prominent role in urban renewal initiative under way in New York City. His remarks caught Clark's attention, and the mayor promptly asked Ylvisaker to join his staff after explaining during their first meeting he was recruiting him to "lead a spiritual battle." Despite reservations, Ylvisaker accepted Clark's offer but also decided to keep his teaching position at Swarthmore.[5]

The significance of the Philadelphia mayor's surprising reference to spirituality quickly became apparent. Like many postwar mayors of large cities, Clark had been elected on a platform that was opposed to the corrupting influence of large political machines, espousing instead rational urban planning based on efficient management and centralized policies. Clark surrounded himself with young college graduates and undertook an expansive program of urban renewal projects. By then, Philadelphia was the nation's third-largest city, with two million residents. The city was in dire need of reform. This was no mean task, however, as complex demographic, economic, and social forces were operating against the background of a powerful racial divide. In Ylvisaker's view, the challenges that the city faced exemplified the transformation of the nation's cities since the turn of the century, compelling him to "deal with people problems, not bricks and mortar or power structure problems."[6]

Ylvisaker imagined urban planning and the discussions that surrounded it as a vehicle for reconciling a commitment to politics with a desire for social justice, but his political activism meshed poorly with a teaching career, while health issues further complicated matters. Clark's election to the U. S. Senate in 1954 heightened tensions at City Hall, leading Ylvisaker to abruptly quit politics; he recalled years later that he "felt inadequate in many ways." In December 1956, he suffered a heart attack and, with Clark's blessing, he began looking for a better-paying and less stressful line of work. He accepted a position as an urban policy specialist at the Ford Foundation, where he joined the public affairs department and participated in a large-scale urban renewal program. The program initially attracted little interest, but his new position allowed him to place his gift for planning into practice while leaving behind the political brouhaha of Philadelphia. He declared, "Planning is politics, but it is even more than that. Politics has the job of reconciling the known past with the known present; planning has to make both the past and present compatible with an unknown future. If politics is the art of the possible, planning comes close to being the art of the impossible."[7]

In a talk that he gave in October 1958 to the American Institute of Planners, Ylvisaker described his approach to the urban crisis, an approach that was innovative in several respects. By the late 1950s, struggling urban neighborhoods were collapsing under the weight of a host of problems, including middle-class suburban flight and an influx of socially and culturally marginalized groups, as well as the effects of technological modernization and the fiscal crisis. A social ghetto was gradually forming in America's cities that were further fueled by ongoing migration from regions with more traditional economies such as the South and Appalachia. This social environment caused deviant behaviors, claimed Ylvisaker. The rise of juvenile delinquency was one of the most discussed issues in postwar Philadelphia. Local judges blamed migration from the South and found fault with African American women for their kids' misbehavior. Fear was closely tied to anti-welfare discourse in the city. For Ylvisaker, it was necessary to reorganize urban planning to put an end to both racial discrimination and urban disorder.[8]

The Ford Foundation provided him with an opportunity to demonstrate that he could design programs that would promote social progress, thus countering this steady social deterioration and halting the decline of communities and the increasing of individual pathologies. His belief that he could do so was driven by his faith that urban planning had access to the tools needed to establish social bonds within urban communities. Notwithstanding this optimism, Ylvisaker found the atmosphere at the foundation to be as negative and tense as they had been at Philadelphia City Hall. Competition between departments was intense, as each vied for administration approval, while the administration in turn deliberately fueled interdepartmental conflict. During his first eighteen months, Ylvisaker left and went back to his job at the Ford Foundation three times to protest against what he saw as endless bureaucratic meddling. He ultimately remained, out of an awareness of the unique access that the foundation provided to financial resources. The tensions and personality conflicts that Ylvisaker observed inside the institution were made even worse by external pressures from Congress and the National Science Foundation.[9]

Institutional Constraints

After World War II, in the context of McCarthyism, social science research was inspiring growing doubts in Congress, which maintained a tight rein on the budget of the National Science Foundation (NSF) and the tax-exempt status of philanthropic foundations. Institutional constraints reinforced the cultural and scientific hegemony of behaviorist theory in the postwar intellectual and academic community, a theoretical slant that had significant impact on the field of poverty research.

In 1950, during congressional testimony concerning the creation of the NSF, Clarence Brown, a representative from Ohio, summarized his colleagues' fears by alleging that "the average American does not want to see people getting mixed up in their lives and private affairs, deciding for them how they should live, and if Congress gets the feeling that the goal of this law is to create an organization where there will be a bunch of short-haired women and long-haired men poking their noses everywhere in people's private lives to know whether they love their wives and whatnot, we will not vote for this law."[10]

In a sign of the anti-intellectual rhetoric of the times, this allusion to the 1948 Kinsey Report on Americans' sexuality was intended as a call to order to the scientific community about the lines that should not be crossed. This distrust led to a form of rejection that confirmed that the hard sciences were superior to the social sciences. When the NSF was created in 1950, the wording of the law officially acknowledged the social sciences under the sibylline formula of "other sciences." This designation was quite ambiguous in terms of poverty research. One natural outcome was that behavioral scientific approaches and studies based on behavioral deficiencies benefited from these changes in the scientific landscape at the expense of income distribution research. In the 1950s, the frontiers of science remained tied to a desire for the kind of fundamental objectivity that was associated with the natural sciences.[11]

Institutional limitations on charitable foundations were similar. After the war, the foundations were subject to increasingly strict congressional oversight. The effort to control science became effective because of the Republican majority in Congress after the 1946 midterm elections. A number of Republicans saw the foundations as the birthplace of New Deal ideas, both domestically and abroad, and they strongly opposed the alliance between the social sciences and federal agencies that had prevailed since the 1930s. Inspired by works such as Gunnar Myrdal's *An American Dilemma* (1944) psychologists and sociologists contributed to the historic struggle to overturn *Plessy v. Ferguson* (1954) in an attempt to show that discrimination influenced African American children's mental and educational development. Tax-exempt status was used as a tool to apply pressure on the foundations.[12]

In charge of tax matters, the House Ways and Means Committee passed new tax legislation in 1950 that strengthened legislative oversight of the tax-exempt approval process. The law allowed tax-exempt status to be revoked if a foundation accumulated funds over a long period or if its expenditures failed to comply with congressional guidelines. In August 1951, a Georgia Democrat named Eugene Cox initiated a detailed investigation to assess foundations' influence in the country and the world. A member of Congress for thirty years, Cox was the leader of a group of conservative southern Democrats who were openly hostile to liberal social engineering policies. The Cox Commission's preliminary report accused the Rockefeller Foundation of introducing communism into Chinese schools, contributing to the communist victory in China by spreading this nefarious ideology before the 1949 revolution. The Guggenheim Foundation was also criticized for fueling the revolution by importing extremism into China. Cox used these political charges to persuade his fellow Congress members that foundations needed to be thoroughly investigated. The tone of the opening discussions was strongly hostile, as William Fulton, a member of the highly conservative American Legion, published a virulent pamphlet fulminating against the foundations and branding them as secretive and as the financiers of "real communists, fellow travelers, socialists, internationalists, and other utopists."[13]

In April 1952, Congress appointed a seven-member commission to explore these questions more closely. The commission's findings were considerably milder than anticipated, partly because foundation directors willingly cooperated, even managing to turn the proceedings to their advantage. In highly polished congressional testimony, Paul Hoffman, representing the Ford Foundation, pleaded for expanded efforts to fight the threat of communism. Charles Dollard, the Carnegie Corporation president, echoed these arguments, while also pointing out that the U.S. Secret Service had not named a single recipient of Carnegie Foundation funds as a "communist." The foundation representatives skillfully used the subject of communist subversion to demonstrate that, contrary to the allegations of the Cox Commission, their organizations promoted American ideals throughout the world and helped spread a view of the Soviets as archenemy. This argument helped justify continued funding for research centers at Columbia and Harvard focused on the communist world. The directors did not totally deny the potential "risks" of political drift, but they successfully argued that the potential benefits outweighed those risks because, as Hoffman put it, research was the only way of guaranteeing continued social progress and Americans' well-being. Hoffman further mollified Congress by pointing to the number of grants to fund behaviorist research.

Because the hearings were conducted amid such a cordial and cooperative atmosphere, the tone of the final report was quite favorable to the foundations. The words it contained put forth the commission's conclusion that accusations of communism were unfounded and counseled the foundations to continue to apply approaches based on social science. Such a consensual tenor did not reflect the position of Tennessee congressman B. Carroll Reece, who claimed that the foundation presidents had cleverly concealed their institutions' permissiveness. Reece called for a new investigation a year later to scrutinize how tax-exempt status was awarded and used. Reece, who presided over the hearings, openly attacked the foundations. A report circulated claiming that communist ideas were widespread among a variety of professional organizations, from the National Research Council and the American Education Council to the John Dewey Society and the American Historical Association. The report prompted Congress to enact a series of laws near the end of the 1954 legislative session mandating stricter oversight of how tax-exempt status was granted and managed.[14]

The situation was made worse by a scandal involving a study of juries in Chicago the following year. The study, which was supported by Ford Foundation grants of four hundred thousand dollars in 1952 and a million dollars in 1953, examined the behavior of jury members during trials and deliberations. When actual jury deliberations were quoted in a scholarly article without the consent of the jury's members, a huge public outcry ensued. An immediate congressional inquiry was ordered and assigned to the National Security Committee, which was led by Mississippi senator James Eastland. Eastland was openly antagonistic toward the foundations because of the 1954 Supreme Court ruling in *Brown v. Board of Education*. In his opinion, the foundations were subverting the courts under the influence of sinister communist tracts, particularly the widely acclaimed *An American Dilemma* (1944), whose author, Gunnar Myrdal, was accused of being a communist agent. Similar accusations were leveled against the academics who had conducted the Chicago jury study. During congressional hearings, Harry Kalven, one of the study's lead researchers, was confronted with copies of a letter that he had written to President Harry S. Truman urging the president to offer clemency to Julius and Ethel Rosenberg, as well as an article defending the physicist J. Robert Oppenheimer, who was also accused of communist ties. The inquiry ultimately led to a 1956 law that proscribed observations of juries under any circumstances, but the broader effect of the Eastland Commission was to further weaken philanthropic foundations.[15]

Congressional pressure had immediate ramifications for the orientation of the foundations' scientific policies. The Ford Foundation took the lead by refusing to fund projects deemed "risky," which included any studies related to American Indians or desegregation. Revealingly, Alfred Kinsey's application for a grant to support a new sexuality study was also rejected despite Kinsey's insistence and the fact that his funding from the Rockefeller Foundation had recently been withdrawn. Although Kinsey's grant application had been initially approved, the opposition of the foundation's board of directors led to the reversal of this decision.[16]

Successive postponement of funding for a revised edition of the *Encyclopedia of the Social Sciences*, whose original 1930 edition had been edited by Edwin Seligman and Alvin Johnson with the help of Ida Merriam, gave further evidence of reservations about funding for the social sciences. The Ford Foundation had agreed to support the project when the update was first proposed. Confirming that the volume was an important resource for scholars and students, the internal report indicated approval, and the foundation saw the encyclopedia as an important voice for the cumulative social science knowledge base before a broader public. The board of directors received an application for a two-million-dollar grant to support the new edition, but in order to avoid further congressional reprisals, the request was ultimately denied.[17]

Philanthropic foundations gradually adapted their research activities to the political environment of the 1950s. In one symptomatic move, the Russell Sage Foundation was reorganized, closing the Department of Industrial Studies that had been directed by Mary Van Kleeck. From then on, foundations funded only behaviorist-oriented research centers, including Talcott Parson's Department of Social Relations at Harvard and Columbia's Office of Applied Research. In this way, the foundations extended already well-established ties between behaviorist psychology and the American political elite. The fact that the Ford Foundation chose to analyze poverty exclusively from the angle of behavioral deviance was powerful proof of this new research environment.[18]

The Ford Foundation and Juvenile Delinquents

Juvenile delinquency had been an important topic of academic research at some American universities ever since the period between the wars, particularly in Chicago and New York. Increased interest in security- and criminality-related issues after World War II and in the 1946 municipal elections increased the appeal of delinquency research. In 1953, a senator known for campaigning against organized crime, Estes Kefauver, decided to shift his focus to juvenile delinquency. The U. S. Senate also held hearings with testimony at which leading criminologists and childhood specialists explained the spread of delinquency while deploring a lack of reliable data and arguing for increased funding for research that would contribute to a better understanding of delinquency. The NSF's refusal to finance delinquency studies left an opening for the foundations to adopt the issue, and the Ford Foundation seized the opportunity to enhance the visibility of its support of behaviorist research.[19]

Founded in 1936 by the Ford family, the foundation's activities expanded significantly after World War II as a result of substantial revenues derived from Ford Motor Company stock. H. Rowan Gaither was named president in 1953, and he formed an interdisciplinary team of social scientists that included Donald Marquis, chair of psychology at the University of Michigan, and Peter Odegard, a University of California political scientist. The team reshaped the direction of the foundation's research and development efforts to encompass promoting peace, education, and scientific knowledge about individual behavior and human relationships. Underprivileged populations, particularly low-income families, were well within the purview of this philanthropic approach. To avoid clashes with Congress, the foundation conformed to NSF's guidelines and promoted the behavioral sciences by focusing on the behavior of the poor, particularly regarding the question of social deviance.[20]

Under Paul Ylvisaker, the public affairs department was responsible for the foundation's research projects. Ylvisaker deliberately dramatized rising delinquency rates, underscoring the fact that between 1948 and 1955, although the younger segment of the population had increased by only 16 percent, the number of juvenile delinquents had jumped by 70 percent. He argued that this increase reflected accelerating modernization, which had caught young people in a vortex of impersonal forces and caused them to lose the reference points necessary for a stable sense of identity, ultimately transforming the nation's large urban centers into what he called "deserts." In the immediate wake of the war, urban policy had focused entirely on new methods of community organization such as those proposed by urban reformers, among them Robert Moses in New York.[21]

Ylvisaker wanted to promote new techniques of community activism that would integrate the poor more effectively into the local community. He used urbanist, modernist arguments that spanned the question of race as well as the urban crisis. Because the foundation president declined to address racial issues directly, however, Ylvisaker was obliged to remain somewhat circumspect on matters touching on race. Terms like *civil liberties* and *racial relations* were deliberately avoided in his presentations and were replaced by coded references to populations "more accustomed to neglect." The project quickly gained approval from the foundation directors. In 1956, the new president, Henry Heald, endorsed this strategy geared toward practical outcomes and jointly assigned the delinquency research program to the departments of public affairs and education.[22]

While Ylvisaker continued to be plagued by the same sorts of personal and bureaucratic rivalries that he had encountered at Philadelphia City Hall, he tried to maintain a close working relationship between the two departments by appointing a joint coordinating committee. The goal of the project was straightforward: urban residents would themselves design educational and social programs that they perceived to be helpful in combating delinquency. The idea was to initiate an autonomous process, nudge the programs along, and evaluate their effectiveness by alleviating the problems in the blighted urban zones that Ylvisaker labeled "gray areas." He argued that this was a break with previous urban management strategies. Because of its outsider status within the community, the foundation was able to play a critical role in social stabilization. Ten local experiments were planned and an official partnership between the Ford Foundation and the Mobilization for Youth Program of New York was signed. Actually implementing the agreement proved difficult, however. The program was originally conceived by social workers and sociologists as a way of ending near-permanent gang wars in Manhattan's Lower East Side.[23]

Two social workers named Helen Hall and Helen Harris had authored the project and were searching for funding from the charitable foundations, particularly the Ford Foundation and the Russell Sage Foundation, but both organizations initially declined to get involved. The Ford Foundation responded that both of the lead researchers' names were on a blacklist created by Norman Dodd in 1954 and were also cited in the Reece Commission hearings as demonstrating the communist infiltration of social workers. Hall and Harris asked for support from sociologists, and two faculty members from Columbia University, Lloyd Ohlin and Richard Cloward, endorsed their proposal. Known for their book, *Delinquency and Opportunity: A Theory of Delinquent Gangs* (1960), they supported a theory that synthesized the Mertonian concept of *anomy* and the Chicago school's structural approach. In other words, delinquency was a rational response to a blocked opportunity. Existing social structures supposedly prevented citizens from gaining access to these opportunities. In terms of prevention, the theory and its implications were innovative because instead of focusing on psychological and psychiatric issues, they stressed social factors like the education system and promoted "community reorganization of the ghettos." Their support for the project reassured the Ford Foundation, which had partly funded the research for their book. Cloward and Ohlin's conclusions were relatively close to Ylvisaker's own thinking, and a partnership was created. The Ford Foundation founded a separate juvenile delinquency office in New York, with David Hunter as director, to ward off accusations of involvement in local controversies.[24]

Similar urban programs to combat juvenile delinquency were created throughout the country, and the Ford Foundation allied itself closely with local organizations, just as Ylvisaker advocated. In most cities in which the foundation was active between 1961 and 1962, mayors and local agencies played decisive roles in the successful operation of the programs, particularly in Oakland, California; New Haven, Connecticut; Boston; and Philadelphia. For each project, Ford provided a four-year operating budget of between $1.5 million and $2 million. The foundation financed a program in Oakland that was developed by the Associated Agencies, an umbrella organization of educators and municipal civil servants designed to lower tensions in the school system by making collaboration easier between social workers inside and outside the system. Out of a total grant of $2 million, the foundation directed $750,000 to new experimental approaches to preventing deviant behaviors. In 1963, a similar project in North Carolina was applied in the state's rural areas and midsized cities. In New Haven, Connecticut, the foundation funded the local union activist Mitchell Sviridoff, whose organization, Community Progress, offered educational, legal, and social services in the city's poorer neighborhoods. Ylvisaker's close relationships with charitable and social organizations in Philadelphia ensured that the City Council for Community Progress received significant financial support.

Embracing the subject of juvenile delinquency allowed the Ford Foundation to maintain a strictly behaviorist stance on poverty and on the phenomenon of social deviance associated with it. At the same time, the fight against delinquency offered a way to promote Ylvisaker's concept of forging new social bonds in prosperous America's "urban deserts." The inevitably reductionist nature of the behaviorist approach to poverty research, however, ultimately narrowed the scope of both research and activism, and the approach remained hotly contested within the poverty community. These conflicting views on the poverty paradox innerved discussions of the Survey Research Center at the University of Michigan.[25]

Debates at the Survey Research Center

In 1946, the University of Michigan created the Institute for Social Research, with psychologist Rensis Likert as director. Likert had worked for the Department of Agriculture during World War II, collaborating with a number of other agencies to compile statistical data for the war effort. With a group of economists and sociologists, he negotiated an agreement with the University of Michigan to create an institute devoted to social sciences. The agreement allowed an unusual degree of financial independence that gave the researchers control over their external funding. To avoid becoming overly specialized, Likert insisted that institute-sponsored research projects be interdisciplinary. In 1948, after the Research Center for Group Dynamics moved from the Massachusetts Institute of Technology to the University of Michigan, the Survey Research Center was created and awarded an operating budget of eight hundred thousand dollars in 1950. The center was particularly interested with consumption and the economic behaviors of consumers.[26]

A research seminar on the incomes of underprivileged populations was created to advance what was known about the behavior of poorer consumers. The diversity of the seminar participants reflected the prevailing interdisciplinary spirit by including sociologists, psychologists, and economists. Among the latest were Kenneth Boulding, Martin David, William Haber, and James Morgan. Monthly meetings began in 1956 with discussions of how to operationalize the construct of poverty. The economists demanded that the crucial question of a lack of income be examined. Three categories of poverty were identified—absolute, relative, and temporary. Although absolute poverty was relatively easy to define, relative poverty was complicated by the problem of defining and measuring a wide range of variables that included household budgets, welfare resources, monetary income, and moral and psychological factors. Temporary poverty proved to be equally complex because of problems in quantifying variables that were by definition exceptional events—accidents, loss of employment, and health problems.[27]

Despite an initial focus on monetary factors, a conceptual shift during the discussions led to an increasing emphasis on more cultural and psychological views of poverty. This behavioral orientation was undeniably reinforced after the center received an additional grant from the Ford Foundation. Under the leadership of a psychologist named David McClelland, some discussions turned on the problem of low "motivation" among the poor. In 1953, McClelland had published *The Achievement Motive,* an edited volume that introduced a method for measuring motivation. Early tests showed a strong positive correlation between motivation and income level, leading to the conclusion that low income could cause the poor to become apathetic and to transmit their resignation across generations. There was a consensus about the implications of this correlation, with economists and sociologists attempting to explain how the poor might be encouraged to break free of a state of inherited torpor. Scholars also argued that social programs should be evaluated according their potential for breaking this vicious cycle.[28]

In December 1956, the economist Thomas Morgan summarized this focus on apathy among the poor: "Political apathy is not unfeelingness; it is non-activity, a failure of the low-income classes to recognize their political interest and the channels through which action can be made effective." He added that it was "problematical however, whether the poor have the power and the skill to organize or whether their inaction is evidence of lack of motivation to organize for political activity." Emphasizing psychological issues removed the debate from the domain of practical solutions because it complicated planning for the mechanisms that government intervention might take and reframed the debate around the notion that poverty might be a permanent condition. In late 1956, the seminar began looking for ways to integrate the poor into society by addressing their psychological blockages. These discussions sparked debates when Wilbur J. Cohen joined the group and recommended solutions that targeted income transfer through the Social Security program.[29]

By 1956, Cohen, a former student of Edwin Witte at the University of Wisconsin, had already had a long, distinguished career at the Social Security Administration, where he was well known for his ability to represent the agency before Congress. Beginning in the 1930s, he was among the chief advocates for a gradualist strategy to expand Social Security benefits. He established close contacts in Congress after the war that included with Wilbur Mills, the chairman of the House Ways and Means Committee, which controlled the federal budget. In 1954, when he was chosen to succeed Isidore Falk as head the Bureau of Research and Statistics (BRS), Cohen abruptly decided to leave the federal government, because he was not interested in research, and decided to let Ida Merriam take command. He lost all remaining interest in working for the government when the former president of Kodak, Marion Folsom, was appointed secretary of health, education, and welfare, and he promptly accepted a faculty position in public administration at the University of Michigan from Fedele Fauri, a friend of his who was dean of social work. Even though he kept contact with Ida Merriam, Cohen moved to Ann Arbor in July 1955 after the new position became official.[30]

Beyond this important transition, Cohen's arrival on campus was a major turning point that led Cohen to shift his research focus onto welfare programs. In December 1956, he delivered an outspoken lecture at the University of California claiming that the federal government needed just ten years to end poverty if it stopped the cautious approach adopted by the administration of Dwight D. Eisenhower. His arguments were new less because they legitimized welfare than because they redefined the ultimate objective of assistance programs. Cohen, however, broke with this monetary approach to transcend the logic of welfare by stressing an investment in human capital, which he saw as an inherent aspect of the concept. He believed that a combination of educational, medical, psychological, and social services could completely alleviate the difficulties faced by low-income families. Cohen summarized his plan on the Madison campus in 1957, urging policymakers to create more schools, roads, hospitals, and public housing projects.[31]

The emphasis on human capital was Cohen's answer to the new socioeconomic conditions created by prosperity, in which welfare was considered to be a stepping-stone toward poor families' integration into mainstream society. When Cohen joined the seminar discussions to promote his approach, the dynamics of the group were altered. Academics also joined the steering committee, including economist Guy Orcutt and Lawrence Klein. A number of federal employees who were members of the poverty community also arrived, including Selma Goldsmith of the Commerce Department, Helen Lamale of the Bureau of Labor Statistics, Ida Merriam of the BRS, and Herman Miller from the Census Bureau.

In 1957, discussions centered on the motivational aspect of poverty, eventually reducing the issue to a simple political question: Should the government promote employment or should it promote welfare? Naturally, Cohen was a forceful proponent of services for underprivileged segments of society that could reinforce existing welfare programs. One outcome of the discussions was an agreement to sponsor a study of low-income families that was to be co-directed by James Morgan, Martin David, Harvey Brazer, and Wilbur Cohen. Their study centered on an assessment of the economic behaviors of three thousand low-income families as they responded to redistribution mechanisms, with a particular emphasis on motivation and on factors that could contribute to a lasting reduction of dependency on assistance. IBM 704 computers helped process the data, and the economists applied a precise definition of poverty that reflected both monetary and nonmonetary sources of income, rent, and tax expenditures to participating families. To establish an empirically based poverty threshold, they adopted a "standard of need" that used data from New

York household budget studies supplied by Eleanor Snyder. The average budget for a family of four was set at $4,330. Using these parameters, poor families were defined as those "whose incomes fall below 90% of budgetary needs." This definition provided the basis for an analysis of national income distribution, but the process of definition and quantification created conflicts after it became clear that only 10 percent of monetary transfers originated with the government. In 1959, it was found that 50 percent of poor families received no welfare assistance at all, a figure with which Cohen, defending Social Security welfare programs, adamantly disagreed.[32]

Although they were not as controversial among the members of the seminar, discussions of the causes of poverty did generate a certain amount of conflict that undermined the final outcomes of the income study. A correlational study compared head-of-household income with length of time worked, number of hours worked, and income from daily wages. Fourteen characteristics were labeled causal variables: sex, age, education, degree of urbanization, migration, location in the Deep South, unemployment rate, supervisory responsibilities, attitude regarding work, level of motivation, geographical mobility, race, physical condition, and school performance. The seminar participants acknowledged that belonging to a subcategory did not automatically signify that an individual belonged in the low-income bracket: "If a family is poor the classification tells something about the type of poverty and the chances that the family may be able to improve its situation."[33]

Still, despite researchers' efforts to find a balance between a psychological definition and a strictly monetarist perspective, their desire for objectivity led to a proliferation of variables that hindered clear conclusions about the nature and causes of poverty: "The difference between expected and actual earnings may reflect underlying variability in the determination of income. Alternatively, it may be associated with differences in ability, motivation, or other factors not adequately measured by the analyses." This vague conclusion weakened the study's explanatory power, and little by little, this conceptual ambivalence corroded the seminar's cohesion. In late 1950s, Cohen left the university and went back to work for the government, distancing himself from the published report.[34]

The final report shows that nagging questions about poverty continued to exist into the early 1960s. It also demonstrates that even a long, empirically sound list of variables failed to point the way to simple solutions. Wisconsin economist Robert Lampman neatly summarized the lack of clear implications of the report: "The meaningfulness of the analysis of determinants of family income for this theme is never made clear." Moreover, he deplored that "there is no representation in detail of how the poor differ from the non-poor in the process of income determination. One is left wondering whether the poor are inherently different from other people; whether they are poor because, while similar to other people, different things have happened to them; or whether, perhaps, different happenings cause them to become basically different, or vice versa." The debates among the members of the Survey Research Center revealed that the strictly behaviorist model was the subject of real scientific questioning.[35]

Ascendancy of the Behavioral Hypothesis

In the 1950s, both the National Science Foundation and the philanthropic foundations consolidated support for behaviorist approaches throughout the American scientific community. As behaviorism became the default orientation in response to congressional opposition, it came to define the research activities in the whole country. Behaviorism was especially influential in shaping how the public perceived poverty. Individual psychological blockages came to be accepted as explanations for the inability of the poor to fully participate in the economic, political, and social spheres of American democracy. At the Ford Foundation, the emphasis on juvenile delinquency was symptomatic of the triumph of this model. Inside the social science research community, the foundations enabled behaviorist perspectives to dominate, defining the institutional landscape of the country's research and its ties to the power elites, while backing explanations of poverty as the result of pathologies that were of "cultural" origin.

Such hegemony paved the way to the dominant hypothesis in the early 1960s of a distinct culture of poverty—pathological behavioral patterns that reproduce poverty from one generation to the next. If sociologist E. Franklin Frazier and social psychologist already used it in the interwar years to analyze the migration of African Americans, it was Oscar Lewis's major works on Mexican and Puerto Ricans that transformed it into a major lens through which to look at the poor. Interestingly, Lewis himself was surprised by its popularity and the fact that it was initially a way to describe poverty in an underdeveloped country, not in the land of plenty. For the poverty community, such behavioral analysis was both an intellectual challenge and a political curse as it modified the explanation of the poverty paradox. It became all the more necessary to construct a different view that focused more on income than on pathology. The time for a new "Wisconsin idea" had come.[36]

3

The New Wisconsin Idea

In 1950, the historian Merle Curti spoke to a group of students about the Golden Age at the University of Wisconsin, warmly recalling animated debates about social issues on the campus earlier in the century. The university archivist, Charles McCarthy, had characterized his "idea" of the university and its place in the American political landscape in 1912 as collaboration between universities, politicians, and union leaders to solve the problems of the working class. As research director of the Committee on Industrial Relations under John Commons, McCarthy had founded the academic field of labor relations and its commitment to place knowledge at the service of society. Such ambition aimed at using existing judicial and institutional frameworks to help regulate labor conflicts and contractualize labor relations.[1]

In 1932, with the critical support of Commons, Edwin Witte, Harold Groves, and Elizabeth Brandeis Raushenbush, the state of Wisconsin implemented the Wisconsin Workmen's Compensation Act, a safety net that guaranteed workers certain rights and anticipated New Deal legislation such as the Social Security Act and the Wagner Act of 1935. The Wisconsin Idea had begun to take hold throughout country because of its novel approach to labor relations. In the 1950s, it had become mainstream politics. The famous Treaty of Detroit signed between Walter Reuther's United Auto Workers and General Motors epitomized such hegemony. For many postwar liberals, industrial democracy was then part of the American way of life.[2]

In concluding his speech, however, Curti urged his young audience to carry the torch of the university's idea, a mission for which the times proved propitious. Robert J. Lampman, a young economist trained by major figures in Wisconsin, agreed with Curti that such an idea was more a principle of reform than a mere treaty or collective bargaining argument—it was a way of remedying the nation's inequalities. Contrary to what many of his fellow economists believed, the elimination of poverty was not part of the postwar American consensus. As a consequence, Lampman focused on income redistribution and tried to make sense of the poverty paradox of persistent poverty in an otherwise affluent society. Solving it was the new Wisconsin Idea. Industrial democracy was not enough; eliminating poverty was necessary.[3]

Robert Lampman and the Wisconsin School

Born in 1921, Lampman was from Plover, in central Wisconsin, and was raised in the progressive atmosphere that prevailed at the turn of the century. His father was a teacher and devout Methodist with an appreciation for history and science that he passed on to his son. As the first family member to attend college, Robert naturally gravitated toward the main campus of the University of Wisconsin at Madison, where he was an active participant in campus life.

He joined the Young Men's Christian Association and the American Student Union, and he was openly pacifist and advocated for social reform. During a holiday trip to the South, he saw firsthand the dire consequences of the 1929 crash and the violent conditions of segregation. His studies of philosophy under Max Otto, a pragmatist influenced by William James and John Dewey, furthered the development of his social and existential thinking, even if he was ultimately more attracted to economics. The powerful teaching styles and social consciences of Selig Perlman and Edwin Witte also made a lasting impression on the young Lampman, and he befriended Elizabeth Brandeis Raushenbush, who became a lifelong influence on his thought and career. The daughter of the progressive reformer Louis Brandeis, who inspired so many New Dealers, Raushenbush served on the University of Wisconsin faculty for forty-two years, following in her father's footsteps in perceiving research as defined by social commitment. An eminent presence in the economics department throughout the 1940s, she provided a bridge between the John Commons era and the rising young guard, among whom Lampman was considered among the most promising.[4]

After obtaining his bachelor's degree in 1942, he served as an air navigator in the U.S. Naval Reserve, first in the Aleutian Islands and later in a Florida-based training squadron. After the war, the citizen-soldier benefited from the GI Bill's provisions and decided to resume his studies at the University of Wisconsin. His doctoral dissertation was supervised by

Figure 3.1. Robert J. Lampman with his flight crew in Alaska in 1944 (third on the right at the forefront). Courtesy of Institute for Research on Poverty.

Perlman and Witte and was completed in 1950. His study examined the conditions for implementing collective bargaining in a particular profession and was fully consistent with the institutional model established by his peers. Armed with a new doctorate, Lampman accepted an assistant professorship at the University of Washington.[5]

While Lampman was substitute teaching for a colleague, he stumbled on information about applying nationwide survey methods to the question of income distribution, a subject that had previously received little attention from Wisconsin economists. Lampman decided to investigate the causes of unequal income distribution by exploring correlations between wealth and family size. He was specifically interested in understanding to what extent higher levels of family fertility exacerbated unequal income distribution. Although the question seemed simple, a variety of answers had been proposed over the years by demographers, social workers, and home economists. Paradoxically, economists have tended to ignore such microeconomic questions, and it is difficult to this day to find accurate data on wealth distribution in the United States. Only the National Bureau of Economic Research (NBER), directed at the time by Simon Kuznets, had attempted to build the database needed to address income-related questions.[6]

Simon Kuznets was originally from Pinsk, a Polish city under Russian control at the time of his birth in 1901, and he studied statistics and economics at the Kharkov Commercial Institute. He worked for the statistics bureau of the new communist government in Russia before moving to Poland in 1921 and immigrated to the United States with his family the following year. He completed a dissertation on cyclical economic fluctuations at Columbia University under Wesley Mitchell. Thanks to Mitchell's influence as its first president, Kuznets joined the NBER, where he conducted research while teaching at the University of Pennsylvania. Kuznets inspired a generation of students, civil servants, and academics throughout the 1930s and 1940s to develop the methodological tools needed to gather and analyze statistics on national income distribution.[7]

Despite Kuznets's scientific and institutional status as president of the American Economic Association, Lampman was highly critical of his analyses of changes in the income curve since the 1930s. According to Kuznets, a "social revolution" in the country during the World War II had triggered a drop in the share of national income held by the richest segment of the population between 1939 and 1948 because of stress on the nation's large fortunes between 1914 and 1945. This phenomenon was part of a global historical shift, with income inequality distributed along a ∩-shaped curve. The curve initially rose under the influence of the agricultural and industrial revolutions, followed by a period of stabilization and a subsequent descending phase. Kuznets contended that the United States had been following this pattern since the end of the nineteenth century by using the tax system to transfer government-sponsored social expenditures.[8]

Lampman was skeptical of the assertion that reduced inequality was inevitable. He argued that increased wealth had in fact not produced more equitably distributed income. Although he did not contest the fact that overall per capita income had increased, he complained that the unreliability of Kuznets's data and procedures—and specifically the weakness of the instruments that were the basis of his calculations—skewed his results. It was true that the only data available to Kuznets came from the limited information from the United Kingdom and Germany used for his 1953 study. Lampman also had reservations about Kuznets's method of calculating revenue, which he defined only as earned income, adjusting the total national income reported by the Commerce Department by using a range of different variables. According to Lampman, this led Kuznets to underestimate capital gains and the role of occasional income in the overall increase in family revenues. As a consequence, he criticized the causes of these changes that Kuznets cited, pointing to a lack of evidence that taxes and social assistance had benefited the poorest of households. Recent studies by the economist Joseph Pechman had reinforced his point by showing that the system primarily helped the middle classes.[9]

While he did not offer a solution to these criticisms, Lampman maintained that a more nuanced approach would be required to substantiate the claim that inequality was diminishing. He published an article in the *American Economic Review* explaining his views that predictably ensured his notoriety among his fellow economists. Based on the belief that he shared with the Wisconsin economist a similar view of how economics could be applied to social issues, Kuznets invited Lampman to participate in a seminar at the NBER that would enable him to refine his arguments. Lampman accepted the invitation, and Kuznets redoubled his

Figure 3.2. Robert J. Lampman reading the *American Economic Review* (1956). Courtesy of the Institute for Research on Poverty.

efforts to comprehend how categories used to analyze the different components of annual income could be rendered more precise. Because the NBER focused on research on both the richest and the poorest populations, Kuznets asked Lampman to supervise a study of the highest income bracket. Lampman continued to refine his earlier analyses, demonstrating that his position complemented that of Kuznets: "Our finding that the share of wealth held by the top two per cent of families fell from about 33 per cent to 29 per cent from 1922 to 1953, or by about one-eight, would seem to be not incompatible with Kuznets' findings and with the general belief that there has been some lessening of economic inequality in the United States in recent decades. Wealth distribution appears to have changed less than income distribution during this period." This gap led Lampman to concentrate on the question of income equality as the core of his future research. When he left the research center, he found a position at the University of Wisconsin, where he discovered that the dynamic environment that he had experienced there earlier had become far more sedate.[10]

The University of Wisconsin at a Crossroads

Actually, when Robert Lampman returned to the Wisconsin campus, he was struck by the sharply diminished profile of the social sciences. Despite repeated efforts to reorganize themselves, the university's social scientists had been unable to revive the earlier academic excitement. This was partly from the ostracism of the social sciences by the National Science Foundation that reduced funding to only a small fraction of the total university research budget. The total 1951–52 budget of the Department of Sociology and Anthropology came to $13,900, while economics received only $8,636. Even this meager funding mostly paid for teaching—77 percent for sociology and anthropology and 100 percent for economics—with a mere 10 percent of the economics budget allocated for research. By contrast, only 40 percent of the budget of the Department of Biochemistry was allocated to teaching, a ratio that prevailed in the other natural sciences. This scientific dichotomy was exacerbated by the Alumni Foundation, which regarded the social sciences with deep suspicion and almost exclusively supported the hard sciences.[11]

An interdisciplinary committee of campus social scientists issued a highly critical, pessimistic report on the state of the social sciences at Wisconsin in 1948. The report listed fourteen critical problems ranging from poor funding and a lack of fund-raising strategies and a dearth of doctoral programs. The committee recommended that a steering committee be established to promote the social sciences within the university, but a number of academics resisted, preferring to increase the power of the university's Social Sciences Division. Entrenched opposition and a lack of administrative support contributed to the failure of this initiative, creating the impression that the university's earlier penchant for social science innovation had been permanently stifled. A Social Sciences Research Committee was eventually formed in 1951, but it failed to generate adequate support either inside or outside the university.[12]

By the late 1950s, a generational changing of the guard among the faculty and the administration began to transform attitudes toward the sciences at the university. Fred Harvey Harrington, who became university vice president in 1958, was to play a key role in improving the outlook for the social sciences. Harrington's ambition was to transform the university into a purveyor of ideas to help the nation's political forces demonstrate the superiority of the American model in the context of the Cold War. He invited the faculty to revive the university's traditional strengths in the social sciences so that Wisconsin could distinguish itself from other universities that were more focused on national defense and the hard sciences. The economics department modified its approach to support this shift.[13]

Economists had become aware since earlier in the decade that the institutional model developed between the wars by the earlier generation of Wisconsin economists was no longer relevant. The 1929 crisis and the spread of Keynesianism had further rendered their thinking mainstream. The Ivy League universities benefited greatly from the Keynesian Revolution, however, and particularly Harvard and Yale, which had helped spread John Maynard Keynes's ideas. In this spirit, the department chair, Edwin Young, implemented curricular reforms requiring doctoral courses in statistics and mathematics. He also recruited young faculty members, among them Robert Lampman. He pinned particular hopes on a new arrival named Guy Orcutt, an economist who left the prestigious Harvard campus to move to the University of Wisconsin, an academic change typical of Orcutt's unusual career path.[14]

There was little in his origins to suggest that Orcutt, born in suburban Detroit in 1917, would become one of the most innovative economists of his time. Fascinated by science from a young age and a born tinkerer—his father was an executive at Alkali, a major electric utility company in Michigan—he dreamed of a career in electrical engineering. Like Elmer Sperry, he was passionate about electrical systems and simulation models, a passion encouraged by his early university experiences. After he had developed an appreciation for basic research and a growing interest in philosophy and logic, however, the 1929 crisis compelled him to turn away from the natural sciences. This was confirmed in 1939 during a two-month stay at a Quaker summer camp in West Virginia that showed him the misery caused by the crisis, an experience that increased his interest in economics.

Orcutt subsequently joined the graduate program in economics at the University of Michigan, where he wrote a dissertation, completed in 1944, that applied statistical procedures and instruments to a search for the "natural" laws of economics. His study laid the foundations for the still-embryonic field of econometrics, and Orcutt joined the faculty at the Massachusetts Institute of Technology, where he continued to refine his statistical regression methodology as part of a research group led by George Wadsworth of the Department of Mathematics. The group collaborated with the U.S. Army to develop a weather forecasting system for the Allied armies. Orcutt then took his expanding theoretical and technical expertise to the Institute of Applied Studies in Cambridge, where he worked under the benevolent reign of John Maynard Keynes. At Cambridge, Orcutt continued to refine his theoretical positions and published a foundational article on economic simulations and the need for reliable data-processing systems to define the mechanisms underlying the economy.[15]

This mathematical and strategic shift in the field of economics continued after the end of the war, as exemplified by studies sponsored by the Cowles Commission, which was founded in June 1949. Conducted by a group of military experts and the RAND Corporation under Tjalling Koopmans, the Cowles studies promoted a view of economics as a rational, objective science that could apprehend and anticipate the activities of economic actors. Orcutt's approach was heavily influenced by this holistic vision, which gained further impetus from the burgeoning revolution in information technology. As a professor at Harvard from 1948 to 1958, he helped create a technology center for New England universities that was funded by IBM and that made IBM 704 computers available to academic researchers. With the help of these second-generation computers and a grant from the Ford Foundation, Orcutt developed a computerized simulation of the demographic and social behaviors of 10,358 individual members of 4,580 families over a ten-year period. Such microeconomic models finally made it possible to describe macroeconomic mechanisms. This was of great importance to the field, because in the absence of simulations, researchers were forced to construct models without full knowledge of their constituent elements. Orcutt encouraged economists not to limit themselves to government statistics, which were too general and macroeconomic in focus, an insightful view that was confirmed during a stint working for the board of directors of the Federal Reserve System between 1954 and 1955.[16]

The University of Wisconsin offered Orcutt support for a completely independent center for basic research that Lampman labeled the "Manhattan Project" of the economics. In 1959, the Social Systems Research

Institute (SSRI) was founded, with funding from the university as well as external sources such as the Ford Foundation, the Brookings Institution, the NBER, and the Russell Sage Foundation. With a 1963 operating budget of a million dollars, the institute included sixty-seven researchers from eleven University of Wisconsin departments. As an economist, Lampman was deeply gratified by the creation of the SSRI, which he envisioned as a crucible for the new Wisconsin Idea.[17]

Recasting the Wisconsin Idea

Immediately after accepting his job at the University of Wisconsin, Robert Lampman energetically embraced an approach conceived of as a reaction to postwar economists' cautiousness that Elizabeth Brandeis Raushenbush labeled "action research." For the American Economic Association, Lampman organized a series of roundtables on the question of capitalism and income distribution. In a choice he deplored, more and more economists declined to take a position on such questions, arguing that the theoretical reasoning behind equality studies was grounded in fallacies and inspired by outdated ideology. This rhetorical stance among his colleagues enabled them to avoid being politicized, a position that Lampman criticized as somewhat facile. Economists' treatment of taxation perfectly illustrates their perennial procrastination on the issue of equality, and many of them simply refused to frame the discussion around the real effectiveness of progressive taxation as a mechanism for redirecting income toward the nation's poorest inhabitants. The idea of a postwar fiscal consensus was an easy way out.

In his view, economics was imprisoned by a professional ethic of objectivity that had been the central tenet of the field since its origins in the late nineteenth century. In the post-McCarthy era, he saw this presumption of neutrality as having mutated into a form of political conservatism that undermined research throughout the field of economics. The Wisconsin economist firmly believed that professional responsibility could be reconciled with political commitment, and he called on his fellow scientists to transcend the "factual level, which is doubtless the level on which the contemporary generation of social scientists has made its most distinctive contribution."[18]

In adopting this perspective, he hoped to discover the fundamental causes of inequality and to go beyond professional and political issues to grasp the essence of the social contract that binds humankind. To take up the social question meant obeying moral and humanistic imperatives that legitimized action: "Finally, interest in economic equalization will diminish if it is believed that further equalization will lead away from rather than toward the 'something more' than equality, namely, the dreams of fraternity and mutual respect which evoke man's deepest responses. Only as these conditions are met with the traditional concern with 'equality and all that be set at rest."[19] In short, Lampman's plan was to measure the poverty paradox in such a way as to defuse potential political controversy. At its incipient stage, the new Wisconsin idea was a moral imperative.

His approach synthesized the different currents of thought that had circulated since earlier in the century at the University of Wisconsin. From the beginnings of the Wisconsin school, when Max Lorenz became one of the first theoreticians to support efforts to measure income distribution at the turn of the century, he borrowed an emphasis on measurement and income transfer. Although Lorenz's 1905 dissertation study at Wisconsin had focused on the economics of the railways, he owed his reputation to the curve that he used to calculate equality of income distribution. The John Commons generation also influenced Lampman, who adopted their emphasis on prevention and finding a solution to the working-class question that would use an institutional safety net to insure workers against the cyclical and structural ups and downs associated with industrialization. In the context of postwar economic growth, however, he believed that the labor question had been solved by New Deal labor policy, notably the Wagner Act. As a consequence, he narrowed his research to low-income people. All the more since the so-called Eisenhower Recession, which started in 1957, put poverty at the forefront. In a few months, unemployment rose above 6 percent and the crisis accelerated plant closures. In such a difficult context, many poor people decided to migrate in search of a decent living.[20]

Lampman framed his research questions around practical ways of limiting income disparities. In his view, three institutions—labor unions, families, and the government—had historically struggled to regulate social inequality. Lampman believed that the American social contract based on free enterprise and recognition of the right to unionize had reached a point of equilibrium after the war in terms of the redistributing wage-based income. However, a recent report from the Roosevelt Foundation, written by Eleanor Snyder, showed the current difficulties for workers in the very low-income bracket.[21]

To bolster her statistical data, Snyder contacted Ida Merriam and Lenore Epstein of the Social Security Administration's Bureau of Research and Statistics (BRS). With their assistance, she drafted a report that once again raised the specter of the poverty paradox—persistent, widespread poverty despite strong economic growth. The study sample consisted of fifty-seven hundred families and fourteen hundred individuals who lived alone. Snyder showed that only 3 percent of the working-class population had an income below two thousand dollars and were employed full time in New York, but that the results rose to 36 percent for the occasionally employed; for the unemployed, the percentage came to a staggering 81 percent. Snyder's study broke with the objectivist methodology of the social science community, and she expressed impatience with the statistical alibi for objectivity routinely cited by economists: "During the next decade I would hope that economists and social investigators will not continue to be handicapped by lack of quantitative data concerning the interrelations between poverty and the distribution of incomes, in terms of employment and labor force status of individuals as family members." Snyder's study confirmed for Lampman that something went wrong for the people in the lower income brackets.[22]

Faithful to the Wisconsin tradition of distrusting unions, however, he complained about unions' conservatism and their inability to promote true income distribution not solely linked to their own interests: "Trade-unionism may be characterized as a reaction to or protest against market direction's threats to well-established differentials in income. It is typically an exclusive movement aimed at giving preference to 'regular' workers and those having seniority. . . . It should be borne in mind that union members are, generally speaking, in the upper half of the income distribution." The postwar contract and the creation of the American Federation of Labor and Congress of Industrial Organizations in 1955 only reinforced such trends.[23]

Since the 1929 crisis, families had lost the ability to help family members who were in short-term difficulty, and deep structural changes in the 1940s, including internal migration, urbanization, and suburbanization, had further weakened family networks' ability to respond to hard times. Between 1940 and 1960 more than three million black men and women moved from the South to northern cities. In Chicago, for example, as Lampman observed, the number of African Americans and poor whites from Appalachia increased in the 1950s. All faced the hostility of Chicagoans. The Appalachian migrants were compared in *The Chicago Tribune* to "a plague of locusts." Beyond moral arguments, Lampman was interested with social and economic factors that explain the poverty of all these groups.[24]

Only the federal government, with its aid and social assistance programs, had the capacity to redistribute income. Yet monthly payments to welfare families were extremely low, especially in the South. They still averaged only one hundred dollars a month. Even though they had increased since World War II, Social Security benefits were also not enough to lift poor people out of poverty. A retired female worker living alone was paid only $626 a year. The moderate expansion of social policies under Dwight D. Eisenhower convinced Lampman that it was necessary to rethink the country's social safety net.[25]

As he carried out his research, he was joined by intellectuals and politicians who also questioned the social and economic policies of the Republican administration. The poverty issue reached new circles. Early in 1957, a left-wing economist named Gabriel Kolko published an article titled "The American 'Income Revolution'" in *Dissent*. Tapping statistics from the poverty community, especially the Bureau of Labor Statistics, the article debunked the myth of the Kuznets curve. Led by Leon Keyserling and Mary Dublin Keyserling, a pamphlet was published by the Conference on Economic Progress in May 1957. The "Eisenhower Recession" transformed the question of depressed areas into a more important question on the extent of poverty in the affluent nation.[26]

Such critical views, however, were still marginal. The extraordinary success of John Kenneth Galbraith's book *The Affluent Society* (1958) reinforced the idea that the world of economic growth and personal affluence was the one virtually all Americans experienced.

The Galbraith Challenge

John Kenneth Galbraith was the archetype of—and even a prototype for—the postwar liberal economist. Galbraith was born in Ontario, the son of a Canadian farmer who was part of a very active agrarian movement and a prominent local figure whose son inherited his interest in agriculture. A brilliant student, Galbraith earned a scholarship to study agricultural economics at Berkeley, where he later held a position as a professor. In 1934, he accepted an offer from Harvard, a geographical shift as well as a theoretical change because he discovered John Maynard Keynes's work, which was beginning to be taken seriously. Galbraith joined Alvin Hansen, Seymour Harris, and Paul Samuelson in transforming the Harvard economics department into a springboard for Keynesianism.[27]

After the war ended, Galbraith committed himself to supporting the Democratic Party, eventually serving as adviser to Adlai Stevenson in the latter's 1956 bid for the presidency. *The Affluent Society* was published two years later and rapidly became a bestseller. Galbraith assailed the "conventional beliefs" of postwar liberals that caused them to support the idea of growth as an absolute panacea. Although Lampman tended to share Galbraith's doubts about this unbridled faith in growth, he took issue with Galbraith's representation of poverty, which he deemed to be no different from the liberal perspective that Galbraith was criticizing. There was something quite ironic in Galbraith's book. In the first place, it was financed by a Carnegie Corporation grant to explain the postwar poverty paradox; in the end, it contributed to strongly underestimating such a paradox and to putting responsibility on poor people's shoulders.[28]

In Galbraith's modern, affluent America, a poor person was at best apathetic and at worst asocial. In his opening paragraphs, he referred to American poverty as an "afterthought" and a "special case." His methodology also drew criticism because he used the absolutely lowest-available estimate of the poverty threshold, one thousand dollars, which had been set by Eisenhower's Council of Economic Advisers in 1955. He ultimately represented poverty somewhat traditionally as a residual phenomenon on a path toward inevitable disappearance. This perception of the poor as an ever-diminishing minority was reinforced by the categories that he employed to divide the poor into isolated cases or specific social domains, such as "case poverty," in which poor people were mentally or socially defective, and "insular poverty," which concerned people in depressed areas who refused to migrate to better places. Although he deplored poverty from a moral and political point of view, Galbraith subscribed to the view that the poor were a permanent residual population in a society defined by abundance: "To put the matter another way, the concern for inequality had vitality only so long as the many suffered privation while a few had much. It did not survive as a burning issue in a time when the many had much even though others had much more. It is our misfortune that when inequality declined as an issue, the slate was not left clean."[29]

Inspired by Thorstein Veblen's theory of the leisure class and its attack on "conspicuous consumption," Galbraith thought that poverty had lost political traction because of the appeal of mass consumption for the middle class. He proposed instead a program of investment in human capital that would prevent the hereditary transmission of poverty while integrating the poor more effectively into the nation's "vital core." Galbraith's book provoked a strong reaction. Lampman saw it as a form of resignation based upon a false method of categorizing the poor. Underlying Galbraith's approach, the Wisconsin economist detected an ambivalence common among economists, whom he believed systematically dissociated cognitive reasoning from practicality whenever the subject of inequality in a capitalist society was broached. The poverty paradox proved that Galbraith wrote an overtly optimistic book that gave a biased view of poverty.[30]

Lampman's Poverty Charts

To avoid having his new research endeavors confined to the academic ivory tower and to respond to Galbraith's overly optimistic view of the country, Lampman agreed to an invitation from Democratic senator Paul Douglas of Illinois to draft a report on the living conditions of low-income families for Congress's Joint Economic Committee (JEC).

Douglas, who was also an economist, was among the more prominent Congress members and was strongly committed to social and economic issues. Douglas had grown up in near-poverty conditions in rural Maine and worked his way through Bowdoin College before attending Columbia University, where he eventually earned a PhD in economics in 1921. Most of his academic career was spent in the interwar University of Chicago economics department. He published extensively and established himself as a leading labor economist and policy intellectual in articles and in books that included *Wages and the Family* (1925), *Real Wages in the United States* (1930), *Standards of Unemployment Insurance* (1933), and *The Theory of Wages* (1934).[31]

After World War II, Douglas was particularly concerned with depressed areas that proved resistant to economic growth. Under the chairmanship of Douglas, the JEC commissioned studies on the consumption of Americans and "low-income families," the euphemism devised to designate poor families. It became a place where researchers of the poverty community and reformers started to regularly meet and set up different poverty lines. In 1949, Ida Merriam and Dorothy Brady participated in hearings that led a study of poor people in the nation. In its final report, the committee set the poverty threshold at two thousand dollars and confirmed another report's conclusion that 10.5 million American families were living below the poverty threshold. Two low-income family populations were identified—one consisting of families who received welfare but lacked an employed head of household and a second group whose wages were too low.[32]

The following year, the JEC decided to collect case studies that would give a "human face" to low-income families. The poverty threshold used for the study was two thousand dollars and was based on self-reports from this nonrandom sample to describe the participants' difficulties in "making ends meet." Eventually, in 1955, the JEC corroborated the reality of the poverty paradox. Lenore Epstein, a member of the Social Security Administration, contributed by helping determine the major characteristics of families with income below one thousand dollars. Despite the growing economy, the number of poor remained essentially stable with an estimated 3.7 million families (and an additional 4.4 million individuals) below the one-thousand-dollar income level. Selma Goldsmith described the nature of poverty associated with this threshold level, arguing that low-income families simply did not benefit from economic growth. In order to transcend this category-based representation of poverty, the committee adopted a higher threshold, particularly because the one-thousand- dollar level had been cited in a recent publication by President Eisenhower's Council of Economic Advisers. Using this new definition of the poverty level, it was estimated that 8.3 million families and 6.2 million Americans were living in poverty.[33]

In 1958, searching for new ideas to strengthen a possible bid for the 1960 Democratic presidential nomination, the then Illinois senator Douglas asked Lampman to use the report to refute the optimistic arguments contained in John Kenneth Galbraith's 1958 book, *The Affluent Society*.

The resulting report drew on the work of a number of economists and was written under the benevolent guidance of Edwin Witte and Elizabeth Brandeis Raushenbush. They all agreed with the Wisconsin economist that Galbraith made a false description of the poverty issue by contending that the low-income population persisted because the poor were either unable or unwilling to leave regions with traditional economies that were being left behind by economic modernization. He cited individual factors such as mental illness, alcoholism, a lack of education, apathy, and having too many children to explain "profound poverty." The idea of poverty as voluntary flowed from ancient prejudices that made a distinction between the "deserving" poor, whose impoverishment is involuntary, from others whose conditions were of their own making. In Lampman's view, Galbraith belonged to this tradition and, as a consequence, tended to vastly oversimplify the complexity and variety of the causes of poverty.

Defining a poverty threshold was the crucial first step. Because his graduate studies had taken place between the wars, Lampman acknowledged that he was unversed in statistics at the time, even in "descriptive" statistics. He decided to define poverty by collapsing two institutional definitions: the monetary definition used by the Commerce Department and the Census Bureau, and the family budget approach of the Bureau of Labor Statistics (BLS). The inadequacy of either method when applied independently was underscored by the significant differences in their estimates of the number of Americans living below the poverty line, with the BLS assigning 36 percent of Americans to the low-income bracket, and the Commerce Department estimating that the figure was as low as 13 percent. Lampman opted for the Census Bureau estimate of 19 percent as a compromise, adding an additional adjustment by using BLS family data from a 1949 budget study that estimated the basic annual income of a family of four as twenty-five hundred dollars. This combined approach allowed Lampman to posit a benchmark poverty threshold that could complement Census Bureau income distribution estimates.[34]

These rudimentary statistics enabled him to estimate that in 1959, 19 million families—some 32.2 million Americans—were living below the poverty threshold. By basing this estimate on aggregate data from the entire country, Lampman had given a name to the social issue that he wanted to cure, and poverty would forever after be perceived as an inescapable national reality. In another break with time-honored practices, even among social reformers, he defined poverty as an "involuntary" phenomenon that was the product of a statistical interaction between six major variables: age, geographical location, ethnicity, jobs, household structure, and educational level.

This scientific approach represented an effort to defuse the political controversy surrounding the poverty phenomenon. Specifically, the data showed that out of a total of 32.2 million poor Americans, 8 million were over sixty-five, and 6.4 million were African Americans. Education and family status were also important factors, with 8 million poor Americans living in single-parent families and 21 million having no education beyond elementary school. Lampman's estimates also showed that 30 percent of poor families lived in rural conditions and that slow economic development was a factor in 40 percent of the South being categorized as poor. More than 70 percent of the poor thus matched at least one of six variables, to which he added others that he described as purely "descriptive."[35]

Unlike studies from earlier in the century that had emphasized individual responsibility for poverty, the Lampman report directly correlated poverty with a cluster of sexual, racial, geographical, professional,

TABLE 3.1. Lampman's poverty charts (1959)

Characteristics	Low-income population	Low-income population	Total population
Total	32.2 million	100%	100%
Aged 65 and over	8 million	25%	8.5%
Nonwhite	6.4 million	20%	10%
Female head of household	8 million	25%	10%
Educated head of household	21.4 million	67%	45%
Rural residence	8 million	25%	10%
Unemployed head of household	11 million	33%	16%
Nonqualified head of household	7 million	21%	25%
Family size (6 and above)	11.2 million	34%	23%
Individuals living alone	4.4 million	16%	6%
Children	11 million	33%	33%

Source: Robert Lampman, *The Low Income Population and Economic Growth*, Study Paper no. 12, Joint Economic Committee, U.S. Congress (Washington, DC: U.S. Government Printing Office, 1959), 12.

familial, and educational variables against the backdrop of widespread abundance in American society. He also gave comparatively lower prominence to economic and employment issues.

One nagging question remained: Why did poverty persist in spite of strong postwar economic growth? Although the raw percentage of low-income families had dropped from 26 percent in 1947 to 19 percent in 1957, and even assuming sustained growth, Lampman projected that in 1977, between 10 percent and 12 percent of the total population would still be poor. In contrast to Kuznets's findings, Lampman's conclusions found that poverty stubbornly resisted periods of economic prosperity. Searching for an explanation for this phenomenon of resistance, Lampman identified three factors that impeded efforts to reduce poverty: family size, age of head of household, and change of profession. In the case of family size, he tempered the latent Malthusianism of some earlier studies by showing that poverty was not automatically correlated with the number of children in a household. Conversely, two factors appeared to help families rise out of poverty: rural flight and professional mobility. Unlike what was seen in the position that was common even among liberals, the poor were thus capable of both autonomy and action, as illustrated by patterns of internal migration. Indeed, between 1947 and 1957, the number of people living in rural conditions plummeted from 6.5 million to 4.8 million as a result of rural flight. Urban migration was more common among the young, who preferred exodus and travel in search of work to the social and political aridity of the countryside. This youthful geographical mobility also helped explain the high proportion of the elderly who remained mired in the low-income bracket.[36]

In delineating these variables, Lampman had also moved closer shifted in the direction of a political insight according to which certain large groups would inevitably be left behind by prosperity, as well as a corollary that a policy to support economic growth would be unable to ensure prosperity for the entire population. By extension, it was clear that the only way to help groups left behind by economic growth was to improve upon the New Deal notion of safety nets to more effectively bring about income redistribution. Drawing on the findings of Selma Goldsmith's Commerce Department study, Lampman complemented his own conclusions during his National Bureau of Economic Research internship three years earlier.

Although inequality in income distribution had decreased over the previous twenty years, the evolution of capital gains revealed that the distribution of wealth remained as unequal as it had ever been. In other words, a viable political program would be to maintain the cap on capital gains established in the 1930s while using fiscal policies to improve the way in which wealth was distributed, using the proceeds of progressive taxation strategies to fund educational and social programs with the potential to break the cycle of poverty. As Lampman insisted, monetary transfers to the poor had increased from 1 percent of national income to 5 percent in the span of thirty years, a contribution that needed to be more accurately directed toward vulnerable populations, especially the elderly and single mothers.[37]

The Lampman report, which came out in 1959, was the first public attempt to measure the poverty paradox. Although it represented a crude statistical blend, it was a historically significant attempt to interpret and synthesize the growing body of research by the poverty community. In spite of Galbraith's optimistic portrayal, the poverty population was still large in the country.

Poverty in the Affluent Society

During the 1950s, which are often described as a period of profound intellectual conformism, an unorthodox idea emerged in academic circles that poverty stubbornly persisted even in the heart of America the Prosperous. The University of Wisconsin's tradition of expertise on social matters played an important role in the development of this new science of poverty. In 1959, economist Robert Lampman was the first member of the poverty community to publish statistics outside the offices of universities and federal agencies.

Although his work was not entirely innovative and often synthesized the research of other poverty researchers, it was a critical moment because he dared to apply labels to ideas and issues that had hitherto been unnamed. At the risk of scientific oversimplification, the Wisconsin economist immersed himself in an effort to define and measure poverty using monetary data while also refusing to become mired in the petty theoretical debates. More important, his work signaled a turning point that made politically committed social science a very real possibility. Paradoxically, Galbraith's *The Affluent Society* sparked a public debate precisely because it tended to downplay poverty. The "Eisenhower Recession" also contributed to enlarge the circles of people interested in the poverty question. It was time for the poverty community to go beyond the myth of an affluent society.

4

Beyond the Affluent Society

By the late 1950s, poverty researchers had begun to consider John Kenneth Galbraith's best-selling book *The Affluent Society* (1958) simultaneously as a challenge and a curse. Inside the poverty community, many feared that the public could be easily misled by Galbraith's optimistic portrayal of the United States, which Robert Lampman called an "illusion" that he hoped "the profession [would] set out to correct." Furthermore, the book came out at a time when public references to poverty were limited to accusations that welfare recipients were cheating. If the country was an affluent society, there was a huge major problem—how could the steady growth in the number of welfare applicants be explained? In Detroit; New Orleans; and Newburgh, New York, to name just a few cities, attacks against chiselers ran high. Public officials defended themselves by contending that taxpayers did not want to support immorality and laziness. How otherwise explain the rise of numbers of people on welfare since the early 1950s? At the end of the decade, as a growing restlessness was bubbling beneath the surface of American society, the poverty paradox became a political issue.[1]

In the context of the fledgling civil rights movement and the decline of McCarthyism, many researchers were prone to go beyond their discrete numeral and statistical work. Upon the influence of social workers, human and personal factors were added to understand the causes of poverty. Such analysis aimed at deemphasizing both the moral responsibility of individuals and the importance of cultural factors. The poverty paradox had its origins in a tangle of social, psychological, and economic factors. By attacking the "mystique of the culture of poverty," the social worker Alvin Schorr followed this path and urged his fellow citizens to go beyond the most prevalent myth of the 1950s—an affluent society for everybody.[2]

Alvin Schorr: From Social Work to Family Issues

In 1933, Frank Bruno, dean of the School of Social Work at Saint Louis University, delivered a speech at the National Conference of Social Work about the impact of the 1929 crash on social workers. In his talk, he argued that recent economic changes had redefined what it meant to be poor for both poor people themselves and individuals in charge of helping them: "It was the experience of defeat, the emotional frustration, the unrewarded effort . . . to gain a foothold upon the slippery industrial banks, which finally broke their spirit. . . . And as if that were not enough, we have erected . . . a condition of eligibility for relief which still further convinces them that struggle is useless." By then, Bruno was a major figure in the field of social work, both as an administrator and as a teacher. As one of his students a few years later, Alvin Schorr heeded Bruno's message by becoming a social worker.[3]

From his earliest years, subsisting on a federal pension for single mothers that was created in 1910 had made Schorr intimately familiar with the workings of the welfare system. Despite occasional hard times, he enrolled at the local university as an English major, developing a strong sense of social justice after the 1929 crisis and, as president of the university student union, rallying for peace and vocally supporting Roosevelt's New Deal. After briefly working for the National Youth Administration—a New Deal program for college students—he enrolled at the School of Social

Work at Saint Louis University in 1941, a complicated career choice in part because, at the time, social work was considered a low-prestige occupation. His mother even tried to warn him against "poorly-paid women's work," a very common gendered misconception of the profession.[4]

Social workers faced a quandary that forced them to adapt to economic upheaval while continuing to pursue an individual-psychological approach to treating poverty. Since the 1920s, the psychological approach had dominated more socially oriented views. That ascendancy was influenced by the "Bible" of a generation of social work students and professionals, Virginia Robinson's book *A Changing Psychology in Social Work* (1934). Robinson contended that the human relationship between patient and social worker afforded patients the greatest degree of autonomy and freedom of expression. *The Compass*, the journal of the American Association of Social Workers, took a similar position.[5]

The financial crisis unleashed by the Great Depression forced the entire profession to support the New Deal, despite contradictions between social work practices and certain federal subsidies and policies. These contradictions generated vocal dissent among a number of social workers, including Mary Van Kleeck, who became the spokesperson for protests against Roosevelt's programs. Van Kleeck charged that some programs were too conservative and primarily intended to generate votes. She also resisted a narrow view of social workers as mere assistants whose principal job was to help less fortunate citizens find work. Despite these controversies, social workers were ultimately able to retain control of Social Security Administration (SSA) welfare programs and to impose the idea that welfare was a right. In 1941, the very year Schorr picked up social work as a career, Jane Hoey, who was the director of the SSA's Bureau of Public Assistance (BPA) pushed social workers to defend it in every part of the country.[6]

During these turbulent times, Schorr completed his degree and worked in a series of positions for St. Louis County. He later worked as a psychiatrist for the Veterans Administration in New Jersey and as director of the Charitable Union of West Hazleton, Pennsylvania, before accepting a position as a family counselor, entering a field undergoing significant change. His diverse jobs gave him a firsthand experience of poverty and the complex relationship between welfare administrators and recipients. Schorr developed a taste for clinical fieldwork and openly expressed a lack of interest in research, publishing only two descriptive articles on services to migrant families. His opinion changed dramatically when in 1958 accepted a position as a family specialist with the Bureau of Research and Statistics (BRS), led by Ida Merriam.[7]

Gaps in his academic background led Schorr to pursue further training; as he put it, "Out of collegiality and, I suspected, anxiety that in some public statement I might embarrass them," people at the BRS gave me "as I went along a high-intensity if sporadic education in their specialties—particularly the proper use of statistics." After he had completed his statistical education, Schorr was asked to oversee a detailed study of the Aid to Dependent Children (ADC) program, which was one of the pillars of the nation's social welfare programs.[8]

ADC was managed by the BPA and attracted increasing attention from both researchers and the general public in the 1950s. The evolution of the program was critical in raising awareness of the poverty paradox, as the number of recipients steadily rose in spite of the increased prosperity of American society. In just five years, the number of recipients expanded from 2,041,000 in 1951 to 2,486,000. In 1952, a study conducted for the American Public Welfare Association by the University of North Carolina Institute for Social Sciences Research revealed some unexpectedly questionable side effects of the program, including the fact that families occasionally deliberately separated in order to be eligible for ADC payments. This increase contradicted the ADC founders' argument that welfare would gradually cease to be necessary. Arthur Altmeyer, one of the principal founders, had even boldly proclaimed in 1948 that the end of welfare programs was imminent. The blatant contrast between such claims and harsher social realities irritated politicians. In 1957, Winfield Denton, a Democratic representative from Indiana, questioned the directorship of the Department of Health, Education, and Welfare about growth in the ADC rolls, asking why the department's officials had assured him in 1951 that the end of welfare was near.[9]

When Schorr was beginning his study, ADC surpassed state aid for the elderly to become the nation's largest welfare program, provoking bitter debate about applicants' motivations and the incidence of fraud. Using data from a 1956 Bureau of Public Assistance survey, Schorr showed that 609,000 families received ADC payments, representing a total of over 2 million individuals—1,682,000 children and 539,000 adults—as well as an increase of 303,000 over what was found in a 1954 survey.

Schorr's conclusions—for example, that paternal absence resulting from death occurred in only 13 percent of families and from abandonment in only 22 percent, whereas divorce accounted for a mere 18 percent—were greeted with considerable consternation inside the SSA.[10]

Schorr's report was sharply critical of ADC's paradoxical effects on families that clearly undermined family cohesion from inside. Created after the 1929 crisis to keep single mothers from being compelled to go to work, the program was obviously poorly suited to the new prosperity and structural changes in women's employment. Schorr insisted on women's social isolation, even though he refused to blame them. With his inner knowledge of poverty, he tried to trace the origins of such deterioration and the reasons why the program failed for both welfare administrators and recipients. Increase in the number of welfare recipients' was met with public outcry, and ADC recipients became scapegoats, especially when they were contrasted with working fathers without federal subsidies struggling to support their children in intact families. For Schorr, the program had become obsolete and was not the modern piece of assistance that social workers envisioned twenty years ago.[11]

Schorr proposed a thorough reorganization of ADC, arguing that it contributed to political problems and was a catalyst for public hostility against welfare programs as a whole. Speaking for the SSA, Jules Berman acknowledged important difficulties in applying the program as well as negative side effects, but he was reluctant to publish the critical report in the *Social Security Bulletin* out of fear of "throwing out the baby with the bathwater," according to Elizabeth Wickenden, a lobbyist for the American Public Welfare Administration. Since the report could not appear in the *Bulletin*, Schorr published it in *Social Work*, thus ensuring his notoriety inside the federal bureaucracy. The article drew positive responses from figures such as Wilbur Cohen, who supported redesigning the program. Schorr pursued his taste for controversy in an iconoclastic essay the following year that reminded families of their responsibilities toward their children and cited the timeless virtues of the "Fifth Commandment." The article also pointed out the weakness of social coverage for the elderly, again appealing to the idea of family responsibility and raising the specter of legal pressure to force children to support their aging parents until the latter were eligible for federal support. His use of religious terms and his recommendations mirrored a widespread desire to end what was perceived as the strong backlash against welfare recipients, a hope that gained urgency in the wake of the Newburgh affair and other scandals.[12]

The Newburgh Affair

The paradoxical evolution of the welfare system began to spark a popular rejection that was fueled by fears of widespread fraud. Inconsistencies in the Social Security system that were the subject of mild debate inside government agencies became the source of a strident outcry from the public. As the Schorr report had observed, women, especially African American women, were vulnerable to criticism for choosing federal payments over work. In Detroit, people criticized the number of people, especially African Americans, on welfare. In a long article that described unwed mothers with illegitimate children, published in April in the *Atlantic Monthly*, Ray Moseley put the blame on individuals and their lack of work ethic. In July 1960, the state of Louisiana further fanned the flames by passing a law that enforced strict eligibility requirements for payments for dependent children, eliminating at a stroke federal support for twenty-two hundred children in six hundred families. Among the provisions of the law was a stipulation that a divorced woman lost support if she gave birth, and another rule that a divorced woman or a woman cohabiting with a male partner was also ineligible. A report requested by Senator Robert Byrd of West Virginia the following year estimated that 60 percent of aid recipients in Washington, DC, were not legally eligible for the program. But it was the "Newburgh affair" that abruptly brought the contradictions and limits of welfare programs dating from the 1930s into the limelight.[13]

Amid this atmosphere of widespread suspicion of welfare recipients, Joseph Mitchell, the city manager of Newburgh, New York—with the approval of the town council—decided to sharply restrict applications for welfare to stem the tide of unregulated migration into the town. Mitchell contended that the federal government had made the issue of poverty worse by creating dependency, rewarding laziness, and encouraging people to migrate. The town of Newburgh claimed that one-third of its total annual budget was being allocated to 1,382 citizens via supplements to federal welfare assistance. Under Mitchell's leadership, in June 1961 the town council approved thirteen new rules to make eligibility more difficult while also mandating that payments be made in food and clothing vouchers. Recipients were also required to accept any offer of employment or risk losing eligibility, and women recipients would be denied custody of their children if they divorced. Another provision imposed time limits on some benefits. All these measures, contended Mitchell, were necessary to debunk "the right of social parasites to breed illegitimate children at the taxpayers' expense."[14]

The Newburgh rulings were primarily motivated by a desire to moralize the poor by codifying the "single mother" classification and forcing able-bodied men to work. In announcing his new policies, Mitchell proclaimed the moralizing, reforming spirit of his policies, refusing to subsidize "crime and out-of-wedlock births." His harsh tone was also an effort to reduce fraud and prevent waste that soon prompted a national investigation of welfare fraud. The fact that some of the Newburgh rules violated the law was widely acknowledged, especially the conversion of payments to the blind, the disabled, and the elderly into vouchers, which was manifestly illegal. In July, the State Welfare Department ordered the mayor of Newburgh to rescind the rules, triggering a public response that revealed strong national support for Mitchell, even among federal bureaucrats.[15]

This anti-welfare position was part of a conservative movement that continued to have a very low media and political profile. A number of anonymous New York Welfare Department employees broke with their colleagues, arguing that the nation's entire welfare system needed top-to-bottom reform. Mitchell's office received hundreds of letters of support, transforming a small-town official into the personification of the fight against federal waste. Conservative political leader Barry Goldwater publicly praised Mitchell as a leading light in efforts to curb the aftermath of the spendthrift New Deal era. The affair became a cause célèbre that was followed by a wave of reports of fraud and abuse. It was no coincidence that the conservative *Wall Street Journal* also rallied to Mitchell's defense and celebrated the mayor's courageous efforts.[16]

Despite widespread conservative support, the New York Supreme Court issued an injunction against twelve of the thirteen Newburgh provisions. Norman Lourie, president of the National Association of Social Workers (NASW), was prompted to publish a pamphlet titled *Will the Newburgh Plan Work in Your City?* intended to counter the Newburgh

WILL THE NEWBURGH PLAN WORK IN YOUR CITY?

I N every city of the United States, people have read about the controversy over public assistance in Newburgh, New York, and asked themselves: "Would the Newburgh Plan work here?" or "Would it help reduce my taxes?" or "Would it hurt helpless people?"

These questions deserve your serious thought as a citizen concerned with the well-being of your neighbors, particularly those not in a position to defend themselves.

You should know that the Newburgh Plan is built not only on false claims but on concepts as old and as harsh as the Poor Laws in the time of Queen Elizabeth of England. They have been argued and rejected by the American people over and over again in the evolution of our present public welfare programs. Such programs are aimed at giving constructive assistance to those honestly in need, with full protection for their dignity and rights as human beings.

Newburgh's Welfare Code is not working — not even in Newburgh. A New York State Court has issued a temporary injunction against application of 12 of the 13 points in the Code — and, in an answer to the court, Newburgh officials have submitted a softer interpretation of them. Yet, the Code is still being discussed in many places as though it offered some new short-cut to progress. It is easy to rail against high welfare costs but the rational citizen will also want to take into account the facts about jobs. Of 150 major labor force areas, 101 have been in the past year "depressed employment areas."

This facts sheet, prepared by an organization representing 30,000 professional social workers, is designed to inform you and other citizens interested in knowing "the other side" of the Newburgh picture as it might apply to the public welfare programs in your own State or city.

We invite you to read it and to pass the facts on.

Norman V. Lourie, *President*
National Association of Social Workers

Figure 4.1. Pamphlet of the NASW. Courtesy of State Historical Society of Wisconsin.

rules before the NASW's thirty thousand members. Lourie's pamphlet maintained that "the Newburgh Plan is built not only on false claims but on concepts as old and as harsh as the Poor Laws in the time of Queen Elizabeth of England." An investigation by the NASW also revealed that Mitchell's regulations relied on flawed data and that only 13 percent of the town's budget was devoted to welfare, as opposed to the 33 percent Mitchell had claimed. In 1960, only a single fraud allegation was filed, and the accused was ultimately acquitted by a local judge. It was also revealed that the state was fully funding the town's welfare payments to immigrants for a total of $205,000.[17]

Although the Newburgh rules were never enacted, their effects extended far beyond the local community, a fact that did not escape the notice of the poverty community. The affair's national repercussions confirmed that the legitimacy of welfare programs was under siege, and it inspired a number of states to impose harsh regulations on their ADC programs. California strengthened existing provisions that terminated allocations to single mothers who refused employment offers, and Oregon declined applications from individuals who had quit their jobs for reasons not approved by a review commission. This period of turmoil offered further evidence that, if it was to avoid becoming completely dismantled, the dual system established in 1935 needed to be redesigned.

Members of the poverty community saw such attempts to moralize the poor as part of an old tradition of poor relief. Welfare has always been seen as a way to modernize the old poor laws that conditioned assistance on drinking habits, sexual behavior, or educational norms. The scandals that regularly resurfaced during the decade endangered the entire welfare system by shaking it to its roots, and the time had come to rebuild the way in which poverty advocates represented their subject in order to relegitimize social activism. Reconciling public opinion with poverty was the crucial first step toward workable proposals for redistributing income.[18]

The Limitations of the Affluent Society

A strong belief in upward social mobility was common among members of the poverty community, many of whose families had participated in waves of immigration into the United States earlier in the century and faced the dire consequences of the economic crisis. The statistician Herman Miller argued that the United States was engaged in a permanent "social revolution" that was highly propitious to social mobility. Citing a pamphlet by U.S. Supreme Court justice William O. Douglas, *Freedom of the Mind*, he expressed concern that the principal consequence of economic prosperity would be to reinforce the power of the nation's elites: "Are we about to return to the feudalism that Europe left behind in the 15th and 16th centuries?" Proposals to redistribute income collided with powerful postwar growth, however, that fueled generalized amnesia about the crushing problems of the 1930s and stifled the potential for reform. As early as 1930, the *Encyclopedia of the Social Sciences*, which Ida Merriam had edited, had underscored the paradox of phases of economic growth during which "an increase in the perception of poverty is a phenomenon that is characteristic of American life."[19]

To transcend this paradox, it was necessary to recast the welfare state as having the potential not only to remedy social inequalities but also to make them "disappear" permanently. This radical change would be possible via the government's newfound capacity for large-scale social action that had been demonstrated during World War II. In a speech in San Francisco in 1954, Merriam articulated the liberal idea that would dominate in the next ten years: poverty could be eliminated in a few decades if it became a government priority. She believed that it was too soon to announce the triumph of opulence and the accompanying idea implied by Kuznets that inequalities would inevitably dwindle. Only the federal government had the power and moral mandate to regulate the excesses of capitalism by guaranteeing a "decent" way of living to every citizen.[20]

This move to find a political critique on a moral imperative was among the poverty community's most important contributions. As its champion in the federal government, Merriam fully subscribed to this traditional component of socially committed Protestantism. She was openly distrustful of the material prosperity that was corroding the social fabric of America and revealed in the increasing number of single-parent families. Her position as a researcher at the SSA provided a pulpit from which to promote a shift in national priorities away from the accumulation of vast stocks of arms and toward a more equitable society. In October 1963, she responded to the Cold War test ban treaty in an article published in the *Social Security Bulletin* that praised this ecumenical ideal:

> Finally, it seems not unreasonable to hope the beginnings of disarmament would release social energies and social inventiveness that today tend to be suppressed and frustrated. Some of the pressure for disarmament is the pressure of fear. But there is also an ethic of concern for others and a moral realization of the meaning of interdependence that must increasingly permeate our thinking about international relations and our willingness to change established institutions before we are likely to achieve either disarmament or greater abundance for all. Disarmament and a more equitable society must go together into mankind's future.

To support her arguments, Merriam asked Alvin Schorr to provide "clinical evidence" that the newly affluent society was also responsible for widespread psychological and individual problems, encouraging him to add the "human" component missing from John Galbraith's 1958 opus.[21]

According to Ida Merriam, crossing the boundary between poverty research and advocacy of policies that favored income distribution would contribute to greater "authenticity" in American society. Statistician Herman Miller concurred with this view, although he was also keenly aware of the risk of losing professional and scientific objectivity that accompanied politicization. As justification for his more fully committed position, he cited the origins of his work in the struggle against the dehumanized world that the British historian Arnold Toynbee had predicted in *Civilization on Trial* in 1948. He contended that while Toynbee claimed that minimum living standards had risen considerably for all of society, this improvement should not stop us from "demanding social justice; and the unequal distribution of the world's goods between a privileged minority and an underprivileged majority has been transformed from an unavoidable evil to an intolerable injustice."[22]

At the heart of their positions was a conviction that postwar societies should not be ruled by economic power and the absolute faith in Keynesianism. In analyzing the causes of the urban crisis in the 1950s, the Ford Foundation urban specialist Paul Ylvisaker placed much of the blame on the postwar erosion of the social bonds that had traditionally bound communities together: "My own personal hunch is that the awakening of self-respect is the most powerful agent for renewing our cities socially, and for that matter, physically. Partly this must be earned; partly—as the saints have taught us—it must be freely given." Ylvisaker did not share many of his contemporaries' optimism concerning the benevolent nature of economic growth. In a lecture at Berkeley in 1948, he distanced himself from the lighter tone of University of California president Clark Kerr in terms of the positive effects of American prosperity and the key role played by universities in the new economy. Ylvisaker argued that, on the contrary, the modern world fostered social and human isolation: "As our relationships become impersonal (a process otherwise called urbanization), the neighborhood, the church, the village, the guild, are eroding, irrelevant, or at best going through the anguish of reformulating their reason for being." By placing human beings and their quest for authenticity at the core of social policy, poverty researchers were reasoning in universal terms, out of a belief that social assistance should be accessible to every member of society. A blend of scientific rigor and moral imperative that drew some of its inspiration from Great Britain, the distant shore of the Atlantic Ocean, this activist position had become the credo of the poverty community.[23]

A Transatlantic Issue

Ever since the late nineteenth century, transatlantic connections among social reformers and researchers were very lively, facilitated by increasingly easy transportation. There was considerable continuity in the positions of Anglo-British and American concerning poverty, and although their exchanges were institutionally framed via international commissions involved in postwar international agencies such as the International Social Security Administration, a certain level of informality did persist and personal interrelations. The successful implementation of the conclusions of the 1942 William Beveridge report provided evidence that social science research could be effectively applied to policy. For the poverty community, Great Britain was a model of "research in action" in Elizabeth Brandeis Raushenbush's own words.[24]

The chilling effects of McCarthyism and the Cold War on the social sciences explained a tendency among Americans at the time to rely on the work of their European colleagues regarding inequality and social justice, subjects that were tending to disappear from American library shelves. Authors such as David Thomson and Bertrand de Jouvenel were frequently read and quoted by Americans. In the early 1920s, the British intellectual and social reformer Richard Tawney, who was also frequently quoted by Merriam and Lampman, already maintained that the acquisition principle—the major force behind capitalism—could not guarantee the emergence of a genuinely just society. Robert Lampman shared Tawney's belief in the need to impose order on the social disorder exuded by capitalism. He felt that social order, ensured by a responsible government, should provide the moral foundation of society. To the extent that American society essentially ignored inequality in the 1950s, the poverty community was influenced by British academics and their expertise as offered to the Labour Party.[25]

The exchange went in both directions, however. There was considerable interest in the work of American researchers in Great Britain, where the idea that poverty no longer existed was as prevalent as in the United States. Jimmy Porter, the hero of John Osborne's celebrated 1956 book, *Look Back in Anger*, complained that there were no more "good causes" to defend in the torpid atmosphere of the 1950s. A few years earlier, at an inaugural Labour Party conference in 1950, a party leader named Sam Watson, who was chairman of the National Executive Committee of the Labour Party, had straight-facedly proclaimed that that "poverty has been abolished." It was such assumptions that rendered poverty invisible across the political spectrum.[26]

Arguably, Richard Titmuss, one of the great British social experts, single-handedly sustained close ties between researchers on the two sides of the Atlantic. Titmuss, who had become well known because of his 1938 book, *Poverty and Population*, joined the London School of Economics (LSE) faculty in 1950, becoming the first member of the prestigious institution to be named specialist in social administration. He formed a cohesive and energetic scientific team at LSE by recruiting a generation of poverty researchers that included Brian Abel-Smith and Peter Townsend. An important figure in the Labour Party and a member of the shadow cabinet, he often served as an expert on the government's different Labour Party committees on matters related to social security and income redistribution.[27]

Ida Merriam and her team of researchers developed a keen interest in the methodology being used to define a poverty threshold by her British counterparts. Under Richard Titmuss, scholars at the LSE abandoned the view that had been dominant since Seebohm Rowntree's pioneering budgetary approach in the early twentieth century. In 1962, Townsend published a definition that reflected postwar economic and social conditions and renounced the budgetary approach that he felt minimized basic human needs. He contended that social researchers tend to isolate the poor as if poverty was "a static concept" and individuals were like "Robinson Crusoe living on a desert island." Poverty became a dynamic process and "[man] as a social animal entangled in a web of relationships—at work and in family and community—which exert complex and changing pressures to which he must respond, as much in his consumption of goods and services as in any other aspect of his behavior." In lieu of traditional definitions of poverty based on the notion of subsistence, Townsend proposed "relative insufficiencies," which took the fundamentally relative nature of poverty into account. Based on this viewpoint, any income under 50 percent of median income was the basis for defining poverty.[28]

Beyond the question of definition, researchers were also interested with concrete solutions to cope with it. In 1962, Alvin Schorr embarked on a Fulbright-sponsored study tour of the French and British social security systems. He was surprised at the connection between allowances and the number of children in each family that was part of the French system. In other words, there was a concordance between welfare and "the fundamental values of the French." He started to ponder the transfer of a family allowance system in the United States. His research enabled him to meet Richard Titmuss, whom he called the "only genius I've ever met" and who exerted a strong intellectual influence on him.[29]

Despite his rather predictable anti-Americanism as a member of the left wing of the Labour Party, where such sentiments were traditional, Titmuss maintained close ties with his American counterparts throughout his career. Anglo-American intellectual exchanges were consistent with the transnational approach that Titmuss advocated as a means of avoiding nationalist tendencies inherent in the core concept of the welfare state. He felt that nationalism was in fundamental contradiction with the universal imperative underlying social policy. Indeed, Titmuss and the American poverty community shared a similar professional culture. Wilbur Cohen found Titmuss's book *Essays on the Welfare State* (1958) very "stimulating." In May 1959, answering Cohen's questions about streamlining definitions between experts on the two sides of the Atlantic, Titmuss referred to significant similarities and expressed "great respect" for the work that Cohen was doing "in combining academic research and social action."[30]

In methodological terms, Titmuss advocated an approach to poverty based on categories. He believed that Beveridge's universal approach had failed to eradicate poverty among the hardest-hit segments of the population. He shared a deep commitment to reform with the American poverty community, and Ida Merriam wholeheartedly embraced his idea that "the gift" is the foundation of all human relations. In a book analyzing blood donations in Western societies, Titmuss demonstrated the authenticity of such an individual practice, which legitimized social policies while minimizing the technical and political thinking involved in creating them. For him, human giving offered a basis for an alternative to the market-based capitalist system, an argument that served as the basis for his critique of the postwar conservative social contract that had evolved in an era dominated by prosperity. The LSE professor emphasized this position in 1960, arguing that economic growth and the postwar welfare state were not the only possible "solution" to the problem of poverty.[31]

Researchers on both sides of the Atlantic were attempting to transcend systems that were in a sense mired in categories in order to integrate all of society's poor, a broader category that encompassed members of every subgroup in society. This viewpoint heralded a conceptual shift toward a new idea of the "poor" that would replace research that had focused on the "unemployed." As leader of these assaults on the myth that the welfare state guaranteed social justice, Titmuss published a brochure in 1962 titled *Income Distribution and Social Change*. He demonstrated that the working class had failed to benefit from postwar income redistribution because many of its members had not enjoyed a noticeable improvement in their financial situation.[32]

In his reading of Titmuss's argument, Lampman joined with Titmuss in gradually abandoning the social question in favor of more equitable distribution of wealth. In a period of affluence, British experts confronted a poverty paradox that was as powerful in Great Britain, where the welfare state created after World War II was failing to alleviate poverty, as it was in the United States. The Wisconsin idea was also a British idea.[33]

Beginning in 1962, a number of publications announced that poverty had been "rediscovered" in Britain and decried the equalization myth promoted by the Labour Party since the 1950s. In a lecture about poverty, Titmuss asserted that "fifteen years after the creation of the Welfare State," there had been no revolution "of income distribution." It was necessary to improve the social contract developed by William Beveridge during the war and adopted by the Labour Party at the end of the war. Beveridge often argued that politicians should go beyond the concept "of freedom from want," a concept that "doesn't mean much if you don't put it in a specific social context." This way of operationalizing "need," which was similar on both sides of the Atlantic, targeted an aspect of the postwar social contract that had previously been immune to questioning.[34]

Poverty researchers in both countries shared a similar notion of their own function, a subject of extensive correspondence between Titmuss and Merriam. They discussed the need to preserve an image of political neutrality, a stance that Titmuss contended was based on an assumption that "the administration can be rational." In the early 1960s, this cautious position among transatlantic researchers was soon to be challenged by the new visibility of poverty and the very research they had conducted since the end of World War II.[35]

From Invisibility to Visibility

In the early 1960s, responsibility for publicizing the groundwork for reform fell to journalists and intellectuals who were more anxious about the accumulation of social and racial issues in the nation. A feeling of restlessness was prevalent among African Americans, women, and young people. Challenges to postwar liberalism questioned the promise of affluence, and John Kenneth Galbraith became the scapegoat of a new generation of writers for considering that poverty was nearly "an afterthought." In 1962 and 1963, the invisible research of researchers came under the limelight. Edward R. Murrow's television documentary *Harvest of Shame* shed new light on migrant workers in the country. It was, however, the work of two intellectuals, Michael Harrington and Dwight McDonald, that made the poverty research visible. Their writings transformed dry statistical and economic analyses into narratives of the misfortunes of the poor, who were presented as having normal social lives or participating in consumer society.[36]

In his 1962 book, *The Other America*, Harrington was the first to re-frame the technical statistics into a story that could appeal to middle-class readers. Strongly influenced by Dorothy Day—a Catholic and a radical militant—Harrington has always paid close attention to the issue of poverty. In New York, he lived close to the Bowery, where inhabitants suffered from disease and neglect. In his articles for the *Catholic Worker*, he regularly questioned the extent of poverty. Estimates of the number of poor people—between forty million and fifty million, or about a fourth of the population—were quite a surprise for many readers. When it reviewed the book, *Newsweek* noted that the presentation of the problem was "impressive." However, the book sold modestly after its publication. Only the review by Dwight Macdonald gave it a broader audience and made poverty a mainstream political issue.[37]

In his popular piece published in the *New Yorker*—a magazine whose average reader earned a mean income of $30,000—Dwight Macdonald praised the work of the poverty community. He confessed that he was himself blind to the poverty question, and without those researchers' impressive body of work, illusions about affluence would have continued forever. Even though from time to time he mocked the ciphered language of academics, he accused Harrington of being a little bit too "impressionistic" as far as statistics were concerned. Macdonald believed in a middle-of-the-road policy that made the plethora of statistics accessible to his middle-class readers. He carefully described the works of the Department of Commerce, the Bureau of Labor Statistics, and the Census Bureau.[38]

In agreeable prose, he made a synthesis of the major debates in the community. First, he endorsed the crucial notion of a poverty paradox by deploring that "it seems likely that mass poverty will continue in this country for a long time." He synthesized the main difficulty: "The more it is reduced, the harder it is to keep on reducing it." Then, he explained how it was difficult to figure out a poverty line: "Statistics on poverty are even trickier than most." Eventually, he agreed with the idea that poverty was relative. If "nobody starves in this country any more," he added in a clear reference to the work of the women of Department of Agriculture, "nobody starves, but who can measure the starvation, not to be calculated by daily intake of proteins and calories, that reduces life for many of our poor to a long vestibule of death." Macdonald's book review made Harrington's book a *New York Times* best seller in 1963. It also made public the remarkable body of work carried out by the poverty community. The moment had come to transform the science of poverty into an operational science, and researchers of the poverty community into experts.

Part II

FROM SCIENCE TO WAR (1963–1974)

5

An Economist at War

Throughout the 1960 Democratic presidential primaries, candidates Hubert Humphrey and John Fitzgerald Kennedy engaged in a prolonged debate about the permanence of endemic poverty in Appalachia. Kennedy, a high-spirited senator from Massachusetts, spoke eloquently of "these cold, impersonal figures which tell a human story—a story of hardship, despair and of personal tragedy and they also tell another story—a story of a government which has the power to help, which has a duty to help, but it has refused to help." His references to poverty were met with public surprise, and journalists asked incredulously how it was possible for there still to be poor people in the United States amid such unprecedented prosperity. Poverty experts, though, saw the arrival of a new liberal administration in 1961 as an opportunity to implement a national war on poverty.[1]

Their hopes evaporated quickly after the administration took office. It rapidly became clear that the New Frontier would not reach the poorest citizens and that Kennedy's team was more interested with depressed areas, juvenile delinquency, and the welfare mess. Chaired by Attorney General Robert F. Kennedy, the President's Committee on Juvenile Delinquency and Youth Crime was inspired by Mobilization for Youth and the Ford Foundation's programs to cope with deviant behaviors. Lauded by John Kenneth Galbraith, aid to depressed areas was supposed to reinvigorate both regions and individuals. Supported by Wilbur Cohen, who took the helm of the Social Security Administration under Kennedy, welfare amendments reinforced control of beneficiaries in 1962.[2]

There was a simple reason for the consensus among the Kennedy team: they were all convinced that economic growth would naturally eliminate poverty. Their main goal was to strengthen the power of the Council of Economic Advisers (CEA). Created in 1946 to advise the president, the CEA promoted such policy and gave economists decisive power to control the nation's economy and future. Walter Heller, the new CEA's chairman, even promoted a tax cut for corporations in order to guarantee prosperity.[3]

Surprisingly, in 1963, the CEA opened a discussion about the best way to combat poverty. The shift resulted from the work of University of Wisconsin economist Robert Lampman. After hiring him as an expert in the field of income distribution, the CEA gave him a platform for transforming the Wisconsin idea into a more concrete program. Close attention of economists to fiscal issues led Lampman to frame the poverty paradox in fiscal terms. In the poverty community, he was once again the first to publicly endorse a national action on moral and economic grounds.

Neo-Keynesians at the Helm

As the Kennedy administration was involved in planning the transition to the White House in 1960, Walter Heller was offered the position of director of the CEA. A faculty member at the University of Minnesota, he initially declined the offer, claiming that he was only an "economist in his ivory tower." With typical wit, Kennedy replied that he himself was after all just a "President in his ivory tower." Heller eventually agreed to think the offer over because he saw it as a unique opportunity to apply neo-Keynesian remedies that would guarantee that the economy would continue to grow.[4]

Heller was born in 1915 to a German immigrant family who had moved to Buffalo, New York, early in the century. After graduating from Oberlin College, he completed a doctorate at the University of Wisconsin. His dissertation explored federal tax policy and was supervised by faculty member Harold Groves. His dissertation research was wholly consistent with the Wisconsin school, which dominated at the university during the interwar period. Following the Japanese attack on Pearl Harbor on December 7, 1941, Heller joined the fiscal research division of the Department of the Treasury, where he became very familiar with the functioning of the American tax system, which had undergone a rapid series of changes since the New Deal began. The Treasury Department was developing a proposal to expand the tax system to finance the government's rapidly growing budget. Although the federal direct income tax had been created in 1913, only 6 percent of the population was paying it at the end of the 1930s. The proposal faced opposition on numerous fronts, prompting the Treasury to polish its public relations strategies to persuade Congress of the advantages of mass taxation. Continued reluctance persisted despite this lobbying effort, however. In 1943, FDR was even forced to confront a friendly Democratic Congress that was balking at an increase in business tax withholding. Except for occasional clashes, the war helped persuade Congress to enact a tax system that raised the number of contributing households from four million to forty-four million between 1939 and 1944. An additional element of increased tax revenues, individual and business taxes, represented only 1 percent of gross national product in 1939 but reached 8 percent by 1944. Heller helped develop a tax system that could help manage the rapid growth of the nation's tax base.[5]

Working with Milton Friedman and other economists who specialized in taxation, Heller explored options for creating a "negative income tax," or tax credit for the poor, but the idea was ultimately abandoned as too experimental. By the end of the war, Heller had accumulated considerable experience in the field of taxation and fiscal policy, and he agreed to use his knowledge to help the government finance the war effort by becoming the director of the U.S. military's finance division in occupied Germany in 1945. After returning to the country, he accepted a position as an economics professor and dean at the University of Minnesota, joining what the historian Julian Zelizer has called the "tax community" that formed in the 1950s in several government agencies. The tax community consisted of academics, politicians, union leaders, and federal researchers who were trying to promote peacetime fiscal Keynesianism in order to support economic growth while paying for higher civilian and military government expenditures. The tax community pressured Eisenhower, who had planned only minor changes to the New Deal–era tax system, to support their initiative. Throughout 1953, Heller monitored congressional debates on revising the tax code.[6]

The congressional Ways and Means Committee oversaw the first important revisions of the tax code since the 1942 Revenue Bill first established a broad-based income tax. The House of Representatives wanted to update the tax system to reflect changes in how businesses functioned, and the Ways and Means Committee asked Treasury officials, including Heller, to help draft the new tax code. In January 1954, they submitted a proposal for over seventeen thousand changes in the tax code, and with help from the Treasury, a new version of the code was completed within three months. The new policies represented a compromise between electoral concerns and progressive principles that maintained similar tax brackets to those of the previous system but granted numerous exemptions to specific categories of taxpayers. The code was sharply criticized by tax experts, who were convinced that the exemptions system was unnecessarily complex and ran the risk of reducing tax revenue.[7]

Heller advised Democratic presidential candidate Adlai Stevenson during the 1956 election campaign about the potential risks faced by the American economy under the new code. A series of short-term crises confirmed the gloomy forecasts of the tax community, and Heller initially backed Hubert Humphrey in the 1960 Democratic primaries because Humphrey incorporated Heller's proposal for fiscal Keynesianism to guard against recession in his platform. The return of a Democrat to the White House enabled Heller to join the CEA. The chairman enlisted two rising neo-Keynesian stars, James Tobin and Kermit Gordon, who were very familiar with the federal government's inner workings. Gordon had worked for the Temporary National Economic Committee and the Office of Price Administration during World War II, and Tobin had served as an adviser to Adlai Stevenson in the latter's 1956 bid for the presidency.[8]

To signal a break with Eisenhower's CEA, the new triumvirate planned to change the way the CEA operated, realigning its objectives to create an esprit de corps, as Tobin phrased it, a necessary step toward shaping a proactive policy in support of economic growth. Heller, Tobin, and Gordon started by assembling a team of fifteen experts to establish a research center and by adding three young economists to the CEA—Kenneth Arrow, Arthur Okun, and Robert Solow. Heller also sought out new Wisconsin graduates, including Robert Lampman, W. Lee Hansen, and Harold Weisbrod, out of a faith in the university's action-oriented approach to economics research, which coincided perfectly with the CEA's new focus.[9]

The team originally shared an unshakable belief in the capacity of economists to help regulate the economy. In Heller's view, economists could surgically intervene in macroeconomic mechanisms. As an example of such an approach, Robert Solow refuted the Keynesian concept of structural unemployment, which he considered obsolete. Heller's more activist philosophy represented a break with the CEA's more cautious approach under his predecessor. When he arrived in 1963, Hansen was surprised by the prevailing optimism, later recalling the thrill of being part of an environment in which "social problems could be solved with a new federal program." Heller accompanied this intense period of scientific activity by continued cultivation of his connections in the Kennedy administration, which would be needed to influence Keynesian fiscal policy so to ensure continued economic growth. In January 1962, the council published its annual report to the president, which Tobin considered the team's magnum opus. In an allusion to *The New Economics*, a 1947 book by Seymour Harris, the report synthesized the ideas of the "new economists," as they came to be called by the press.[10]

The 1962 report was a successful example of the ability of the triumvirate to persuade President John F. Kennedy to soften a dogmatic focus on a balanced budget and to back the idea of reducing corporate taxes in order to support economic growth. Tobin in particular promoted the view that there was an automatic connection between fiscal policy and growth. The CEA specialized in issuing forecasts, and Tobin predicted that lowering taxes would make it possible to achieve 5 percent economic growth while maintaining unemployment below the 4 percent level.[11]

Okun had observed a correlation between lower unemployment and an increase in gross national product (GNP), specifically showing that a 1 percent drop in the unemployment rate corresponded to a 3 percent increase in GNP. "Okun's law" impressed the president's team and softened opposition at the Treasury Department. Heller's sense of conviction and his communications skills, which Arthur Okun called those of a "great advertising agent" and a "good salesman" clearly helped rally the president to the cause. Their chief concern was that the Berlin crisis and more generally Cold War tensions might cause a major increase in military credits, with negative effects on growth. At one point, Heller asked Paul Samuelson to visit the Kennedy home at Hyannis Port to try to impress the president with what Heller considered economic priorities.[12]

In a speech at Yale in June 1962, Kennedy officially announced that he intended to cut income tax rates. Heller's ideas and Okun's law holding that prosperity would represent the "rising tide lifting all boats" had heavily influenced the government's new policies. The question of poverty had become sidelined, meaning that, as Heller's adviser, Robert Lampman would be compelled to build a strong case in favor of antipoverty policies.[13]

Lampman's Strategy

Heller, after assuming the leadership of the CEA, contacted Lampman, in whose work on income distribution he was particularly interested. They had first met during the 1960 presidential election, when, like most academics, they supported Humphrey in the primaries but eventually rallied to Kennedy. Even after he joined the CEA, Lampman initially continued to teach at the University of Wisconsin. Heller planned to ask him to work on diverse topics. During his first months, Lampman chose to focus on consumer rights, in addition to publishing a series of fiscal reports. His adaptability and efficiency rapidly caught Heller's attention. In June 1962, Heller asked him to join the council as a full member. The position offered the Wisconsin economist an ideal opportunity to become more familiar with macroeconomic and fiscal mechanisms.[14]

Lampman was a quick learner, and he enjoyed working in Washington, DC. He rapidly applied his new knowledge to his interest in poverty. Inspired by the metaphor of the "missile gap" used by Kennedy during the presidential campaign to deplore the inaction of the Eisenhower administration, in 1962 he coined the term "poverty income gap," which he defined as "the aggregate amount by which the present poor population's income falls short of $3,000 per family or $1,000 per unrelated individuals." He estimated that this gap was estimated at twelve billion dollars annually, the equivalent of 2 percent of GNP. This concept allowed him to accurately assess the poverty rate and the poverty income gap, pointing to the need for sustained federal social and economic efforts to reduce the poverty rate. Lampman was also searching for redistribution mechanisms that would make it possible to strategically inject the funds needed to narrow the poverty income gap. This quest for solutions led him to scrutinize the idea of a negative income tax, which was regaining attention among economists at the time.[15]

Such a proposal had resurfaced among economists in 1962 under the influence of conservative economists Milton and Rose Friedman. Milton Friedman was a familiar figure for Lampman and other economists at the CEA. After earning a PhD from Columbia University, he had trouble finding a job and accused the University of Wisconsin of an anti-Semitic plot. However, Friedman enjoyed an excellent reputation among economists, especially for his research carried out with Simon Kuznets on national income. It was while searching for a political alternative to the New Deal that he returned to the idea of the negative income tax.[16]

During a seminar series at Wabash College in 1956, Friedman publicly embraced a negative income tax policy with the near-term goal of simplifying the federal welfare process. His longer-term objective would ultimately be to eliminate welfare entirely by substituting tax policies in order to offer a simpler means of redistributing wealth. The system would be based on reported income and would grant a tax credit to families whose income fell below a fixed tax threshold. In his best-selling book, *Capitalism and Freedom* (1962), he devoted a chapter to the transformation of the welfare state and proposed a negative income tax to replace all existing aids to poor people. The simplicity of the tax mechanism was supposed to eliminate costly bureaucracy and to make recipients more responsible. If Lampman agreed with Friedman that existing welfare programs do not "keep families out of poverty," he regarded the negative income tax as a supplementary mechanism, not as the sole one. In 1962, he repeatedly brought up the proposal in discussions with Tobin. The two agreed that it would be possible to use a tax credit to transfer a "poverty income gap" of twelve billion dollars. The increasing interest in poverty issues gave hope that his research could turn into something more concrete.[17]

The success of Michael Harrington's *The Other America* (1962) was an important step. Lampman praised the way in which Harrington underscored the paradoxes inherent in a society defined by abundance: "There is also the irony that some poverty is created by 'progress,' and the further irony that unionism and welfare statism do not benefit the really poor. And there is the ultimate irony that we now have the material ability to solve the problem of the minority poor, but lack the will to do. Indeed, we even lack the social conscience to recognize the existence of the problem: the 50 million are invisible to the rest of the nation." This paradox began attracting more interest in early 1963, and Dwight McDonald's review of Harrington's book in the *New Yorker* reflected growing awareness of the issue. By emphasizing the forgotten face of the United States, the author was attacking the conservative foundations of fiscal Keynesianism. By then, some members of the poverty community had started to promote their view outside the government's offices. In January, statistician Herman Miller wrote a long article for the middle-class readership of *The Nation* to expose poverty to a larger public.[18]

Beginning in March 1963, Lampman rode this wave of liberal political turmoil to promote his plan to help the poor. In a report drafted for Heller titled *Reasons for the Lack of Enthusiasm of Liberals on Tax Cuts*, he pointed out that liberals were deeply divided about lowering taxes and asked whether a coalition among liberals might not rally around a tax-based approach to supporting the nation's poor. Actually, he was facing a twofold problem: On the one hand, he needed to demonstrate the limitations of Okun's law as it applied to the poor and, on the other, he had to persuade Heller to back a new, potentially costly program at a time when everyone was focused on lowering taxes. In other words, he had to make a political case of the poverty paradox.[19]

To bring in more and recent evidence, he used a survey carried out by Oscar Ornati for the Twentieth Century Fund. Lampman was a member of the fund's scientific committee. Ornati was a young economist at the New School for Social Research in New York whose previous work had examined the living conditions of the working class and the role of unions, and he brought a new, "objective" perspective on poverty, as he put it. Ornati immediately confronted the problem of definitions, and he decided to define poverty on an exclusively monetary basis, based on his assertion that poverty reflected primarily a gap between an individual's resources and his or her basic needs. He was well aware that this argument might be seen as subjective, and his review of the various definitions used since the turn of the century in household budgets increased his awareness of the delicacy of the question of a viable definition.[20]

To correct for this statistical magnification, Ornati changed existing calculations inside the poverty community to reflect three poverty levels: a "subsistence" level of under five hundred dollars, an "adequate" level of two thousand dollars, and a "minimum comfort" level of six thousand dollars. He used past surveys to create charts showing change in the three groups over time, ultimately finding that a significant percentage of Americans remained poor, with nineteen million individuals in the first group, forty-six million in the second, and seventy million in the third.[21]

In his efforts to identify and account for every characteristic, Ornati developed a grid composed of fourteen variables. His system accounted for skin color, sex, old age (over sixty-five)/youth (between fourteen and twenty-four), rurality of residence, geographic residence, lack of a breadwinner head of household, part-time employment, family size, educational level, and the number weeks worked per year (at two levels: 0–26 weeks and 27–49 weeks). This enabled him to show that poverty was essentially an urban phenomenon and that it was particularly prevalent in midsized cities. Regional geography was also a significant variable, with 30 percent of the nation's poor families and 25 percent of the individuals residing in the South. Ornati nevertheless considered economic variables to be the most important means of comprehending the mechanisms of poverty, particularly the amount of time worked. Lack of work qualifications was also shown to be an important factor in under- or unemployment and hence financial vulnerability. A further factor was the increasing employment instability among lower-qualified workers. Such data and categorizations showed not only the extent but the also the transformation of poverty in the past few years.

During a bus ride in April 1963, Lampman confided to Rashi Fein, a friend who was strongly involved in health care issues, that he planned to submit a report that revealed the significant deterioration of the living conditions of the poorest layers of American society. Because of agitation among the members of the CEA and fear that there was not enough time to win over the president, Fein attempted to dissuade him. The Wisconsin economist replied that his professional ethics required him to oppose prevailing wisdom.[22]

On April 25, he submitted a study showing a significant slowing in the reduction of poverty rates in the country. Specifically, his report demonstrated that while the percentage of poor families had diminished from 33 percent to 23 percent between 1947 and 1957, the decrease had since slowed, with the poverty rate stagnating since the early 1960s at 21 percent. Heller sent the report back to Lampman two days later with a handwritten note saying that it was "very illuminating!" Heller urged him to draft a simplified version for the president. Lampman was encouraged by such reaction and forwarded a second, more detailed report for the president's entourage that included an introduction by Heller, who deliberately dramatized the portrait of poverty: "The results are distressing—they offer one more demonstration of the costs of economic slack. And they therefore, also provide another dimension of what's at stake in the proposed tax cut." Heller was well aware of his own political interest in such a program, since it justified the tax cut while also igniting a backlash against agitation by the left wing of the Democratic Party.[23]

Heller asked Lampman and a fellow economist, William Capron, to bring together an informal working group of federal researchers and academics to evaluate proposals for a federal program that would combat poverty. Capron had been among the most highly visible of the CEA's economists ever since he had persuaded Theodore Sorensen—Kennedy's speechwriter and main adviser—of the merits of a tax cut. In addition to Lampman and Capron, the working group gathered many members of the poverty community, including David Martin from the University of Wisconsin, James Morgan from Michigan, Ida Merriam from the Bureau of Research and Statistics, and Wilbur Cohen. Disagreements quickly arose once concrete solutions were pondered over. During the Saturday morning informal brown-bag lunches, the bureaucrats were especially irritated by the economists' optimistic belief that poverty could be rapidly eliminated. Opposition was fueled by Lampman's insistence that the Social Security safety net was insufficient to the task of helping the poor rise out of poverty. Wilbur Cohen strongly opposed him, accusing the Wisconsin economist of dishonesty when he argued that Social Security was of no help. Furthermore, he believed that a program for the poor was a "poor political program" and would never obtain congressional support.[24]

In parallel to these internal squabbles and discussions, Lampman and Heller were cultivating political connections beyond the halls of government. On May 20, 1963, Heller gave a speech at the annual meeting of the polygraph industry in New York lamenting the negative public perception of poverty. He asserted that "the notion that poverty is a spur to

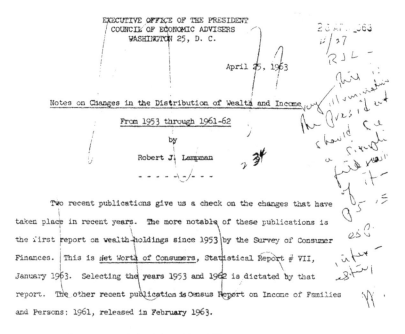

EXECUTIVE OFFICE OF THE PRESIDENT
COUNCIL OF ECONOMIC ADVISERS
WASHINGTON 25, D. C.

April 25, 1963

Notes on Changes in the Distribution of Wealth and Income

From 1953 through 1961-62

by

Robert J. Lampman

- - - - - - - - - - -

Two recent publications give us a check on the changes that have taken place in recent years. The more notable of these publications is the first report on wealth-holdings since 1953 by the Survey of Consumer Finances. This is Net Worth of Consumers, Statistical Report # VII, January 1963. Selecting the years 1953 and 1962 is dictated by that report. The other recent publication is Census Report on Income of Families and Persons: 1961, released in February 1963.

A quick summary of the information follows:

-- the data on income by type show a "profit squeeze," which is offset, in a way, by increasing capital consumption allowances. They also show the rising importance of trans-fers.

-- the size distribution of income data show a slight drift toward greater inequality, accompanied by a shift toward a less progressive tax effect.

-- the net worth data show a shift toward greater inequality. They also show that net worth increased more slowly than income, and that consumer debt increased much faster than net worth. They also show that the lowest fifth of income receivers now hold a much lower share of net worth than they once did.

-- the figures on poverty show a drastic slowdown in the rate at which the economy is taking people out of poverty. The rate in the last five years is far below that for the earlier postwar years.

Figure 5.1. Memo from Robert Lampman with Heller's remarks (1963). Courtesy of the Institute for Research on Poverty.

progress, and must be a penalty for laziness, error, or failure, persists as an almost unconscious hangover of attitudes conditioned by a wholly different set of economic facts." Hoping to counter prejudice against the poor, he proposed a vast investment program that would help the lowest income levels. In an effort to inspire union activism in June 1963, Lampman spoke publicly about the harsh fate of the poor before the convention of the Communications Workers of America. These outreach efforts by Heller and Lampman's disappointment about them reminded the Wisconsin economist of a claim made by Selig Perlman, one of his mentors, that the unions perceived the poor as a threat. Efforts to promote the cause of poverty inside the federal government proved equally frustrating, and Lampman was forced to face the hostility of the "Irish mafia," Kennedy's closest political advisers, who believed that the potential appeal of poverty to the nation's voters was negligible.[25]

In early August, Lampman gave up on the struggle to promote his plan and returned to his post at the University of Wisconsin. Heller urgently recalled him after his return from the summer political break, however. The success of the March on Washington changed the political situation. In his brilliant "I Have a Dream" speech, delivered on August 28, 1963, Martin Luther King Jr. adopted the metaphor of the poverty paradox to describe the fate of African Americans: "The Negro lives on a lonely island of poverty in the midst of a vast ocean of material prosperity." Furthermore, King urged policymakers to give African Americans something other than "a bad check; a check which has come back marked 'insufficient funds.'"[26]

As they were preparing Kennedy's reelection campaign, the president's team had become increasingly concerned about strong liberal opposition to tax-reduction policies. Sorensen was looking for a topic to enhance the president's appeal on social issues and to attract votes among women and the young. Poverty, which had recently developed a higher press profile, seemed like it could be tailor-made for this purpose. Lampman worked on developing a politically workable definition of poverty, using Heller's original principles for inspiration. Acutely aware of Americans' reluctance to address poverty, he decided to avoid references to wealth redistribution and income inequalities. He developed a somewhat euphemistic slogan—"widening participation in prosperity"—that meshed perfectly with the pro-growth orientation of the CEA. Any program would have to be gradually phased in and targeted in order to avoid what Heller called a "shotgun approach."[27]

Skeptics in Kennedy's cabinet focused on the high cost of the project, which would compete with other domestic programs and the ongoing global struggle against the Soviet Union. In an informal meeting in November in Robert Kennedy's office to prepare for the following year's elections, the diplomat George Kennan argued that the poor, like the Bible, "will always be with us" and that it would be best to concentrate on fighting Communists. Kennan's fatalism was not shared by every member of the president's team, however.[28]

A few days later, with CEA backing, President Kennedy narrowed plans for a poverty program in Appalachia. In collaboration with the Center for Appalachian Studies at the University of Pittsburgh, the idea was to concentrate on a forty-four-county region of Eastern Kentucky, using 1960 census data to rank order the counties by per capita income and unemployment rate. The richest county in the region was Boyd County, with an average per capita income of $1,553. There were several reasons for selecting Appalachia, including Kennedy's strong political ties in the region since the 1960 primary elections. He named the deputy secretary of the Treasury Department, Franklin Delano Roosevelt Jr., to direct the new program. The public's interest in the plan was fueled by articles by Homer Bigart in the *New York Times* in which he portrayed a region devastated by poverty and afflicted by bitter-cold winters. It helped the cause that the region's population was primarily white—demonstrating that poverty was not a purely African American phenomenon—particularly because Kennedy wanted to avoid further alienating southern Democrats amid tensions over civil rights.[29]

The War on Poverty thus began with modest goals and in a limited geographical area. Lampman and the other members of the CEA considered Eastern Kentucky to be a living laboratory where their policies would be tested. The folkloric representation of poverty nevertheless irritated the Wisconsin economist, who was firmly convinced that this portrayal did not reflect the statistical reality of economic hardship in the nation. In November, as interest in the program mounted, Heller met with President Kennedy to personally lobby him to broaden the scope of the program. But Kennedy's assassination in Dallas on November 22, 1963, would alter the course of events in an unexpected way.[30]

President Johnson's War on Poverty

Immediately after he returned to Washington from Dallas, Lyndon Baines Johnson met with Walter Heller to review the late president's domestic policy objectives, including the War on Poverty. Even though he

announced his decision to resign, Heller made a very convincing presentation of Kennedy's unfinished project. From the outset, however, Johnson's
startling vision of the program contrasted sharply with poverty researchers' perspectives. Heller explained later that Johnson had in mind very
concrete ideas, with "bulldozers, tractors, and people using heavy equip-
ment." Because he was concerned about balancing the budget, Johnson
was also adamant that he would not be a "budget slasher." As a result, he
envisioned a program that entirely avoided any form of direct financial assistance but focused entirely on providing services to the poor. Johnson's
model was the New Deal, not the new Wisconsin idea.[31]

In the winter of 1963, under the leadership of the CEA, all members
of the poverty community gathered for meetings that had to transform
their ideas into concrete programs. Still in charge of research at the Social
Security Administration, Ida Merriam suggested enhancing the welfare
component of the Social Security program, and the idea of a national
payment scale across every welfare programs started to circulate. She provided technical assistance for CEA initiatives. In November, she furnished
the statistics for the first series of reports. In December, she also rewrote
part of a report that she considered technically weak. The Census Bureau
statistician Herman Miller and Social Security officials Wilbur Cohen and
Lenore Epstein were asked to generate a definition of poverty, while Alvin
Schorr joined the working group that concentrated on the poverty program's more concrete aspects.[32]

A number of experts outside the administration were invited to participate in the design phase; among them were Robert Lampman, David
Martin, James Morgan, and the sociologist Lloyd Ohlin. In early December 1963, they agreed to attempt to operationally define poverty, also
establishing the different categories of the population concerned. The
project's final phase was motivated by a single basic question: How can
the number of poor in the nation be reduced? The president's team expressed disappointment in the results, and CEA economist William Capron claimed that every one of the proposals should be tossed in the trash.
By its very nature, the poverty expert community was closely linked with
federal research, and many members were still working in the same agencies and departments where they had participated in the early moments of
the science of poverty in the 1950s. But this intimate relationship between
science and government was a handicap when concrete decisions were

imperative. As a result, the administration began to limit their roles to scientific work.[33]

In December, Lampman agreed to draft a text that would constitute the basis of the CEA's annual report, which was scheduled for January 1964, allowing the president to formally announce a national war on poverty. In order to simplify technical difficulties, he arbitrarily fixed the poverty threshold at three thousand dollars for a family of four, in hopes that a round figure would have the necessary impact. The idea of a higher poverty threshold was the result of intense debate. Beginning in May 1963, the Wisconsin economist applied his new threshold in reports to Heller, citing its tidiness and the fact that it mirrored three other key federal indexes: the minimum annual salary, the lowest taxable income bracket, and the maximum allowable income for eligibility for Social Security assistance. Lampman was optimistic about this politically credible level of clarity, asserting that there was "no such thing as a clear definition of minimum income."[34]

Embracing a specific threshold level of poverty reveals the care taken by the program's designers in crafting a plan that was acceptable both to the Johnson administration and to the broader public. The president had made his distaste for the term *poverty*, which he considered too negative, abundantly clear. In December, Johnson's advisers started looking for a new term. The move to pull the program toward the political and social center grew out of a political need to package poverty as attractively as possible to avoid a perception expressed by one of the president's advisers, Adam Yarmolinsky, of "a program to help only blacks."[35]

By then, Lampman did not feel that he betrayed his support for the civil rights movement by emphasizing a more universal and color-blind vision of poverty. He insisted on the fact that "the 'poor' are not all 'nonwhite'—more than 79 percent of the poor families in 1960 were white! The poor are not simply in the South—54 percent were in other parts of the country. Even in the South, two thirds of the poor are white. The poor are not simply the aged—69 percent were under 65 (age of head). Nor are they the young—only 8 percent were under 25." Revealingly, Lampman had strayed from an earlier 1959 position that targeted low-income families. He was therefore abandoning his earlier propensity to rank the population according to handicapping criteria from only five years earlier. Compared with his earlier views, his 1964 criteria presented a quite different face of poverty.[36]

TABLE 5.1. Robert Lampman's 1964 poverty charts

Selected characteristics	Total number of families (millions)	Total number of poor families (millions)	Total number of families (percent)	Total number of poor families (percent)
Total	47	9.3	100	100
Age of head of household				
15–24	2.5	0.8	5	8
25–54	30.4	3.9	65	42
55–64	7.3	1.4	16	15
65 and older	6.8	3.2	14	34
Educational level of head of household				
8 years or less	16.3	6	35	61
9–11 years	8.6	1.7	19	17
12 years	12.2	1.5	26	15
Over 12 years	9.3	0.7	20	7
Gender of head of household				
Male	42.3	7	90	75
Female	4.7	2.3	10	25
Professional status of head of household				
Not in civilian labor force	8.4	4.1	18	44
Employed	36.9	4.6	78	49
Unemployed	1.7	0.6	4	6
Color of family				
White	42.4	7.3	90	78
Non-white	4.6	2	10	22
Number of children under 18 years of age				
None	18.8	4.9	40	52
1 to 3	22.7	3.3	48	36
More than 4	5.5	1.1	12	11
Wage-earning family members				
None	3.8	2.8	8	30
One	21.1	4.3	45	46
Two or more	22.1	2.2	47	23
Family geographical location				
Northeast	11.5	1.6	25	17
North-Central	13.1	2.3	29	25
South	13.5	4.3	30	47
West	7	1	16	11
Zone of family residence				
Rural Zone	3.3	1.5	7	16
Rural Zone (nonfarm)	9.9	2.7	22	30
Urban Zone	31.9	5	71	54

Source: Council of Economic Advisers, *Economic Report of the President Transmitted to the Congress January 1964 Together with the Annual Report of the Council of Economic Advisers* (Washington, DC: U.S. Government Printing Office, 1964).

Lampman demonstrated that more than nine million American families were living beneath the three-thousand-dollar poverty level, most of them white and with an employed head of household. By using broader categories, Lampman was seeking to avoid a pair of binary distinctions that had undermined earlier efforts to combat poverty—first, the division between the "deserving" poor and the rest and, second, the dichotomy between the working class and the poor. In fact, the stark truth was that his analyses showed that the majority of the country actually worked. At the president's request, he also cited Burton Weisbrod and Capron's work on human capital investment theories.[37]

The action plan that Lampman ultimately proposed followed a single consensual line by avoiding any reference to a negative income tax. This explicit omission was explained, naturally, by his about-face on the issue in December 1963 in his section of the report, which lacked almost any reference to practical aspects of the fight against poverty. On the other hand, Capron and Weisbrod actively promoted their theory of human capital in discussions with other government agencies. Concretely, the final plan as it was envisioned would primarily reinforce existing programs to assist populations who remained in a state of poverty but were not covered by existing programs. Three types of assistance received the most attention, but the program also needed to be flexible while also providing for prevention, rehabilitation, and social assistance. By late December, the CEA formally delegated responsibility for actually executing the war on poverty to the various federal departments involved. This date marked the end of Lampman's leadership in the War on Poverty.[38]

The Birth of an Operational Science

The agency responsible for regulating the American economy—the Council of Economic Advisers—was thus the home of the scientific research about poverty that formed the basis for a workable, operational science that became the basis of actual social programs. Although often criticized for fiscal conservatism—lowering taxes and refusing to attack the structural causes of the problems of the economy—the CEA nevertheless functioned as the crucible of one of the Johnson administration's most ambitious initiatives: the permanent eradication of relative poverty on American soil. Robert Lampman was the architect of this redeployment of neo-Keynesianism. In a few months, he became "a good salesman" of the Wisconsin idea in a way that was consistent with Walter Heller's political strategies. Sidestepping the statistical dithering of poverty experts, he embraced an arbitrary poverty threshold to push the project through the political process. Lampman was a strong believer in the political relevance of a program that the southern element in Congress was not expected to oppose, since the poor were predominately white and lived in northern cities. Poverty had been transformed into an undeniable American reality amid modernity and abundance. Lampman, whose contemporaries were intrigued by the idea that technology might solve economic problems, personally believed that through modifying the tax system, poverty could be eliminated. However, he muffled his work on the negative income tax and hence on ideas for the direct transfer of income, a silence at a decisive moment that would have serious consequences for subsequent efforts to combat persistent, grinding American poverty and that was one reason why the War on Poverty ultimately proved to be a Pyrrhic victory for the poverty community.[39]

6

A PYRRHIC VICTORY

In 1964, poor people were visible everywhere in the mainstream media. In a long article for *Look*, Michael Harrington portrayed the millions of American families who were still "ill-housed, ill-clothed, ill-nourished." He focused on the O'Haire family in Boston and explained that Earl and Mary O'Haire worked for long hours but could not make ends meet. Harrington deplored that "the American dream does not apply in the Boston slum." In an echo to the theory of a culture of poverty, he added that "poverty telescopes youth; it is a system of adult education for children." To his reader, Harrington explained that it was a question of civic responsibility to help them enter into the affluent society. Lyndon Baines Johnson's War on Poverty was an answer to these "poverty-haunted families."[1]

For poverty experts, such sudden visibility was not a complete victory. In a couple of months, they became very skeptical of the way the president's advisers waged the war against poverty. When President Johnson announced this effort in his 1964 State of the Union Address, he endorsed the behavioral view of poverty and refused income distribution. In front of members of Congress, he explained that "the lack of jobs and money is not the cause of poverty, but the symptom," even though the poverty community argued the exact opposite. To cure such symptoms, the Texan president endorsed the new idea of Community Action Programs (CAPs) to put an end to the denial of opportunity for poor in the nation. By participating in local structures, the poor would be empowered and eventually would find their place in the affluent society. The War on Poverty turned into an unexpected Pyrrhic victory.[2]

Marginalization of Poverty Experts

Like all members of the poverty community, Robert Lampman was "extraordinarily surprised" by the unexpected turn of events, all the more so since the administration "went to the Pentagon to get people" instead of calling the best and the brightest in the field of poverty. President Johnson still nostalgically confided that his role model, Franklin Delano Roosevelt, had always brought "new ideas" and "new bureaucracies." As a consequence, he chose President Kennedy's brother-in-law Sargent Shriver, to run the War on Poverty Task Force. A graduate of Yale University and Yale Law School, Shriver had worked with the Joseph P. Kennedy Jr. Foundation, a job that familiarized him with educational and mental health programs. It gave him a sense that it was necessary to involve people in the planning administration of programs designed to help them. The Peace Corps, which he had launched, was a success. Its implementation proved Shriver's ability to lobby Congress.[3]

Poverty experts were held at arm's length from the outset, a policy confirmed after Johnson assigned management of the program to the military, asking them to apply the technological know-how used to conduct the Cold War. The appeal of modernization that caused Johnson to choose the military to run the program was shared among the nation's top liberals in the 1960s, and it was highly influential in the decision-making process that was supposed to translate the science of poverty into a series of practical solutions.[4]

Preoccupied with setting up the program and drumming up congressional support, Shriver asked a Department of Defense (DoD) official named Adam Yarmolinsky to fine-tune the contents and wording of the law.

A former attorney for philanthropic foundations and a former law clerk for Supreme Court justice Stanley F. Reed, Yarmolinsky had joined the Kennedy team to recruit young talent for the administration immediately after the election. He was attracted by Robert McNamara's zeal for modernization and soon joined the DoD. Yarmolinsky learned the ropes of the DoD by helping plan civil defense measures in the event of a nuclear attack. McNamara, a former Ford Motor Company executive, immediately announced plans to apply the same management approach to the federal government that had proved so effective at Ford. Soon after McNamara was appointed, the DoD adopted a rationalized management program suggested to him by RAND Corporation consultants that he called the Planning, Programming, and Budgeting System.[5]

In the beginning, Yarmolinsky often reminded participants of the budgetary constraints imposed by the president and his categorical ban on any type of income distribution. In other words, Johnson urged his advisers to design a "hand up," not a "handout," an approach he saw as consistent with what he termed "American ideals." Budgetary restrictions also meant that the debate focused on a cultural rather than a monetary approach. In fact, Yarmolinsky contended that monetary definitions of poverty were reductionist because they neglected economic and social realities: "You see my definition makes it a little harder. You can't just look at income size. Somebody who is suffering temporary reversals is not a member of the underclass, and I'm not sure what proportion of the poor are in that situation. Somebody who has given up the notion that he can do enough for a society so that he can make a decent living is a member of the underclass." In other words, the War on Poverty could be achieved without structural economic reform and income redistribution. Both Johnson and Yarmolinsky defended self-support and an emphasis on services designed to prepare individuals for the workforce.[6]

It came as no surprise that Yarmolinsky rapidly accepted his new assignment to wage a war against poverty. He was aware that the new position gave him the freedom to fully implement the DoD's rational management approach to this new area of federal intervention. Poverty experts were astonished not to be full-time members of the group, a decision for which Sargent Shriver took full responsibility, out of a belief that experts were overly focused on technical and scientific matters. He believed that they were also too closely linked to the federal administration and that their ideas were therefore already obsolete. In his zeal for advancing innovative ideas, Yarmolinsky hit upon the solution implemented to cope with juvenile delinquency in the past few years: a community-based program that would be supervised by a coalition of attorneys, bureaucrats, and foundation members. A belief in such a solution was the result of preliminary discussions in the winter following President Johnson's decision to help the poor in the nation.

Beginning in December 1963, a series of informal meetings were held with the president's advisers. For many of those involved, the idea of integrating the poor into community-based organizations seemed to offer a visionary way of dispelling the psychological blockages that impeded their full participation in society. Yarmolinsky's closest advisers agreed that strengthening a sense of empowerment among the poor was a fundamental step in socializing them. A former journalist and Peace Corps administrator in Peru, Frank Mankiewicz, further suggested that the system would ideally be present in every American city and that the national network of community centers could be staffed by young college graduates.[7]

With William Capron's backing, even the Council of Economic Advisors (CEA) rallied somewhat around the idea of a program based on local action, which was consistent with their initiatives to develop human capital. The appeal of this new line of thinking to some CEA members is also explained by internal dissent, with some members seeking to distance themselves from Heller's strict embrace of Keynesian principles. Capron was also highly annoyed by the linguistic understatements that Lampman used to designate poverty, especially the slogan "Widening Participation in Prosperity" that was being considered at one time in place of the War on Poverty.[8]

As the idea of a community-based approach took hold inside the administration, small-scale applications were initially envisioned. During a meeting in mid-December, officials from several federal agencies asked for experiments to be modeled on Saul Alinsky's integration studies in the 1940s in Chicago's Back of the Yards neighborhood. The president's speechwriter, Theodore Sorensen, expressed a belief that Johnson might readily approve this simple and practical idea. During Christmas week, 1963, Heller and Kermit Gordon, director of the Bureau of the Budget, traveled to Johnson's ranch in Texas to submit the plan to include a community-based component alongside more traditional measures for his consideration. The president was initially skeptical and asked for more time to consider the question. After he returned to Washington, however, he gave his consent, and Sargent Shriver's group began to meet daily in early February 1964. The poverty community was on the margin of the war it had advocated for so many years.[9]

The Triumph of Community Action Programs

The Poverty Task Force was primarily composed of urban experts, particularly from the field of juvenile delinquency, and Department of Justice officials. When asked by the task force for his views on urban deviance, the sociologist Lloyd Ohlin confirmed the relevance of this conception of poverty, stressing the importance of the key notion of a "culture of poverty." Edgar May, the author of a book about poverty, *The Wasted Americans*, was invited to explain it. For writing his study, he took the place of a Buffalo caseworker in the Welfare Department of Buffalo. Like most members of the Task Force, he agreed that poor people shared a distinct culture and similar pathologies.[10]

As Shriver struggled to refocus the discussion, he found allies in the Labor Department, among them Labor Secretary Willard Wirtz and his assistants, Jack Conway and Daniel Patrick Moynihan. The previous year, Moynihan had written an important report on armed forces draft rejects, *One-Third of a Nation*. The report analyzed the physical and mental condition of young military draftees and had a significant influence on the debate. Moynihan had found that fully half the draftees who participated in his study were found to have mental and physical deficiencies that rendered them unfit for military service. Generalizing this finding to the draftees' age group suggested that fully one-third could be categorized as having deficiencies. For Moynihan and officials from the Labor Department, the only solution was to find jobs for the poorest Americans, especially African Americans.[11]

Virulently criticizing the notion of "eliminating poverty," they saw the "poverty" category as an entirely statistical invention that ultimately masked the economic problems that afflicted American workers. This was a long-standing debate between the CEA and the Department of Labor. Lampman recalled that during informal discussions that poverty experts were asked to attend, they faced bitter criticism and "perpetual attack," particularly by Jack Conway, who even "slammed the door to the meeting room." At one point, the Wisconsin economist said that he was personally singled out for asserting that reducing unemployment would not necessarily reduce poverty, a clear indication that the idea of the "working poor" was an alien concept inside the Department of Labor.[12]

The alliance between Yarmolinsky and Labor Department officials also grew out of a shared hope of integrating the poor not only economically but also culturally and socially. The prevailing view was that if the poor could not be completely integrated, the nation risked the development of a permanent underclass unable to meet the challenges of the Cold War. Yarmolinsky believed that Moynihan's report confirmed the existence of an apathetic segment of the population that was a source of weakness for American democracy. In his mind, structures that could combat this endemic social ill were urgently needed, and drawing on the RAND Corporation's notion of a geographical grid, he imagined a nationwide network of evenly distributed community centers. The proposal was an ideal example of the DoD's systematic management methods in which budgeting provided the theoretical framework, planification rationally channeled the drive to break the poverty cycle, and programming created the necessary structures for integrating the poor.[13]

The short time frame imposed by the president, who planned to introduce a draft of the law in Congress in March, led Yarmolinsky to entrust a few participants with narrow research responsibilities, while the rest of the group worked on drafting the law. As one observer of the debates and a CEA member, William Cannon, recalled, there was unanimous agreement not to merely modify existing programs. Cannon believed that most people wanted to avoid repeating the mistakes made with Social Security amendments in 1962 that had culminated in adding punitive measures onto existing welfare programs. For the Social Security Administration (SSA), Wilbur Cohen virulently objected to these criticisms, baldly claiming that it was pointless to try to fight poverty by destroying existing welfare programs. CEA proposals for investment in human capital were also judged as too traditional, while income redistribution advocates were also sidelined. As a result of the elimination of these long-standing, research-based proposals, the Labor Department plan for a community-based approach was the only remaining alternative.[14]

For Labor's officials, a program to combat poverty needed to focus on employment, and while both opposed income distribution as a solution, Wirtz and Yarmolinsky were quickly at odds on this issue. With Daniel Patrick Moynihan as an intermediary, the secretary of labor proclaimed that community-based proposals were misguided and proposed to fund a vast job creation program that would be paid for by a tax on cigarette manufacturers. Wirtz's vehemence can be explained by the growing momentum of the idea of community-based action under the leadership of David Hackett and Richard Boone, two members of the Presidential Committee on Juvenile Delinquency and Youth Crime. Moynihan deplored the paradox of the president's message in his State of the Union Address: "Trying to cure poverty" without a more structural approach, he explained, was like "treating the symptoms and not the disease." Moynihan's doubts were not heard by the administration.[15]

With the help of Yarmolinsky, Boone was able to assuage Shriver's doubts by stressing the flexibility of the concept of "maximum feasible participation." The lawyer and Yale graduate Norbert Schlei, who was in charge of composing the text of the law, argued that the idea allowed for multiple interpretations because it was a concept that "no more than two people were in agreement about the exact meaning of." The program was initially seen as a modest affair with a budget of fifty million dollars, but it quickly turned into a larger-scale project with an anti-delinquency component. Yarmolinsky recommended also integrating Aid to Dependent Children in order to constitute a broad program that included training and community-based components. Wilbur Cohen firmly opposed the plan, arguing that expanding the program to incorporate more categories would entail straying from the original mission of the project. For Cohen, it was unthinkable to remove the program from the SSA. Supporters of a pragmatic approach also suggested an educational component, with Moynihan arguing for preschool education and Hackett proclaiming the Ford Foundation's successes with urban action and juvenile delinquents.[16]

In synthesizing this range of suggestions on February 22, Horowitz described a program present in every rural and urban zone in the country that would encourage the largest-possible number of poor citizens to participate while allowing flexibility in how individual facilities were managed that included the poor themselves. Richard Boone echoed the

Figure 6.1. President Lyndon's Johnson Poverty Tour in May 1964.
Courtesy of the LBJ Library.

idea, imagining community centers entirely run by the poor. In late February, Shriver submitted an initial full draft that integrated both a National Youth Corps and a Community Action Program. By early March, the training program was assigned a name—Job Corps. To ease bureaucratic tensions and to present a united front to Congress, Shriver continued to assign program components to different federal agencies, although Job Corps and Community Action Programs would ultimately be the Office of Economic Opportunity's responsibility. The president was regularly updated, and he abandoned resistance to a community-based plan that adapted the spirit of FDR's New Deal to the more prosperous 1960s.[17]

On April 24, 1964, the Texan was proud to announce from the porch of a white coal miner in Inez, Kentucky, that the country had "declared a national war on poverty" with one major objective: "total victory." When in August 1964 he signed the Economic Opportunity Act, he was proud to allocate a budget of $947 million for creating opportunities for the poor. The intellectual foundation of the War on Poverty was "maximum feasible participation" that was supposed to assist poor people in developing autonomous capacity, not income distribution. If the Wisconsin idea disappeared from the table, the War on Poverty was the cornerstone of the Great Society envisioned by the Texan reformer. If it was the consequence of twenty years of invisible research, this victory paradoxically led to further marginalization of poverty experts, whose proposals were confined to administration task forces that accelerated divisions in the community. If Daniel Patrick Moynihan started to work on his controversial report, *The Negro Family*, to promote jobs programs and income redistribution, experts tried to promote similar alternative solutions from within the Johnson administration.[18]

The Rise of Internal Opposition

From the beginning, relations were strained between the newly founded Office of Economic Opportunity (OEO) and other federal departments. Arguing that the community-based component had overshadowed other viable options, Labor Secretary Willard Wirtz refused to cooperate with the new agency and forbade his staff from offering assistance. Wilbur Cohen vainly attempted to persuade President Johnson not to create the new agency and to assign the new programs to Social Security. Nevertheless, for most experts, the conflict stemmed more from the fundamental approach to the War on Poverty than from how it was organized.[19]

Actually, they were in a delicate position, however, because, although they supported fighting poverty, they were adamant that it needed to include more income redistribution. Their discomfort steadily mounted, but it was difficult to openly condemn the project because the Republican opposition vehemently opposed any proposal that smacked of social engineering. Although Lampman agreed to work as a consultant for the OEO and drafted occasional reports for Shriver, he did little to conceal his disappointment with an agency that he found "extraordinarily chaotic." He ultimately quit the OEO and went back to his faculty position at the University of Wisconsin, where he applied for a Ford Foundation grant to study the economic structures of the Philippines. His parting criticisms targeted Shriver's "intellectual dilettantism" and his "high school girl's enthusiasm." Following in Lampman's footsteps, Herman Miller also took a sabbatical year to teach at the University of California, Los Angeles. He published a book, *Poor Man, Rich Man*, that was openly skeptical and attempted to inform the general public about the country's widespread problem of poverty. Using the 1959 statistics contained in the Lampman report, he tried to present figures and charts that gave a more scientific approach toward the poverty paradox. Poverty was not limited to Appalachia and was strongly correlated to income distribution.[20]

Remaining uninvolved in this process was excruciating for the SSA, particularly for the Bureau of Research and Statistics. Wilbur Cohen kept Ida Merriam informed about Yarmolinsky's task force, but she quickly lost interest. She voiced reservations about "feasible participation," the core concept of the War on Poverty, arguing instead for income redistribution in order to refine the existing welfare system. Summarizing the prevailing views within the SSA, Merriam confided to Robert Ball in February 1964 her lack of appreciation of the "tendency to always want to develop something new rather than carry through on a full application of the good ideas we already have." These voices of dissent would soon reach the ears of the president.[21]

Although poverty experts presented a united front against the idea of Community Action Programs, divisions surfaced when it came time to suggest alternatives, and opponents quickly made their voices heard in the administration. In July 1964, President Johnson approved the formation of a task force open to outsiders that would examine the question of income distribution, which had been largely neglected during previous discussions. Princeton professor John Corson was invited to lead the new group, which included the main members of the poverty expert community, notably Robert Lampman, Ida Merriam, and Alvin Schorr. He also invited a Labor Department official named Stanley Ruttenberg; the president of the University of New Hampshire, John McConnell; and a Harvard economics professor named Arthur Smithies. Two officials from the Bureau of the Budget, Charles Schultze and Michael March, provided a liaison with the White House. A veteran social worker who was close to Wilbur Cohen, Elizabeth Wickenden, was also asked to participate.[22]

Following Johnson administration rules, all discussions were secret, with any communication about the contents of discussions outside the committee banned. Between July and November 1964, the group worked to create mechanisms to enhance existing federal programs involved in redistributing income, which amounted to approximately thirty-two billion dollars in 1962. Near the end of August, Corson issued a first working document titled "Sharing Opportunity" that summarized the broad principles of the American social security system and the dichotomy between its insurance function and its welfare assistance function. The report argued that welfare was a fundamental right of Americans and that the welfare state needed to be redesigned.[23]

Corson's report was criticized by officials inside the SSA, including Wilbur Cohen, Ida Merriam, and Elizabeth Wickenden, for not emphasizing the agency's central role clearly enough. Corson agreed to modify the report, and the second draft reaffirmed that "the task force shows the original objectives of the architects of our social security system—that a small and declining minority of Americans should find it necessary to turn to public assistance for essential support." It also confirmed citizens' rights to welfare assistance. Having established this framework, Corson asked the group to evaluate existing programs and possible alternatives, heightening tensions in the group. Wickenden quickly lost patience with the constant search for novel solutions, which she described as mere recycled paternalism: "It seems to me that we are currently distracted from the real goal which is to create an institutional structure—by protecting and serving everyone—that minimizes poverty, need, deprivation, income deficiency, call it what you will."[24]

Similarly, Merriam, voicing the agency's point of view, argued in favor of changing the existing welfare system to allow the federal government to set applicants' resource requirements and payment amounts. To her surprise, Cohen and Wickenden rejected her proposal as infeasible, fearing disastrous effects on public opinion and strong opposition from Southern Congress members. Wickenden was afraid that "they [had] not fully understood the risk implicit in this proposal in the light of current confusions concerning the role of social insurance." Ironically, in October, Corson asked Wickenden to assess the viability and feasibility of a national welfare program. She expressed deep distaste for this mission, stating that "since I continue to be unalterably opposed to a national assistance program (as posing a real threat to social insurance, as well as public welfare programs) I could scarcely do a good job of presenting this as even a possible alternative nor will I agree to it without dissent in a final report." Cohen's laconic remark about Corson's way of managing the task force was that "this fellow is surely going to drive me to drink."[25]

Difficulties grew out of an absence of proposals that might outweigh the community approach. Merriam forwarded a report by Alvin Schorr to Cohen from early 1964 in which Schorr envisioned a family assistance system based on the European approach that he studied during his Fulbright trip in France and England. Schorr's preference for a family allowance reflected his belief that the family was the basic unit and that larger families needed additional support. He also clearly saw, however, that a similar program in the United States would face a variety of obstacles, where a federal program that explicitly encouraged having children might be interpreted as urging people to remain poor because of a popular American belief that family size was correlated with poverty. Schorr was specifically concerned that a family allowance program would be construed as encouraging specific minority groups such as African Americans and Catholics to have more children. He even asked a group of demographers at the Bureau of Research and Statistics to study the question, but their findings indicated no causal connection between income transfers and birth rate.[26]

Lampman offered another new antipoverty proposal. After learning that he was nominated to the task force, he started campaigning in favor of a tax credit and intended this time to make a better case for it. In September 1964, Lampman summarized his views in a speech at the National Tax Association convention in Pittsburgh, forcefully asserting that the American tax system had paradoxically been shown to discriminate against poor families. Because it was based on a three-thousand-dollar minimum income tax threshold, the system incorporated a cluster of deductions that benefited only families and individuals who paid taxes. In effect, as he repeatedly pointed out, this amounted to an indirect system of payments of $120 per child to middle-class families through the per child tax deduction; a total of seven billion dollars was thus being redistributed to middle-class families via this mechanism. There was a hidden welfare state for the middle class based upon a system of income transfer. Why not implement the same for the poorest citizens?[27]

On the heels of the recent tax cut for corporations, the incoherence of the system drew this remark from Lampman: "This irony had special poignancy in the 1964 tax cut which reduced the taxes of the non-poor by about $10 billion—but did little for those at the low end of the scale. The introduction of a minimum standard deduction for $300 per taxpayer and $100 per dependent, for the most part merely added to the redundancy of already unused deductions and exclusions." To remediate this inherent unfairness without challenging its progressive intentions, Lampman suggested a tax credit for poor families who paid no taxes, to compensate for their lack of deductions: "This plan would not bring people over the poverty line, but it has the great merit of striking at two of the relatively uncovered risks that relate to income deficiency—the risk of being born in a large family, and the risk of loss of income and large medical expenses associated with temporary, non-occupational disability." To avoid repeating his earlier mistake, he collaborated with the Department of the Treasury to ensure that the proposal incorporated a feasible tax redistribution system, although he continued to vacillate between a universal tax credit and a version that varied according to family size.[28]

Three versions of the universal tax credit were ultimately proposed: first, a credit equal to the exemption amount; second, a credit equivalent to one-seventh of the exemption that would limit the overall cost of the tax credit program; and third and eventually, a credit based on the current base tax rate of 14 percent. Each plan applied to a family of five.

The plan was seductively simple. In a report that she addressed to Cohen, Merriam underscored the force that the tax credit derived from novelty and claimed that it could appeal to outside researchers who believed that "social insurance is not a glittering new idea."[29]

TABLE 6.1. The tax credit: Lampman's negative income tax (September 1964)

Base income	Base tax credit	Payments (1)	After-tax income (1)	Payments (2)	After-tax income (2)	Payments (3)	After-tax income (3)
$0	$3,700	$3,700	$3,700	$528	$528	$569	$569
200	3,500	3,500	3,700	500	700	535	735
900	2,800	2,800	3,700	400	1,300	418	1,318
1,600	2,100	2,100	3,700	300	1,900	306	1,906
2,300	1,400	1,400	3,700	200	2,500	200	2,500
3,000	700	700	3,700	100	3,100	98	3,098
3,700	0	0	3,700		3,700	0	3,700
4,400	−700	0	4,302		4,300	0	4,302
5,100	−1,400	0	4,900		4,900	0	4,900

Source: Treasury Discussion Paper for Task Force on Income Maintenance Meeting, 01/09/1964, Folder 1 Task Force on Income Maintenance, Box 189, Wilbur J. Cohen Papers.

Pleased by the response to the tax credit proposal, and aware of the growing number of single mothers, Lampman submitted an additional tax credit proposal to replace welfare for single-parent families that used the tax system in a way similar to how the universal tax credit was used. Under his proposal, a single-parent family with four children would be able to deduct thirty-seven hundred dollars, the equivalent of an allocation of seven hundred dollars per child for families that earned no taxable income.[30]

The task force unanimously supported the new proposal, despite the fact that they entertained little hope that Wilbur Mills's Ways and Means Committee would approve a tax credit program. In a strategic turn, Cohen and Wickenden even preferred to allow the debate to center on this issue instead of an overhaul of existing national welfare programs. This diversion strategy was all the more effective in that Corson proved unable to refocus the discussions to preserve the group's cohesion, to the point that either few members were present at the last few meetings or they spent them squabbling.[31]

In the end, the final version submitted to the president in November 1964 was blandly consensual. Its single innovation was Corson's suggestion that the program focus on children who were not covered by the empowerment strategy, with the exception of preschool educational programs such as Head Start. The other proposals entailed additions to existing insurance and social welfare programs, particularly providing social services to the poor. As for a national public welfare program, the final plan avoided the question of regional disparities by settling for standardized nationwide criteria for existing programs. To avoid a political firestorm, Corson kept proposals that would redistribute income through a tax credit or family allowances under his hat. The landslide victory of President Johnson the very same month calmed down opposition to the Community Action Programs, and strongly reduced support to alternatives in the Johnson administration.[32]

Marginalized Experts

In late August 1964, Herman Miller, who had just left the Census Bureau, gave a talk at the RAND Conference on Urban Economics in Santa

Monica, California. Contrary to what might have been expected from one of the pioneers of income distribution studies, he expressed dissatisfaction with the War on Poverty. He defined it as "an election-year gimmick" adopted by President Lyndon Johnson to win the upcoming election. He also complained that "the new focus on poverty . . . , with its emphasis on underprivileged youth, many of whom are members of minority groups, may in part be a device that the middle-class has created to defend itself from the poor and to avert more drastic consequences." The very month in which Congress members endorsed the Economic Opportunity Act and Community Action Programs, Miller was skeptical about their objectives and deplored it as pointless and paternalistic. As community action agencies opened up everywhere in the nation, the very architects of the War on Poverty expressed strong doubts about it.[33]

Following President Johnson's resounding call for a full-fledged, nationwide War on Poverty, experts became caught up in a rapidly accelerating series of political events throughout 1964. The time for careful scientific measurements was over, and the moment for practical thinking had arrived as experts at last faced the concrete problem of eliminating

Figure 6.2. War on Poverty Baltimore Community Action Agency (1965). Courtesy of Library of Congress, Prints and Photographs Division, LC-DIG-ppmsca-49925.

poverty. The president's proclamation made it urgent to find solutions, and although the experts had spent the previous decade clamoring for precisely this turn of events, they were nevertheless caught off guard. In a meeting several years after the War on Poverty was launched in the fall of 1963, many experts were still trying to understand what had caused the scales to tip toward a service-based approach to addressing poverty at the crucial moment despite their strong preferences for a structural, income-based approach. Although most of them had framed the debate around economic and monetary questions, a behaviorist perspective ultimately prevailed among the different task forces in the administration, and the idea that only a community service–based approach could help remove the mental blockages afflicting the poor had rapidly taken precedence.[34]

If some political analysts tend to invoke scientific rationality as an important factor in the administrative decision-making process, the triumph of an empowerment strategy based on community services illustrates the ascendancy of cultural and political factors. Johnson's closest advisers controlled the decision-making process from beginning to end and explicitly excluded any solution that involved income distribution. The Texan president even mistrusted his own administration and therefore consigned the management of the War on Poverty to officials from the Department of Defense, based on his belief that they were better able to develop innovative methods for fighting the social scourge of poverty. The delight of poverty experts that the administration had embraced their cause quickly soured when it became evident that they exerted little tactical influence over the president's team of advisers, who enthusiastically espoused a behaviorist position on eliminating poverty. The experts' marginalization compelled them to propose more concrete ways to fight against poverty, inevitably increasing tensions in the poverty community.[35]

Uncertainty of Numbers, Certainty of Decisions

In 1964, a heated debate unfolded in the columns of the *New Leader* between two intellectuals, Irving Kristol and Michael Harrington, about poor people in the United States. Kristol mocked liberals' statistical blunders, asking how anyone could seriously contend that there was still poverty in the richest nation in the world. He declared that "the poor in America are not an oppressed social class but a statistical segment." In a withering response, Harrington offered the following advice to his adversary: "If [Kristol] thinks this a relativist, statistically tricky definition, I suggest he go have less than nine-tenths of a welfare meal for dinner and then rewrite his original article." Harrington reasserted the views that he had expressed in his landmark book, *The Other America* (1962), arguing that poverty was primarily a psychological phenomenon and was therefore inherently both relative and fundamentally subjective.[1]

Beyond the personal and political stakes behind it, this war of words marked the beginning of public debate on the statistical definition of poverty. Up to that point, discussions on the subject had tended to remain somewhat vague, but the official launching of the War on Poverty made systematic, public debate an urgent necessity. The ensuing publicity caused irremediable divisions among poverty experts, while conservative critics were eager to pounce on every statistical glitch. The poverty paradox was then publicly and politically questioned outside the community.

This conflict over numbers reflects the central question of measurement. Although it had ancient roots, new life was breathed into the "trust in numbers," in historian Theodore Porter's words, when the entire federal government adopted a centralized system of programming, planning, and budgeting. Alan Enthoven, the RAND Corporation analyst who spearheaded its adoption by the Department of Defense, observed that "numbers belong to our language . . . , *even if they are a source of uncertainty.*" In a surprising turn, tables of poverty increased the likelihood of uncertainty, and the effort to establish a poverty threshold became a battle of numbers that perfectly illustrated politicization of the science of poverty. The design of an official poverty line was a way to put an end to the debates and to give a more stable foundation to the War on Poverty by using this new poverty threshold as the central tenet of the fight for a guaranteed income for poor people.

Poverty Line at Stake

When in 1964, for the Council of Economic Advisers (CEA), Robert Lampman set the poverty level for a family of four at three thousand dollars, it was a completely arbitrary figure motivated more by public relations than by science. To create his own scale, Lampman drew on research conducted by the poverty community, especially the poverty tables made up by Mollie Orshansky, an employee of the Bureau of Research and Statistics (BRS). His poverty tables, however, caused a major debate on the very number of poor people in the country, not only among the public, but also within the community. If the disagreement remained secret in the first place, Orshansky cast doubts on Lampman's poverty line and methodology. Professional and gender divisions caused a chain reaction that undermined the community's cohesion and enabled conservatives to criticize the whole statistical architecture of the War on Poverty.[2]

Orshansky, who was appointed by Ida Merriam to determine the number of American children living in poverty, immediately realized that the first hurdle was finding a means of quantifying poverty. The eighth child of an immigrant Jewish family who fled persecution in czarist Russia and arrived in New York in 1918, Orshansky grew up in Brooklyn, familiar with the consequences of financial difficulty. Two academic scholarships enabled her to enroll at Hunter College, where she majored in mathematics and statistics. After a first job as a statistician with the New York Department of Health, she joined the federal Children's Bureau. Primarily staffed by women, the bureau played a crucial role in creating turn-of-the-century social policies and helped establish the "maternalist" side of the American welfare state. Staff shortages during World War II created a demand for statistical expertise, and Orshansky worked for both the Weight Stabilization Board and the War Labor Board. These temporary positions were open to her, as a woman, only because of wartime male labor shortages. Nevertheless, such employment familiarized her with statistical methods and initiated her into large-scale survey research.[3]

Orshansky joined the Bureau of Home Economics and Human Nutrition of the Department of Agriculture after the war, working under the leadership of Hazel Stiebeling. In 1952, she participated in an extremely large-scale study of food consumption in the rural North. Among the findings of the study was that approximately one-third of rural families' revenues was spent on food. In 1955, she participated in a second household consumption survey intended to update the database as part of a nutritional planning initiative. Her background in household budget estimates brought her to the attention of the BRS, where she followed in Merriam's footsteps in working on low-income family budgets. Soon after joining the research team, she worked with Lenore Epstein to conduct a study of the budgets of the elderly, a complex subject because of the target population's vast geographical distribution. The basic needs of the elderly needed to be preestablished, a problem for which Orshansky, drawing on earlier work estimating rural food expenditures, developed a novel calculation method that led her to conclude that any family budget below twenty-four hundred to twenty-five hundred dollars was "very low."[4]

At Merriam's request, Orshansky used the same methodology in a study of poverty levels among children. As is true of any research orientation, ethical choices inevitably lay behind this project, and Orshansky sensed that the nation was in the midst of a profound crisis that was intricately connected to the consequences of economic modernization. As she wrote in the *Social Security Bulletin*, "We live in a time of rapid change. The wonders of science and technology applied to a generous endowment of natural resources have wrought a way of life our grandfathers never knew. . . . Yet there is an underlying disquietude reflected in our current social literature, an uncomfortable realization that an expanding economy has not brought gains to all in equal measure." The assumption that children were the first victims of this crisis in a seemingly prosperous nation added impetus to Orshansky's determination to accurately determine the number of American children living in poverty. Contrary to many members of the poverty community, she was not hostile to Oscar Lewis's "cycle of poverty." After scrutinizing the statistics, she contended that "the children of the poor today are themselves destined to be the impoverished parents of tomorrow" and urged "some social intervention . . . to break the cycle, to interrupt the circuits of hunger and hopelessness that link generation to generation."[5]

Because of significant difficulties involved in collecting new data, she decided to base her new study on recent Census Bureau data reporting family income as a function of family size. Although the data did not directly reflect the poverty level, Orshansky decided to extrapolate them using Engel's law, which Dorothy Brady had previously employed in urban studies at the Bureau of Labor Statistics (BLS). Orshansky knew that every government statistician and economist was familiar with this principle, which she had learned to appreciate during her stint at the Agriculture Department. She therefore turned to the Agriculture Department's updated 1962 nutritional budgets to address the additional problem of specifying the basic primary needs of an American family.[6]

Previous research had tended to distinguish between three nutritional budget levels—*moderate, low cost,* and *economical.* Orshansky chose to use the two lowest levels, which she believed reflected real poverty, as the basis for calculating the poverty threshold. To determine the proportion of total income that urban families devoted to nutrition, Orshansky turned to the BLS's studies conducted by Helen Lamale. In her careful work, Lamale had estimated that a family's food expenditures represented approximately one-fourth of their total income, but Orshansky found these studies to be less reliable than Department of Agriculture studies because in her view they underestimated food expenditures. Orshansky decided to use Department of Agriculture rural budget data that

Figure 7.1. Mollie Orshansky in her office at the Social Security Administration (1967). Courtesy Social Security Administration Historian's Office.

had found that rural families used one-third of their income on food pur-
chases. She extrapolated this percentage to Census Bureau data and, mul-
tiplying by three, arrived at an estimate of the poverty threshold. This led
to her to the conclusion that a family of four needed $3,165 based on the
lower nutritional category and $3,955 for the higher category. When she
applied these estimates to different family categories, the results allowed
her to calculate the number of American children living in poverty with
relative accuracy.[7]

In choosing this method of calculation, Orshansky was proclaiming
that children's basic primary needs were critical to society, a position
that she unabashedly attributed to her status as a member of the "female
branch of research," as she put it.[8]

Orshansky synthesized twenty years of budget studies that she sifted
from the morass of poverty research, attaining unexpected notoriety in
the fall of 1963 and early 1964 when the War on Poverty was launched.
Indeed, because it represented the first concrete estimate of the poverty
threshold, Orshansky's article in the *Social Security Bulletin* went from
being a modest report to constituting the centerpiece in a wide-reaching,
highly public debate. Although Robert Lampman and the CEA did not cite

TABLE 7.1. Mollie Orshansky's 1963 poverty charts

Residence and parental status	Total number of families with children	Poor by low-cost diet	Poor by economy diet	Total children in families	Poor by low-cost diet	Poor by economy diet
Total number	26,227	6,936	4,805	62,655	21,996	15,859
Mother and father	23,748	5,256	3,375	57,109	17,481	11,725
Mother only	2,225	1,578	1,355	5,108	4,333	4,012
Father only	254	102	75	438	182	122
Nonrural	24,349	6,237	4,239	57,425	19,634	13,932
Mother and father	21,953	4,610	2,854	52,072	15,202	9,866
Mother only	2,163	1,536	1,320	4,951	4,268	3,962
Father only	233	91	65	402	164	104
Rural	1,878	699	566	5,230	2,362	1,927

Source: Mollie Orshansky, "Children of the Poor," *Social Security Bulletin* 26, no. 7 (1963): 10.

her data directly, because the data were too specific, they nevertheless acknowledged that Orshansky had established a reasonable annual base-level monetary income of around three thousand dollars. Orshansky's method of measuring poverty had launched a discussion that would become an extended, prolonged, and at times controversial statistical debate.[9]

The Conservative Countercharge

The methodology that lay behind Orshansky's way of defining poverty quickly attracted criticism, referred to by Herman Miller in September 1964 in a series of lectures that he gave in Los Angeles. He observed that "these data suggest that many families included in the poor category actually have a satisfactory standard of living." Although Miller did not question the underlying quantitative criteria, his purpose was to refine the methodology used to establish the poverty threshold. The anthropologist Margaret Mead weighed in on the debate, arguing in favor of extreme scientific caution in defining poverty in a nation defined by abundance and even inquiring whether Orshansky had not fallen victim to an exaggerated reliance on statistics.[10]

The most virulent criticisms, however, came from political opponents of the War on Poverty, who quickly seized on the statistical complexity of Orshansky's quantitative methodology. In February 1965, Rose Friedman authored an American Enterprise Institute pamphlet denouncing these poverty tables as a statistical illusion. Founded in 1943, the institute was part of the conservative intellectual machinery to find alternatives to the New Deal. As it enjoyed a modest research budget of less than a million dollars, it relied primarily on the Department of Economics at the University of Chicago to help spread his political, economic, and social views. A few days after the launching of the War on Poverty, Milton Friedman asked his wife, Rose, to conduct an evaluation of the government's poverty statistics. In his book *Capitalism and Freedom* (1962), he had already cast his doubts about the expansion of welfarism in the country. He had chosen his wife not out of mere expediency but because, like her husband, she had worked as an economist since the 1930s inside the deep recesses of the federal government. As they recalled somewhat provocatively years later, "Ironically, the New Deal saved our lives." While Milton went to work for the Commission on National Resources, Rose took a job with the Department of Agriculture as a researcher, which she found to be a stimulating scientific environment where she became familiar with the inner workings of nutritional budgets. She also worked closely with Dorothy Brady on income distribution. In other words, she became highly familiar with the scientific and bureaucratic organizations around which the poverty community revolved. If Friedman and Lampman competed on the issue of the negative income tax, Rose Friedman and Mollie Orshansky disagreed on the very definition of a poverty line.[11]

Actually, the conservative economist began a counterstudy of government poverty figures by criticizing the political instrumentalization of scientific data that "did not provide either then or now guidelines for assisting families in obtaining better nutrition by spending less money." Rose Friedman also challenged the arbitrary nature of Orshansky's multiplier, which she contended underestimated nonmonetary income, particularly in rural areas. She argued that flawed scientific assumptions biased the conclusions and exaggerated the problem of poverty. As she put it, "To sum up: Miss Orshansky's crude criteria of income adequacy correspond neither to the minimum cost at which families *could* get an adequate diet nor to the income level at which three-fourths of the families do in fact achieve adequate nutrition." Friedman added that such "criteria yield incomes that are far higher than the first and 20 to 50 percent higher than the second." The methodological choices, according to her, led to a profound political and intellectual mistake. The poverty paradox was just a statistical construction.[12]

To clarify her position and make comparison easier, Rose Friedman used a similar quantification system to perform a new set of calculations based on a 1955 Department of Agriculture survey that had focused less on emergency assistance programs than had the 1962 study used by Orshansky. Friedman also chose the most costly of the three plans as the basis for her calculations, and instead of 33 percent, she estimated that a family spent an average of 60 percent of its income on food. Her new calculations yielded an average income for a family of four of twenty-two hundred dollars, which indicated a significantly lower estimate of the number of families and individuals living beneath the poverty level.

Friedman's criteria produced an estimate of only 4.8 million poor citizens and even fewer poor families in 1962—approximately 10 percent of

TABLE 7.2. Rose Friedman's 1965 poverty estimates

Family size	Poverty threshold
2 members	$1,295
3 members	$1,785
4 members	$2,195
5 members	$2,550
6 members	$2,855
7 members	$3,155

Source: Rose Friedman, *Poverty: Definition and Perspective* (Washington, DC: American Enterprise Institute, 1965), 28.

American families. Friedman also focused on a minor scientific detail to criticize the lack of reliability of the January 1964 CEA report—Lampman's failure to take family size into consideration. She saw this as a foolish basic error that rendered estimates of median income meaningless because it failed to take the number of members in a family into account. As a result, the statistics overestimated the proportion of elderly families in the population, at the expense of larger families. She also argued that using data for a single year skewed results and inflated the proportions of both the young and the elderly. Friedman demanded improved statistical procedures, particularly concerning these two segments of the population. In the first, "families with young heads are just beginning their income cycle," while in the second, "the aged are at the opposite end of the income cycle from the young families" because "they have passed their peak earnings and are on their way down." For these reasons, errors and differences "are so large that little confidence can be placed in the Council's characterization of the poor." The whole War on Poverty was based upon false premises.[13]

Rose Friedman's article was openly critical and one sided, but it echoed questions that had been mooted since the 1950s inside the poverty community. Statistical reconsideration further discredited the OEO's plans at a time when the agency was experiencing difficulty in applying the pragmatist empowerment strategy. By undermining from inside the scientific consensus about measuring poverty, Friedman deliberately exacerbated existing internal turmoil. In effect, she was pursuing a political objective that mirrored her husband's agenda as a faithful supporter and adviser to Barry Goldwater in the 1964 presidential campaign, in which the Arizona senator denounced liberals' misguided social engineering efforts and taxpayers' efforts to finance it. When Friedman asked how a war could be waged based on false premises, his main conservative targets were the War on Poverty and the OEO. The failure of Goldwater did not put an end to critics.[14]

Orshansky Strikes Back

Rose Friedman's tract intensified the search among poverty experts for a more unassailable poverty threshold. Amid the politically correct three-thousand-dollar level suggested by the CEA, Mollie Orshansky's budgetary threshold, and Rose Friedman's conservative proposals, there was a state of true statistical confusion that led Ida Merriam to ask Orshansky to focus on the key question of categories. Orshansky agreed to revise her poverty tables, which was easy because in 1963 she was focused on children and her calculations did not seek to cover the whole population. She was profoundly troubled by the fact that the welfare of children had become politicized, and she argued that the quest for a fundamentally relative definition of poverty was not only futile but also indecent. The poverty paradox was not an illusion, and it questioned our sense of solidarity. As she put it in a new article published in the *Social Security Bulletin*, "And if it is not possible to state unequivocally 'how much is enough,' it should be possible to assert with confidence how much, on an average, is too little." Her new poverty tables would focus on the little budget of poor people in the affluent nation.[15]

In other words, Orshansky believed that her definition of poverty was not "unreasonable," even if it was admittedly arbitrary, as long as it was calculated using the multiplier inspired by Engel's law. She held her ground and defended both the relativity of her approach and her method of using budgetary methodology. Orshansky disagreed with economists' approach that tended to use only monetary elements. Their work neglected the fact that poverty was not experienced by the poor themselves as relative and that the actual experience of having only seventy cents a day for food versus one dollar and forty cents was not the same and was not at all a relative matter for a particular individual. Orshansky confirmed her preference for a nutrition-based method of calculating poverty, adding a biting criticism of the political calculations behind Lampman's method. She maintained that by refusing to account for the diversity of families, the Wisconsin economist was indirectly favoring elderly and rural populations and underestimating the proportion of large families and urban families. In her opinion, this kind of method reflected a traditional tendency among economists to use economies of scale to argue that nutritional expenditures by families were not proportional to the number of children. According to this view, economists were victim of their own professional prejudices who viewed family life through the lens of abstract aggregates. In other words, as Orshansky put it, "economizing inside the family doesn't go even-Steven," and the idea that if a family had insufficient funds, the housewife would just stretch a food dollar was thoroughly unconvincing. Nor did this assumption stand up to the facts, and the myth of the economy of scale only reflected "a lowering of dietary standards enforced by insufficient funds." She also maintained that numerous studies had shown that "families with large numbers of children do indeed have lower incomes than smaller families." That is, economists lose sight of the daily experience of the poor and of the financial irrationality associated with their condition. As a woman who had known poverty, Orshansky adamantly opposed a rationalist and overly theoretical perspective on human misery.[16]

In order to document her position, Orshansky asked Herman Miller of the Census Bureau for fresh data about households and low-income individuals. She refined her statistical studies of poverty throughout 1964, using sixty-two different familial variables in urban and rural versions, including fifty-two variables for families and four specific to individuals living alone. These 124 entries were calculated for both economical and low-cost budgets. For each family, Orshansky applied the multiplier approach, leading to her estimate that the nutritional budget represented 27 percent of the total household budget of a family of four. This application of a familial variable adapted to family type complicated the operation, because Department of Agriculture studies employed only nineteen gender and family variables. As a result, there were no data that corresponded to Orshansky's variables for a range of categories, forcing her to apply a statistical patchwork to produce her results. Furthermore, for large families, available data did not include children's exact ages, which meant that she was forced postulate that children were in growth phases and had high nutritional needs.[17]

The expenditures and needs of individuals living alone were similarly complex to calculate because existing data did not identify the proportion of the elderly. Orshansky decided not to use the multiplier with this specific group. Using percentages from the Bureau of Labor Statistics, she arbitrarily estimated family consumption as 72 percent for the low-cost budget and as 80 percent for the economical budget. Orshansky also distinguished urban families from rural families by incorporating differences into family budgets. For example, she took into account food production in rural settings in the home, which recent Department of Agriculture studies had shown did not exceed 40 percent, a significant drop since the turn of the century. Orshansky concluded that the poverty threshold for a rural family corresponded to 60 percent of that of an urban family.[18]

Orshansky used these data sets to draft a chart that incorporated 124 entries for families and individuals living below the poverty threshold. In an effort to make the tables clear enough to present the public, she simplified the presentation by using the two different thresholds that she had developed. This new quantification method proved that a significant number of children in the United States were living in poverty, while also showing

TABLE 7.3. Mollie Orshansky's 1965 poverty charts

Family size	Threshold with an "economical" budget	Threshold with an "low-cost" budget
1 individual	$1,539	—
1 individual under 65	$1,580	$1,885
1 individual over 65	$1,470	$1,745
2 individuals	$1,988	—
2 individuals w/head of household under 65	$2,050	$2,715
2 individuals w/head of household over 65	$1,850	$2,460
3 individuals	$2,440	$3,160
4 individuals	$3,130	$4,005
5 individuals	$3,685	$4,675
6 individuals	$4,135	$5,250
7 individuals	$5,090	$6,395

Source: Mollie Orshansky, "Counting the Poor: Another Look at the Poverty Profile," *Social Security Bulletin* 28, no. 1 (1965): 7.

TABLE 7.4. A comparison between the Council of Economic Advisers and the Bureau of Research and Statistics

Type of unit	CEA (millions)	BRS (millions)	Total population
Total number of individuals	34	34.6	187.2
Rural	6.4	3.2	12.6
Nonrural	27.6	31.4	174.6
Individuals living alone	4	4.9	11.2
Rural	1.4	0.1	0.4
Nonrural	2.6	4.8	10.8
Number of family units	30	29.7	176
Rural	5	3.1	12.2
Nonrural	25	26.6	163.8
Children under 18	15.7	18	68.8
Rural	2.4	1.5	4.8
Nonrural	13.3	16.5	64

Source: Mollie Orshansky, "Counting the Poor: Another Look at the Poverty Profile," *Social Security Bulletin* 28, no. 1 (1965): 14.

that the elderly represented a smaller share than previously thought. The new poverty table profoundly altered the visibility of American poverty, and more important, Orshansky had added more than two million children to Lampman's earlier calculations.

By late 1964, Orshansky's poverty tables began to circulate inside the government. In January 1965, the CEA annual report included a paragraph citing them in a description of differences according to family size. In March 1965, the OEO also expressed interest in Orshansky's results. Leon Gilgoff, director of the Office of Research, Programs, Planning, and Evaluation, asked Orshansky for a full report that would allow the agency to use her tables as its official guideline for program funding levels. On March 12, the two poverty thresholds were presented to the OEO administration, and it was unanimously agreed that they made it easier to target the poorest social categories. In May, Orshansky's poverty tables were adopted as the official federal poverty threshold.[19]

Thanks to the careful work of Mollie Orshansky, the adoption of a poverty line provided a more stable scientific foundation to the War on Poverty. In the summer of 1965, it proved to be crucial as other foundations

Figure 7.2. Danny Kaye, Lady Bird Johnson, Mrs. Lou Maginn (director of a Head Start project in East Fairfield, Vermont), and Sargent Shriver on June 30, 1965. Courtesy of the Lyndon Baines Johnson Library.

became very shaky. The Watts riots and the Moynihan report on black pathology caused major turmoil inside the administration and in the country. Despite the popularity of the Head Start program, Community Action Programs quickly became controversial.

If they completely endorsed such a program for preschool education, poverty experts believed it was the right time to promote their vision of an income transfer program, and they decided to invest the very place of decision making—the OEO.[20]

The OEO's Alternatives

Under economist Joseph Kershaw, the OEO's Office of Research, Planning, Programs, and Evaluation developed an alternative to the empowerment-based approach. In accepting Sargent Shriver's plan, Kershaw was primarily interested in improving the planning dimension of the War on Poverty, and he enlisted the assistance of Robert Levine. Levine was an economist by training who had worked as a military analyst with the RAND Corporation. Together, Kershaw and Levine immediately concentrated on improving the agency's recruitment by engaging more poverty experts, particularly economists. Robert Lampman helped them compose a new team of experts, and among the new hires were Harold Watts, Walter Williams, and Robinson Hollister.[21]

The agency began an evaluation project to assess the impact of the War on Poverty that was consistent with the OEO's commitment to modernized planning. Kershaw had planned to designate responsibility for evaluation to independent research centers, but internal disagreement—certain departments refused to divulge their results—caused him to relent in early October 1965 and to assure programs like the Job Corps that the OEO would not use external evaluations. Beginning in 1966, Shriver made funding available for independent research on the empowerment strategy. For Levine and Kershaw, the problems associated with using this approach stemmed more from the impossibility of modeling than from its results. Revealingly, the concept of "maximum feasible participation" proved too vague to be truly operationalized. The economists also distanced themselves from a cultural definition of poverty, preferring what they believed was a more rational, income-based approach. One outcome of this view was that it prompted poverty experts to launch a search for a viable alternative.[22]

Because most its members were economists, the group quickly rallied around the concept of a tax credit, with Lampman again the intellectual mediator. Kershaw and Levine made it easier for Lampman to work with the OEO, and although he had no official role because of his preference to remain intellectually and professionally detached, he indirectly participated by contributing to the development of a viable tax credit proposal. Kershaw and Levine soon assigned Walter Williams and a young assistant, the economist James Lyday, to conduct a study of fiscal redistribution. Williams and Lyday drew heavily on a report that the Wisconsin economist had drafted earlier in the year for the OEO that reviewed the conclusions of John Corson's 1964 task force. The process yielded two versions of the tax credit proposal: one that would apply across the board to families under the poverty threshold, and another that applied only to families with children under eighteen years of age. The federal government would administer the program without state involvement, and costs were estimated at $6.5 billion for the across-the-board scheme and $3.5 billion for the more selective version.

Although an income ceiling limited eligibility to the across-the-board plan, the group expressed reservations about its viability. Levine was particularly concerned that Americans hesitate to provide welfare assistance to "able-bodied men." The economist David Grossman also voiced doubts, arguing that the proposal was based on an idealized view of poverty and that not all the poor had an established fixed residence and they often lacked even a fiscal address. Grossman also pointed out gaps in how resources were allocated and the likelihood of fraud. Alvin Schorr remained the fiercest opponent of the tax credit plan, adamantly defending a system of family allowances based on European programs. Schorr complained about the arbitrariness of the plan, which, by numerically establishing a poverty—and hence tax-rebate—threshold, excluded certain segments of the population, thus potentially damaging the program's popularity. He insisted that the universal character of a system that was based on family allowances could be targeted more equitably, and he threw his support behind this approach.[23]

After his first proposal in the Corson commission, Schorr started to gather more data and concrete solutions to the idea of a transfer. The social worker expressed his belief that family allowances would foster genuinely equal opportunity that would enable poor children to "take off." In practical terms, he hesitated between the universal and the more focused approach, ultimately offering three different proposals: first, a tax credit for poor children; second, a system of family allowances; and third, eventually a program for fatherless children. Schorr felt that the political viability of the program ultimately selected would depend on its acceptability to the general population, low cost (between two and three billion dollars), and administrative simplicity.[24]

Schorr's proposals to his fellow economists prompted lively debates. Levine criticized the family allowances approach on the grounds that it was just as selective and arbitrary as a tax credit. Because he lacked strong support in the agency's administration, Schorr quickly found himself isolated. For his part, the Social Security director, Wilbur Cohen, continued to quip that a program for the poor made for a "poor" political platform. The tax credit option found some support among other agencies, though, especially the CEA and the Bureau of the Budget, where Kershaw and Levine had established friendly ties because they shared professional backgrounds with members of the agency. A former CEA member who had maintained professional ties after Walter Heller left, economist James Tobin, offered public support of the tax credit option. Contacts in other departments also managed to attract Shriver's support, and, as he told Robert Levine, he was only too happy to entertain a novel "idea" that could give new impetus to the War on Poverty. In May 1965, Shriver told the president's team that he was in the process of preparing an ambitious and innovative budget plan. Hoping to benefit from the emotional atmosphere inside the administration in the wake of the recent Watts riots, Kershaw and Levine presented their national plan to fight poverty in October 1965.[25]

Five-Year Plans

A few weeks after the Watts riots, which strongly shook the foundations of Lyndon Baines Johnson's Great Society, Shriver introduced a five-year plan to the president's team that would reset the War on Poverty. This piece of expertise called for the end of poverty in 1976, to coincide with the two hundredth anniversary of the Declaration of Independence. It put forth the three major dimensions in the War on Poverty that included an economic policy that supported full employment, massive investment in human capital, and continued community-based programs. The proposal incorporated a new twist by arguing for monetary transfers to poor families that were based on a tax credit. The obvious advantages of a tax credit plan included flexibility and low cost. Following the usual approach used by proponents of the programming, planning, and budget approach, diagrams illustrating how the three axes complemented each other provided visual support for oral presentations. Projections that assumed the continuation of both economic growth and the empowerment approach predicted that only 10 percent of the nation's population would be poor by 1975, and that even this residual segment of the population would be eliminated by a tax credit. In keeping with the upbeat spirit of the CEA, economists recycled Lampman's idea of a "poverty gap." In terms of the budget, the five-year plan estimated that the tax credit program would cost $4.7 billion, with an additional $4 billion earmarked

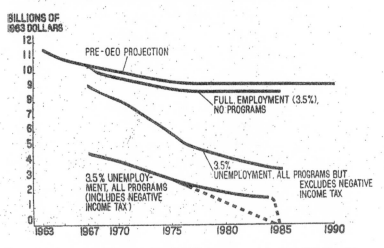

PROJECTIONS OF THE POVERTY GAP

Figure 7.3. Lampman's Poverty Gap (1965). Courtesy of the Social Welfare History Archives, University of Minnesota Libraries.

for other programs and allocated to the OEO (a $2.5 billion increase), $534 million for other federal programs, and $5 billion for Social Security welfare programs.[26]

Despite Kershaw's compelling presentation and Shriver's enthusiasm, the president's advisers gave the plan a cool reception. Officials from the Bureau of the Budget were the only group who seemed to be convinced to support a budget increase to fund the project by the presentation. Experts faced a politically difficult period, with the government forced to limit social engineering projects to finance the war in Vietnam while they also tried to avoid fueling inflation. This complicated balancing act was the origin of the celebrated "guns or butter" argument that ultimately hobbled the Johnson administration for the remainder of the president's term in office. The controversy surrounding Community Action Programs also worried Johnson, who was alarmed by increasing opposition among numerous mayors, which Vice President Hubert Humphrey had relayed to him. But the negative reaction to antipoverty proposals was largely caused by the fact that, by breaking with a system based on social categories, the experts had revealed the fundamental character of social welfare. Johnson had refused all along to back a plan involving direct monetary assistance with no strings attached. As a connoisseur of the inner workings of the Congress, he believed that any plan that included universal coverage was doomed to fail and was especially vulnerable to the disapproval of the Ways and Means Committee. In terms of social policy, Johnson continued to prefer what Wilbur Cohen called a "salami slicing" approach, meaning that the government spread responsibility among several departments. The cost of the tax credit would have forced priorities to be significantly changed, a move that Johnson refused to support. After the Watts riots, the president decided instead to continue to "sprinkle" programs among different bureaucracies and programs, reinforcing the salami-slicing approach, which gave targeted support to a range of groups that included African Americans but that ultimately diluted the universal intentions behind the five-year plan.[27]

In early February 1966, Kershaw and Levine presented a new version of the proposal, a version that reflected fiscal realities. Levine used a new method that took budgetary constraints into account before action plans were even created. Compared with the 1965 plan, the new plan relied more heavily on existing bureaucratic structures, particularly Community Action Programs, which he planned to streamline. In tandem with these efforts, Levine collaborated with the Social Security Administration (SSA) to promote the tax credit in an obvious effort to obtain Wilbur Cohen's approval. In the new version, the tax credit was presented as a way of supplementing Social Security programs in a significantly modified system. For budgetary reasons, the plan proposed dispensing completely with the welfare component of the current system. Together, the OEO and the SSA would cover 100 percent of the "poverty gap" in social categories covered by the welfare program and 50 percent for populations not covered by the current system. Levine's reconfigured proposal gave him the confidence to predict that poverty would be entirely eliminated by 1976.[28]

Despite a consensus about Levine's proposal, however, the second five-year plan met with a polite but reserved response from the president's team. Johnson continued to refuse to back any proposal that included monetary distribution, out of fear of fueling inflation. Some of his advisers even argued that the most seriously underprivileged households would be hardest hit by a rise in inflation, an assertion directly contradicted by

experts from the Bureau of the Budget, led by Harold Watts and Robinson
Hollister. A last draft of the proposal failed once again to gain traction.
The only consolation was that the budgetary functions of the OEO were
transferred to the bureau, a shift that allowed the staff to work closely with
Congress and that ended the institutional isolation that had so clearly hindered the effectiveness of the OEO. Kershaw quit the OEO to resume his
faculty position at Williams College following the administration's failure
to back the proposal, and Robert Levine stepped into Kershaw's position.
Most experts had finally embraced the tax credit idea, which persisted
inside the agency, as the most effective way of reaching the poor. The idea
was soon to gain momentum in the federal government, especially at the
Department of Health, Education, and Welfare.

Time for a BIG Idea

As a consequence of the Great Society, expansion of social policies in the
mid-1960s led the Department of Health, Education, and Welfare to improve its research capacity and its assessment of existing programs. In
1966, it redistributed twenty-four billion dollars to the American population, twenty-one billion dollars alone through the SSA. The majority of the
department's officials opposed Community Action Programs and the idea
of empowering the poor. SSA's members traditionally backed institutional
reforms of existing welfare programs, but the new generation of experts
whose mission was to streamline programs advocated a solution centered
on a tax credit as a way of breaking with what they perceived as an outdated system dating from the 1930s. They considered Community Action
Programs a waste of money and remained convinced that the best way of
helping the poor was to strengthen social services. He wholeheartedly supported the educational component of the Great Society, with its idea of helping young children and high school and university students as well as adults
to pursue their schooling. Under Alvin Schorr's leadership, these "Young
Turks," as Cohen called them, refused to back a strategy defined in terms of
services for the poor and clamored for complete reorganization of welfare.
One of these Young Turks was a woman with the name of Alice Rivlin.[29]

Rivlin, an economist and graduate of the Brookings Institution who
was trained by Wisconsin economist Guy Orcutt, was given the mission

of improving the department's budget process. She advocated a "silent revolution" in budget projections and management as a way to break governmental inertia and end the tendency for "random innovation" that had reigned since the early 1960s. She promoted "systematic experimentation" of new programs before they were adopted in lieu of a random approach, a strategy that involved testing several alternatives and assuming neither the success nor the failure of different options. The idea was to systematically examine different solutions without institutional bias, with the sole criteria being rationality and the ability of a particular solution to benefit targeted groups. It was no accident that the first project chosen by the analysts involved the complex question of the effectiveness of welfare programs, with the goal of creating a scientific approach to welfare.

During 1967, a consensus began to emerge surrounding the idea of a guaranteed minimum income, which under Rivlin's leadership received particular support in the department. Rivlin was nevertheless forced to respect the budgetary guidelines governing the department's operations that she herself had implemented. In order to justify costs, Rivlin pointed out that the cost of a system of family allowances, according to some estimates (which differed from Schorr's), would amount to twenty-eight billion dollars. Rivlin established a more realistic cost ceiling of between four billion and six billion dollars, meaning that the tax credit would be selective and would target the population below two-thirds of the poverty threshold. In the wake of the Newark and Detroit riots, the idea of a shift in the empowerment strategy gained momentum.[30]

Conducted to assess poor people's behavior in case of income distribution, the experiment in an African American neighborhood of Gary, Indiana, was a particular source of optimism for Rivlin and her team. An old bastion of the working class, Gary had become a model city during the Johnson administration, and as a consequence, its underprivileged populations enjoyed access to a range of services. The experiment, which was conducted by two researchers, Terence Kelly and Leslie Singer, was an attempt to analyze the consequences of financial assistance on household incomes and budgetary behaviors. Kelly and Singer granted a two-level tax credit to each of sixteen hundred families, who received either forty-two hundred or twenty-seven hundred dollars per family of four. They created an experimental group and a control group within each family, one of which also received day care subsidies while the other group did not.

These variables were intended to analyze the respective weight of services and monetary income in determining families' reactions. Similar experiments were conducted in rural Indiana and Oregon.[31]

Throughout 1968, Alice Rivlin argued that the time for a change in the scale of the fiscal strategy had arrived, and she developed a program called BIG (Basic Income Guarantee) to conduct a nationwide test of the concept of a guaranteed minimum income. The project distilled Rivlin's hopes of unifying existing social welfare programs and ending the disparities among existing programs in individual states while simplifying administrative procedures. The BIG project was supposed to be the first decisive step toward a minimum income program for the poor, especially the working poor.[32]

Empowerment Limited

During the closing months of the Johnson administration, there was a prevailing feeling of political powerlessness among the members of the poverty community. In one further indication that the War on Poverty had come to a standstill, the empowerment approach was completely abandoned. The apparent excesses of a few agencies damaged its image and undermined local supports. A series of controversies had caused mayors of the larger cities to openly criticize community action centers. One rumor suggested that Lyndon Johnson had stated that the OEO had been managed by "kooks" and sociologists. The president asked his domestic policy adviser, Joseph Califano, to neutralize the agency by moving away from the Community Action Program's strategy, which was judged responsible for the program's excesses. Such failure, however, did not translate into victory for alternative plans.[33]

After their initial hesitation, poverty experts clarified both their statistical measures and their concrete programs of action. It was no coincidence that conservatives should strongly assail the scientific foundation of the whole attack against poverty by opening a debate on the poverty paradox. Rose Friedman accused experts of inventing a fantasy by contending that a so-important segment of the American population was poor. Mollie Orshansky took the task of defining a poverty line that was soon adopted in all federal agencies. Such reordering caused tensions among experts along gender and professional lines. It also pushed them to indicate more specific measures to fight against poverty. Within the OEO, Robert Lampman deployed his concept of a poverty gap that could easily be reduced if the government wanted to this to happen, while Alvin Schorr defended a system of family allowances inspired by European models. In both cases, these proposals were out of sight of the rest of the population. To some extent, poverty experts became prisoners of the very places where they elaborated their science of poverty. As more and more grassroots organizations defended welfare rights, the gap between experts and citizens grew wider in the violent context of the last months of Lyndon Baines Johnson's presidency.

8

A Doomed Alternative

The year 1968 was a difficult time to be a liberal. Domestic reforms faced an array of obstacles, the protest movement was becoming increasingly radicalized, compounding the effects of the ongoing Vietnam fiasco. The War on Poverty appeared to be at a dead end. The failure of the Poor People's Campaign and the assassination of Robert Kennedy ruined the last hopes of the poverty community to build a strong coalition to defend welfare as a right. Conflicting strands of liberalism seemed to be definitively irreconcilable. It was one more failure for experts after their inability to persuade President Lyndon Johnson and his advisers to replace Community Action Programs with what they believed was a more effective means of combating poverty. This resistance reflected a broader political turning point, as rejection of the Great Society spread across the country and helped Richard Nixon to take the White House.[1]

Poverty experts meanwhile faced an untenable situation within their own ranks, and political allegiances began to waver when President Nixon submitted a family assistance plan to Congress that was based on a federally guaranteed minimum income, a program for which they had been clamoring for years. Robert Lampman believed that the plan would challenge the "tenets of America's conventional wisdom" and put an end to Aid to Families with Dependent Children (AFDC) programs, which, citing James Tobin, he dubbed "an insane piece of social engineering." Although some members of the poverty community, including Alvin Schorr, turned their backs on the struggle and left the administration, there was continued interest in the family assistance project, even though the legislative process transformed a supposedly simple and apolitical measure into an intricate and racially biased proposal.[2]

An outgrowth of the 1950s liberal movement that had long operated in the background, the poverty community was abruptly thrust into the spotlight, and political loyalties became a determining factor as the search for alternative ways of fighting poverty intensified. While the idea of an income guarantee began to gain traction in some political and intellectual circles, the nature and significance of this approach to income redistribution was a key element in the fierce political tug-of-war that culminated in Nixon's reelection in 1972 and in the failure of the Democratic candidate, George McGovern, as well as the last shred of hope for many poverty experts.

A Missed Opportunity

A short time before he was assassinated on April 4, 1968, Martin Luther King Jr. shared a final dream with his fellow citizens—the elimination of poverty on American soil that would at last make the constitutional promise of the "pursuit of happiness" available to every citizen. King's assassination meant that his entourage was left to organize the Poor People's Campaign without his charismatic leadership. On behalf of the Southern Christian Leadership Conference (SCLC), Ralph David Abernathy took the lead. In May, demonstrators headed toward Washington, DC, from multiple states, and set up a camp on the Washington Mall. The camp was to hold no more than three thousand people and was called Resurrection City—an urban area taking up fifteen acres near the Mall's Reflecting Pool.[3]

The Committee of 100, which coordinated all organizations, set up a list of grievances in a "Declaration" that invoked the Declaration of

Figure 8.1. Poor People's March at Lafayette Park and on Connecticut Avenue on June 18, 1968. Courtesy of Library of Congress, Prints and Photographs Division, LC-DIG-ppmsca-04302.

Independence. Abernathy denounced the inhumanity of federal welfare programs and vilified the methods used to humiliate the poor and to dissuade them from asking for help. Abernathy also bitterly described aberrant federal policies that granted nine dollars a month to a poor child in Mississippi but paid a senator from the same state thirteen thousand dollars a month to reduce the state's agricultural production. Organizers of the Poor People's Campaign proposed nothing less than a complete redesign of the welfare system in order to correct these obvious incongruities. Rev. Walter E. Fauntroy, Washington director for the SCLC, did not mince his words to criticize "the preferential treatment given to high salaried administrators, to antiquated racist state departments of education, and to politicians who generally respond only to white, middle-class constituencies and the pampered schools of suburbia." A right to both a living and a secure and adequate income was the main priority of Dr. King's posthumous campaign. The Committee of 100 endorsed the development of experimental income maintenance programs in both urban and rural areas. In other words, the platform of the Poor

People's Campaign was not so different from the internal campaign of the poverty community.[4]

If activists met all department officials, they paid close to attention to the Department of Health, Education, and Welfare (HEW), located southeast of the Mall near the Reflecting Pool. The Poor People's Campaign and their representatives held meetings with government officials who had been authorized by the new secretary of HEW, Wilbur Cohen, to attend them. A HEW longtime civil servant, Mary Switzer, was asked to organize such meetings and to coordinate help for poor people. Alvin Schorr and his assistant Nancy Amidei took the opportunity to establish links with welfare organizations and poor people. Each day, they brought blankets, money, and food to Resurrection City. They also created a group called Federal Employees for Democratic Society that endorsed many of protesters' claims, especially in terms of jobs and incomes.[5]

What emerged from discussions was a strong rejection of moralism among the public welfare administration. As Switzer explained, "One of the most frequent complaints is the failure to use courtesy titles (Mr., Mrs., and Miss) in addressing certain applicants, recipients, and others having dealings with the agency." There were many complaints about "arbitrary treatment or unjust actions" by local social workers. Jesse Jackson lambasted the system for making it difficult for poor families to stay together. Demonstrators deplored the behavior of many social workers who scrutinized recipients' moral behavior and showed a strong lack of respect. For experts, it was a major concern, as they all believed that such practices should not be a trait of modern relief, but instead resembled the old poor laws of the past.[6]

Jackson and other activists particularly decried the 1967 amendments to the Social Security Act that froze earnings for recipients, implemented a "man-in-the-house rule," and imposed compulsory work provisions. Welfare rights organizations called them the Law of Anti-welfare. Requests were also made to change the date on which AFDC payments began. After entitlement for Social Security was established, payment was made retroactive to the first day of the month in which application was made. This was not the case with AFDC. Furthermore, in many states, payments did not begin until eligibility was established. Representatives of the Poor People's Campaign demanded that this delay be corrected. Activists also

<u>FEDERAL EMPLOYEES FOR DEMOCRATIC SOCIETY ENDORSE</u>
<u>THE GOALS OF THE POOR PEOPLE'S CAMPAIGN</u>

1. A MEANINGFUL job at a living wage for every employable citizen.

2. A secure and adequate income for all who cannot find jobs or for whom employment is inappropriate.

3. Access to land as a means to income and livelihood.

4. Access to capital as a means of full participation in the economic life of America.

5. Recognition by law of the right of people affected by government programs to play a truly significant role in determining how they are designed and carried out.

<u>ALL FEDERAL EMPLOYEES ARE URGED TO JOIN WITH</u>
<u>THE POOR PEOPLE'S CAMPAIGN. VOLUNTEERS ARE</u>
<u>NEEDED FOR</u>:

____ Alternate Housing

____ Office Work

____ Babysitting

____ Maintenance assistance

____ Transportation (for individuals as well as food & supplies)

____ Medical assistance

____ Other various needs as they arise.

TO VOLUNTEER CALL: NA-8-9544 from 9 a.m. to 8 p.m.
For information about meetings in your local area as well as other activities call: 628-0555.

ALL DONATIONS should be sent to: SCLC,
1401 "U" Street, N.W.,
Washington, D.C. 20009

Federal Employees for Democratic Society will meet at 8 p.m.
Thursday, May 23, 1968 and alternate Thursdays thereafter,
at LINCOLN TEMPLE, 11th and R St. N.W. If you work for the
Federal government, you are invited to attend.

Figure 8.2. Endorsement by Federal Employees for Democratic Society of Poor People's Campaign (1968). Courtesy of the Social Welfare History Archives.

proposed that mothers who had no available child care services be exempt from the work requirement.[7]

To prepare meetings between representatives from the Poor People's Campaign and HEW's directorship, Schorr explained how to deal with the poorest of the poor to Wilbur Cohen. For one thing, he said, it is important not to use pejorative terms: "For any discussions with the Poor

People, may I make these suggestions about terminology. Do *not* say 'Negro,' but 'Black,' *not 'illegitimate*,' as in illegitimate child, not 'out of wedlock' or even 'illegal,' *not 'you people,'* but 'you' or 'all of you' or anything else."[8]

When the secretary arrived, the crowd sang and expressed their concern with the federal government's inaction:

> Tired of drinking from a ghetto cup,
> Don't give a damn,
> Ain't gonna give up.
> Do right, white man,
> Do right,
> Before I get mad.
> Before I get mad.[9]

After discussions with poor people and their representatives, experts were disappointed. Alvin Schorr urged Secretary Cohen to "spell out in more detail what you have in mind in speaking of a Federal program of public assistance." Welfare organizations and poor people defended the idea that welfare was a right and that it was crucial to put an end to the double-tracks system of the Social Security Act. The National Welfare Rights Organization (NWRO) pushed for a guaranteed income as the only possible alternative and urged Congressmen to endorse the proposal written by liberal senator Fred Harris. Eventually, Cohen refused and thereby increased resentment against welfare programs among people living in Resurrection City.[10]

Despite the hopes of civil rights organizations and the activism of some experts, the Poor People's Campaign was ultimately a failure, one that for many participants marked the end of hopes for reform in the Johnson administration. An independent journalist, Charles Fager, asserted that the failure was "due at least as much to SCLC's own mistakes as it was to any Machiavellian machinations of the Administration and the mass media." In a time of strong tensions within the liberal coalition, experts' concerns showed that they were less powerless than Machiavellian. The assassination of Robert Kennedy, who had supported major reforms defended by the poverty community, and the election of Richard Nixon increased troubles and disarray.[11]

Richard Nixon's Aid to Families

When the new president elect decided to make welfare reform a priority, many experts were surprised. During the campaign, Nixon repeatedly lambasted social workers and mocked the foolish Community Action Programs as typical liberals' wrongdoing. During the summer of 1969, he kept on denouncing what he described as a "dangerous decline into welfarism" at the expense of the working poor. The main target of his diatribe was AFDC, which he argued was fraught with dangerous social side effects that the War on Poverty had failed to remedy. Despite Nixon's violent rhetoric, his proposal of a guaranteed income for poor families was a complete surprise to the poverty community. Tricky Dick eventually endorsed what liberal advisers and politicians had refused to support for so many years.[12]

To promote this new vision of welfare, Nixon named Robert Finch secretary of health, education, and welfare. He also invited Daniel Patrick Moynihan, whose iconoclastic views he appreciated, to become his adviser on urban affairs. Moynihan had long called Community Action Programs absurd and dangerous and supported replacing them with a system of direct allowances. With the help of Nixon's adviser John Ehrlichman, Finch and Moynihan began to completely redesign antipoverty programs. They enjoyed an unusual degree of latitude because Nixon preferred to delegate social policy issues, and before long they were asked to present their proposals for a revised and improved War on Poverty. In March 1969, the General Accounting Office published an evaluation of the Office of Economic Opportunity that cited Community Action Programs as an example of the agency's uneven performance. Donald Rumsfeld was appointed to head the agency. Rumsfeld's first step was to increase the agency's research division. Although Robert Levine resigned, his inquiring spirit continued and he showered his successors with praise. Two economists named John Wilson and Thomas Glennan were put in charge of research, partly based on Glennan's earlier work as social science research coordinator at the RAND Corporation. The mandate of the expanded research team was to develop a way to completely overhaul the welfare system.[13]

Among Nixon's major goals was to improve coordination between the various welfare programs, which had deteriorated during 1969. New York City found itself in the center of controversy as welfare rights organizations mobilized poor people and lawyers fought for their rights. In response to steady increases in the welfare rolls and a growing budget deficit, Mayor John Lindsay announced that he was tightening eligibility requirements for special assistance programs, a move that triggered massive rioting and led to the occupation of City Hall by an estimated six hundred protesters. Militants in Brooklyn chanted, "Lindsay and Rockefeller you just lost our vote because you took from us our overcoat." Mass arrests and the ensuing turmoil gave the Nixon administration further evidence that the welfare system was in serious disrepair. The migration of poor people from the South to the North, where benefits where higher, was cited to explain New York's welfare crisis. The specter of a welfare mess that had caused a white backlash in Newburgh nine years ago reappeared on the streets of New York City.[14]

Richard P. Nathan of the Brookings Institution was asked to form a committee to investigate the deeper causes of social unrest. Nathan had previously worked for the Kerner Commission analyzing the factors underlying urban riots and had recommended significant social reforms. Nathan's plan would allow aid in those states with the lowest payments to be increased while at the same time limiting targeted aid to particular groups, thus avoiding bankrupting local governments. His report reflected Nixon's desire for a new form of federalism, although it left responsibility for administering the programs to the individual states. The federal government would guarantee thirty dollars in average monthly payments, plus half of any additional payments up to a fixed limit of forty dollars for recipients of AFDC, sixty-five dollars for the elderly, and ninety dollars for the vision impaired and disabled. However, Arthur Burns, a conservative economic adviser to Nixon, voiced strong disapproval of the plan, urging Nixon to make reducing the welfare rolls a priority, reminding the president that he had been elected on the strength of his promises to reduce welfare.[15]

Moynihan was meanwhile orchestrating a patient campaign to win the president over by comparing the United States to Victorian England and persuading Nixon to reconcile the "two nations" with a minimum guaranteed income for poor families. He also argued that a guaranteed income would give families an incentive to stay together and remain employed. In February 1969, Nixon rejected Burns's views and agreed to consider reforming the welfare system according to the Nathan report's recommendations. This in turn enabled officials at the Department of Health, Education and Welfare to promote their proposal for a tax credit for poor families. A long-term proponent of the tax credit and a member of the research team, Worth Bateman, started investigating the plan's technical implications and invited James Lyday to join HEW. As an Office of Economic Opportunity staff member and the author of several reports on minimum income, Lyday had drafted the text of a law to implement a federally guaranteed minimum income for William Ryan, a New York State representative. With the assistance of Jodie Allen, Bateman and Lyday used computerized simulations and hired the Hendrickson Corporation to collect data. The plan's total cost was projected to be two billion dollars, roughly six hundred million higher than the Nathan plan. Despite the additional costs, Bateman and Lyday convinced their superiors that their plan was better. In March, they were able to pitch it to John Ehrlichman and Moynihan. Presidential approval was needed, and they presented the family allowance system to President Nixon as a break with the "ineffective" approaches of the past. Moynihan also threw his support behind this novel proposal.[16]

Nixon was keenly aware that he faced a key domestic policy decision, and he asked his labor secretary, George Schultz, to evaluate the proposal. A former colleague of Milton Friedman at the University of Chicago, Schultz was a conservative economist, and he advised the president to focus on work incentives in order to avoid the errors of past programs by encouraging recipients to be employed. Nixon gave his agreement and asked the team to draft legislation to place before Congress as soon as possible. Computerized simulations helped set payments to families with dependent children at sixteen hundred dollars, which therefore became the official minimum guaranteed income. At a last meeting at Camp David on August 6, 1969, Nixon agreed to call the program the "family assistance plan," and two days later Nixon publicly announced new welfare reforms in a speech in Miami Beach, promising that they would be consistent with the American work ethic while also helping the "forgotten Americans."[17]

The plan would provide an annual family income of five hundred dollars for two parents and three hundred additional dollars for every child. Unlike for AFDC, aid levels were to be set by the federal government with no input from the states. Supplemental income would be allowed in the form of other payments and wages. Eligibility was based on exclusively incomes that fell below the poverty threshold whether or not the head of household worked. The marginal tax rate for supplemental income was set at 50 percent, and a digressive system encouraged working rather than remaining on welfare. Some reservations about the program persisted inside the administration, and to avoid alienating voters, Nixon made contradictory promises not to lower welfare payments but to replace the payment program for families with dependent children. Still, the plan was conceived in a way that addressed what were perceived as the "perverse incentives" of the welfare system.

The text of the law was forwarded to Congress in October 1969. It included an additional provision that states would be responsible for payments that exceeded the federal family assistance plan. Families retained the right to earn an income of 720 dollars, but families that earned over 3,920 dollars would become ineligible. With Moynihan's guidance, Nixon had steered a path between the different plans proposed by the poverty community since the early 1960s. It came as a surprise for many experts that even Wilbur Cohen praised its simplicity, while under cover of anonymity, another former department official confided to the political scientist Edward Burke in 1971 that he "almost threw his beer at the television when he heard Cohen supported the plan." Only social workers—notably Alvin Schorr, who left the administration for a position at New York University—spoke out against Nixon's contempt for social workers and his efforts to blame the victims, particularly African American women.[18]

One final crucial step remained: winning congressional backing. The timing was ideal for the publication of the initial findings of an experiment conducted in New Jersey by the University of Wisconsin's Institute for Research on Poverty (IRP). IRP was the product of Lampman's effort to convince Office of Economic Opportunity (OEO) officials to finance research before developing new social programs. Economist Harold Watts became his first director. The most important IRP project, the New Jersey experiment, was conducted in partnership with the OEO. The purpose of the study, which OEO staffer Joseph Kershaw helped Watts design and analyze, was to understand how the poor would respond to a guaranteed income. Once again, in a confrontation familiar to the poverty community, the behavior of the poor conflicted with the issue of income distribution. By then, it was supposed to demonstrate the viability of Nixon's family assistance plan.[19]

New Jersey Experiment

From the very beginning, the New Jersey experiment ran into a number of problems transferring money to participating families required close co-operation between the Internal Revenue Service (IRS) and local agencies. The IRP negotiated with the IRS to ensure that the income paid to families as part of the study was tax exempt. The IRS reluctantly agreed, but it insisted on the right to audit selected families. Participating families were matched according to certain criteria. Every participating family would have a male head of household between eighteen and fifty years of age who was neither a student nor disabled and lived with at least one other person. Four guaranteed income levels were established using the Social Security Administration's poverty tables.[20]

These data helped researchers divide families into groups that would receive 50, 75, 100, or 125 percent of the poverty threshold. Supplemental income would be taxed at varying rates—some at 50 percent and others at 70 percent—to test the hypothesis that tax rates could influence motivation to work.

In practice, it proved to be quite complicated to select families to participate in the experiment. As many as sixty-two families declined to participate for fear of losing money or simply out of distrust. The burden of participating also contributed to some families' reluctance to participate and attrition. There were additional problems in selecting a representative

TABLE 8.1. The poverty threshold set by the Institute for Research on Poverty (1968)

Family size	Federal poverty threshold (Social Security, 1967)	Amount of income for the experiment
2	$2,130	$2,000
3	$2,610	$2,750
4	$3,335	$3,300
5	$3,930	$3,700
6	$4,410	$4,050
7	$4,925	$4,350
More than 8	$5,440	$4,600

Source: Harold Watts, "Graduated Work Incentives: An Experiment in Negative Taxation," *American Economic Review* 59 (1969): 462.

TABLE 8.2. Level of guaranteed income—the New Jersey experiment (1968)

Level of guaranteed income	Family size (2)	Family size (3)	Family size (4)	Family size (5)	Family size (6)	Family size (7)	Family size (8)
50% of poverty level	$1,055	$1,450	$1,741	$1,952	$2,136	$2,294	$2,426
75% of poverty level	$1,582	$2,175	$2,611	$2,928	$3,204	$3,441	$3,639
100% of poverty level	$2,110	$2,901	$3,482	$3,904	$4,273	$4,589	$4,853
125% of poverty level	$2,637	$3,626	$4,352	$4,880	$5,341	$5,736	$6,066

Source: Larry Orr, Robinson Hollister, and Myron Lefcowitz, *Income Maintenance: Interdisciplinary Approaches to Research* (Chicago: IRP Monograph Series, 1971), 27.

sample of families that reflected American poverty; African Americans and Puerto Ricans were systematically overrepresented. Every family was required to be interviewed three times a month. The African American population in Trenton, New Jersey, was 22.4 percent, but the percentage of the city's African American welfare recipients was 66 percent, compared with only 18 percent white and 16 percent Puerto Rican. In Paterson, Passaic, and Jersey City, Puerto Ricans were equally overrepresented. In Paterson, the original sample included 50 percent Puerto Ricans, 40 percent African Americans, and only 10 percent whites. The difficulty of establishing representative samples led researchers to include the city of Scranton, Pennsylvania, which had a higher percentage of poor, white, working-class families. The researchers also broadened the operational definition of poverty to include families with incomes that exceeded 50 percent of the official threshold. The experiment became even more complicated after the state of New Jersey expanded eligibility criteria for payments for dependent children, which forced Watts and Kershaw to ask families to choose between state family payments and the minimum income to avoid skewing study results.[21]

The IRP was finally able to establish a sample of 1,375 poor families that was divided into experimental and control groups. In October 1970, only ninety-one families had to be excluded from the experiment because their incomes surpassed the poverty threshold. Initial results were mildly encouraging in showing that the tax credit did exert a marginal effect on the sample families' behavior and that it did not cause men to stop working. The results were interpreted cautiously by the research team at first,

but increasingly intense congressional debates surrounding the family assistance program soon forced them to abandon their scientific reservations
as pressure from the president's team pushed the OEO and IRP to publish
provisional results.

By early 1970, the OEO agreed to publish the provisional data and
to ask the lead researchers to present them to Congress. Congressional
hearings on the Nixon welfare reform plan began in January. It would
be critical to win the support of Wilbur Mills's House Ways and Means
Committee, especially during a period of fiscal conservatism. Watts testified before the committee, but the hearings were a disappointment to the
researchers and the administration. Watts's testimony caused turmoil after
Senator John Williams tried to force him to admit to a conflict of interest
because of his position as IRP director. In an atmosphere of latent hostility,
Watts was very reserved in his interpretation of the effects of the tax credit
on participants' motivation to work. Moynihan was infuriated by what he
saw as the researchers' procrastination and openly voiced his annoyance
with the economists on the research team to the OEO directors. He accused the economists of failing to give accurate information beforehand,
and "after that it's too late." The OEO asked Watts to filter the results in
a way that might encourage the plan to pass, and under pressure Watts
agreed to selectively cull the data for favorable results. The published text
supported the New Jersey experiment, and therefore indirectly the family
assistance plan, with IRP experts claiming that there was no evidence that
assistance caused participants' motivation to work to diminish.

In June, a group of Congress members publicly lambasted the study,
claiming that the study duration was too short to allow for credible conclusions. They also argued that participants may have modified their
behaviors simply because they knew they were being studied. The OEO
soon answered these allegations of a "Hawthorne effect" with a new report that confirmed the preliminary published findings. Watts was caught
up in this institutional turmoil. Summoned to respond to the Congress
members' attacks, he finally published data from a larger sample of four
hundred families in Trenton and Patterson-Passaic that again showed no
negative effects of payments on participants' motivation to work. Watts
reiterated the encouraging conclusions of the OEO report despite his personal belief that the findings were incomplete. The political spin on the

New Jersey findings was ultimately insufficient to propel Moynihan's plan to legislative victory.[22]

FAP Fails

The early hopes of economists who had backed the guaranteed income plan were quickly dashed as the reform effort failed to resist political escalation in Congress. In March 1970, the Ways and Means Committee issued an initially favorable opinion of the family assistance plan, however. During the hearings, conservative economists, including Milton Friedman, urged legislators to keep marginal tax rates on supplementary income as low as possible to sustain recipients' motivation to work. Despite the reservations of some legislators, on April 16, 1970, the House of Representatives voted to approve the law. But the law hit a snag in the Senate committee responsible for final approval. In early May, the Senate Finance Committee asked for more information about the provisions that governed supplemental income.[23]

Primarily composed of senators from the rural South, the committee was deeply suspicious of this most recent social engineering project, and officials at HEW struggled to convince them that the plan had no negative social side effects. Moynihan was afraid that the senators were convinced that the program provided a disincentive to work, but he felt that "it could be demonstrated" that this was not the case. Russell Long, who chaired the Senate committee, called the family assistance plan the "Welfare Expansion and Mess Perpetuation Bill." Long saw the program as an inducement to idleness and preferred a program that targeted the elderly. Delaware senator John Williams also vigorously attacked what he claimed were the negative social consequences of the plan. For Georgia senator Herman Talmadge, the FAP would give poor people the opportunity to "do a little casual labor on somebody's yard from time to time and maybe sell a little heroin or do a little burglary." The southerners unanimously expressed a fear that the FAP would have negative effects on the African American labor force in the South.[24]

The liberal senator Eugene McCarthy responded to their concerns by submitting the fifty-five-hundred-dollar plan proposed by the NWRO and by inviting mothers who were welfare recipients to testify before the committee. The NWRO's vice president, Beulah Sanders, baldly told the senators that they could not "force her to work"! The hearings caused a conservative swing among the committee's more moderate members. On November 20, 1970, they voted to oppose the plan. Liberal senators Fred Harris and Eugene McCarthy joined the opposition, expressing a preference for the minimum guaranteed income plan and stating that the social assistance proposal was too liberal. Senators Abraham Ribicoff of Connecticut and Wallace Bennett of Utah proposed a revised version with a higher minimum income level. In short, instead of improving the social welfare system, the idea of a minimum income had unleashed a political firestorm. "Zap FAP" became the new slogan of the NWRO, which denounced the workfare provision and the misconceptions about race and gender that it promoted.[25]

The Nixon administration responded by attempting to revise the proposal. The debates had highlighted the importance of addressing the crucial connection between eligibility and work. Social welfare had the undesirable potential consequence of providing a pathway out of poverty that discouraged people from working, and the solution was to remove the disincentive effect of the minimum guaranteed income. In January 1971, Wilbur Mills led discussions and oversaw the final version of the legislation. The Ways and Means Committee submitted a new version to the Senate that incorporated threshold effects to encourage work and curtail the possibility of accumulating payments. Beneficiaries of the family assistance plan, for example, would be ineligible for food stamps.[26]

Under the plan's new version, a family of four would receive 2,400 dollars annually, and supplemental income up to 720 dollars was allowed without deductions. To encourage recipients to work, the new plan would exclude only one-third of income—instead of one-half—in excess of the threshold. The earlier plan had a threshold effect beginning at $3,290, but that figure increased to $4,140 in the new version. To manage the program more efficiently, families would be divided into two groups, one group in which family members who worked would be the responsibility of the Department of Labor, and another group of families with no working members. To address concerns about fraud, the committee tightened conditions for eligibility. The total cost of the plan was estimated at $4 billion.[27]

The Senate remained hostile despite these modifications, which Russell Long claimed failed to mitigate a deleterious influence on recipients' motivation to work, asking his colleagues why the government should "give $5,000 to legitimate illegitimacy." The conservative majority on the Senate Finance Committee united against the proposal, claiming that it was supposed to replace traditional welfare with a minimum guaranteed income. The liberal opposition under Fred Harris and Abraham Ribicoff criticized problems with the program, particularly the lack of adequate funding, adding that it was cynical to guarantee a minimum income of twenty-four hundred dollars when the poverty threshold was thirty-nine hundred dollars. They further maintained that it was illogical to allocate the same income to a retired couple as to a family of four.

To counter the conservative trend of the proceedings, Senator Ribicoff organized a bipartisan committee of governors, mayors, and welfare administrators in the month of October. The cause received a boost when Massachusetts governor Francis Sargent promised his support, and Sargent and Ribicoff established an estimated minimum guaranteed income of three thousand dollars for a family of four. The income threshold remained the same as in Nixon's proposal, but their version softened the provision requiring women with children under six years old to work. In January 1972, twenty-two senators and fifteen governors offered their support for the proposal, at which point Nixon and Ribicoff called a meeting and negotiated a compromise. The executive branch agreed to conduct experiments on the guaranteed income that were modeled on the New Jersey experiment before assigning an income level, and in return, Ribicoff agreed to abide by the studies' results.[28]

The administration's caution was justified by budgetary calculations indicating that the Ribicoff plan would cost $11.3 billion, significantly more than the Finance Committee plan, which would not exceed $6.5 billion. In April 1972, Ribicoff and Sargent drafted a new version that incorporated the results of studies of poor families ordered by the Nixon administration. The approach of the elections slowed the committee's discussions, however, with the conservative wing deliberately dragging its feet so that hearings continued into the period leading up to the election. It denounced the family assistance program as an "abomination." In April, Ribicoff and Sargent proposed appending an arsenal of measures to combat fraud and to force mothers to work. Then, on April 28,

1972, they voted to replace the Ways and Means Committee plan with a guaranteed employment program for welfare recipients. The plan stipulated that families with able-bodied fathers or mothers with no children under the age of six would be ineligible for family assistance payments but would be eligible for guaranteed employment. In June, the Senate approved a series of amendments further limiting eligibility for families with dependent children and increasing verification procedures. The Nixon administration hesitated between the Ways and Means Committee plan and the Ribicoff-Sargent plan. The administration increasingly appeared to be stuck at an institutional impasse.[29]

Efforts to redirect the War on Poverty had triggered an unexpected series of changes. Ironically, although the original goal of the minimum guaranteed income had been to simplify the welfare system, the institutional review process had instead made it hugely complicated by grafting it onto existing welfare payment programs. The family assistance plan had become a cumbersome affair so loaded with multiple threshold effects that it was too complex to understand. A catalog of amendments had transformed a program praised for simplicity into a byzantine, technical text that hindered both legislative review and the likelihood of public support. For the poverty community, there was one last hope: George McGovern's presidential campaign.

Demogrant for All?

During the 1972 presidential campaign, the epilogue to the War on Poverty was in the hands of poverty experts. As a social worker and longtime advocate of reforming the welfare system, Alvin Schorr was appointed as one of the top advisers to South Dakota senator George McGovern, who had decided to enter the presidential campaign. McGovern was highly supportive of welfare, but he faced a choice between the universal tax credit and a family allowance scheme. In the wake of Robert Kennedy's premature death and Hubert Humphrey's failed 1968 candidacy, McGovern had become the standard bearer for Democrats' revived hopes. As a believer in the "new politics," he intended to use welfare as the symbol of a renewed social contract and shared the idea that welfare was a right.[30]

Since the end of the Johnson administration, McGovern had repeatedly promoted alternatives to the minimum income and contrasted his proposals with the Nixon plan. In a January 1970 speech to the Citizen's Committee for Children, which included social workers and academics, among them Alvin Schorr, McGovern announced his support for a family assistance program that would provide a monthly allowance of fifty to sixty-five dollars per family and would be paid for by repealing the dependent child tax deduction. He saw the plan as a clear alternative to current realities, arguing that social programs dating from the 1960s had become "a catastrophe" and were mocked as products of "welfare liberals."[31]

As a senator in 1970, McGovern criticized the Nixon plan as too narrowly targeted and therefore harmful to underprivileged populations. He proposed an alternative, four-part plan that would include payments for children, a guaranteed employment program, and higher Social Security payments for the elderly and disabled, as well as specific targeted assistance for those not covered by other measures. His proposals fluctuated somewhat depending on the audience, however. The following year, he came out in support of the tax credit plan, citing a proposal for a minimum guaranteed income of four thousand dollars for a family of four.[32]

McGovern intended to launch a genuine debate on the future of welfare in 1972 as part of his presidential campaign. By then, Alvin Schorr was a professor at New York University and accepted to co-chair a committee on taxation and welfare for McGovern. The committee suggested that the candidate advocate for complete reform of the nation's welfare programs instead of just another "gadget." McGovern's advisers agreed on the need for a guaranteed income for American citizens, but divisions among the experts were worsened by the campaign environment. The senator asked Schorr to assist him after declining an offer of help from Wilbur Cohen, whom he believed to be too obtuse and who had supported Nixon's family assistance plan. The social worker continued to argue in favor of a system of family allowances.[33]

To further the cause, Schorr's group of reformers created an organization to bring together local associations such as the Atlanta Council of Social Agencies and the New York Citizen's Committee for Children. In 1970, Schorr submitted his family allowance proposal to McGovern, who was looking for new campaign topics for the 1972 primaries and had expressed interest in a major reform. The social worker proposed a universal social contract, "not a duplex but a unitary society," and argued that the plan should synthesize the various solutions that the poverty expert community had proposed over the course of the previous decade, and he made detailed proposals to guarantee greater social justice. His first proposal was for McGovern to convert the $750 minimum tax exemption into guaranteed income while increasing Social Security payments to the elderly, the disabled, and widows. He also proposed a program for the long-term unemployed and recommended deeper reforms, especially means testing for Social Security. Schorr envisioned an independent agency to supervise this cluster of measures, and he vigorously opposed the idea of a universal tax credit, which he believed was a "poor political choice," an expression borrowed from Cohen.[34]

Any proposal that remotely resembled Nixon's family assistance program would not help McGovern differentiate himself from his opponent. Relying on his distrust of a two-level program, with one level for the poor and another for the rest of the population, Schorr pointed out British reforms that had helped middle-class families more than the poor. In setting the financial conditions for eligibility and a single fiscal incentive to work, the tax credit would be complicated to apply in practical terms, and it also risked being worse than the existing system for the poor. Furthermore, this kind of program also raised an institutional question, and Schorr wondered whether the views of conservative senators would be likely to change under a new president.[35]

It came as no surprise that Schorr found advocates for a negative income tax among the economists advising McGovern. By then, secret opposition had become public, and it raged during the whole campaign. Within the McGovern campaign staff, tax-related matters were the responsibility of a New York lawyer named Adrian De Wind, whose entourage included economists and attorneys from the Lyndon Johnson administration, including Joseph Pechman and Stanley Surrey. James Tobin from Yale University also contributed technical skills to the campaign. Faced with the stalled family assistance plan and the escalating reaction in liberal circles, the economists needed a genuine alternative to demarcate their candidate's position. The experts initially submitted the idea of a capital gains tax like that on ordinary income that they estimated would reap as much as twenty-two billion dollars. As a counterpoint to this fiscal pressure on capital, they supported the concept of a universal income, a "demogrant," in the form of a federally guaranteed minimum income of one thousand dollars per person for every man, woman, and child, with no conditions for eligibility. This plan was intended to remedy the injustices of both the social welfare system and the tax system.[36]

McGovern's closest advisers were hesitating between Tobin's demogrant and Schorr's more gradual reforms. The demogrant ultimately won, especially under pressure from Jesse Jackson, who was skeptical about the viability of the family allowance plan. In a speech at the University of Iowa in January 1972, McGovern announced that the social welfare system would be replaced by a revolutionary new measure. The plan that he presented included a guaranteed income for every man, woman, and child in the country. At one point in the Democratic primaries, McGovern was facing Hubert Humphrey during a debate in California when Humphrey called the measure pure demagoguery, estimating the program's cost to be $210 billion annually. McGovern lost himself in data in attempting to respond and had difficulty stating the program's precise costs. Within the Democratic Party, the proposal raised as many questions as it attracted supporters. Former president Johnson called it a "stupid idea" and still deplored income distribution as contrary to American ideals.[37]

While he was creating his campaign team after the primaries, McGovern consulted a wider range of experts about welfare and, increasingly aware of his responsibilities if he were elected, he invited Wilbur Cohen to join the discussions. Overcoming his skepticism about some of McGovern's foreign policy positions, Cohen agreed. In August 1972, he joined a meeting of advisers that McGovern organized to help him frame his position on the guaranteed minimum income. Cohen once again complained about the extent of economists' influence on McGovern, especially James Tobin, Arthur Okun, Joseph Pechman, and Charles Schultz. They stuck to their proposal, however, complaining bitterly about the lukewarm reform proposals from Schorr and pointing out that thirty years of Social Security had failed to eliminate poverty. Still, the demogrant's high costs worked against them. McGovern was looking for ways to reduce the scope of the tax credit proposal by targeting only the poor, but the revised plan risked looking too similar to Nixon's proposal.[38]

In late August, McGovern announced that he was abandoning the universal payment plan in a speech to a Wall Street market analysis firm. Cohen believed that his appeals to reason might had struck home.

McGovern's turnaround can also be understood in light of his penchant for fiscal realism. Because any further increases would spell certain electoral disaster, he decided to drop the project. Nixon's team repeatedly attacked the project. A political ad financed by a group called Democrats for Nixon portrayed a white working class very skeptical about the disappearance of the work ethic and the explosion of the number of people on welfare.

Despite this shift, the McGovern campaign remained haunted by the demogrant, which McGovern's Republican adversaries systematically cited to discredit him. McGovern's defeat in November signaled the definitive end of payment plans for children or large-scale tax reform. In more than one way, 1972 also spelled the end of the War on Poverty that poverty experts had been dreaming about for years and a victory for a more cautious, conservative approach like that championed by Cohen. For proponents of welfare reform, McGovern's hesitation had catastrophic consequences, a sentiment summarized neatly by Abraham Ribicoff when he stated that McGovern's proposal changed the way senators thought about welfare reforms. There can be no question that Ribicoff's pessimism reflected the end of a political and scientific era.[39]

War Ends?

In September 1972, the Senate Finance Committee passed a minimum guaranteed income for three specific categories—the elderly, the vision impaired, and the disabled—as part of a set of amendments to the 1935 Social Security law—the Supplemental Security Income (SSI). This initiative by the Senate effectively ended the debate about the Nixon plan. Relations between proponents of a moderate version of the family assistance program, particularly Ribicoff's, and the administration had become strained during the campaign. During the summer of 1972, Nixon asked one of his close advisers to "kill" the plan in Congress and divert blame for its failure onto the Democrats. In October, with the tacit consent of the president's entourage, both houses of Congress approved a law that included category-based assistance but not a single measure to reform aid to families with dependent children. Moynihan resigned his position with the Nixon administration in protest, expressing intense regret that efforts to transform the welfare system that he had been part of since the late 1960s had abysmally failed.[40]

In tandem with SSI, a terminological shift also took place in the ranks of the administration. As soon as he had been elected, Nixon asked his cabinet members to replace the terms *poverty* and *the poor* with *low-income families*, a return to a label in use in the 1950s. Twenty years later, Carol Khosrovi, the OEO congressional liaison officer, formally asked that "low-income individuals become the official category." Donald Rumsfeld, the OEO director, was obliged to calm the ensuing uproar inside the agency to avoid a bureaucratic rebellion.[41]

These semantic debates were just a prelude to the behind-the-scenes dismantling of the War on Poverty, however, and the OEO was disbanded by the Nixon administration in 1973. The scientific category *poverty* that had been empirically created by the experts in the poverty community began to disappear from politics, and when the findings of the New Jersey study were published in 1973, they were greeted with indifference. The results showed that the effects of measures to encourage the poor to work were insignificant, except for Hispanics, an exception that remained unexplained by the experts. Just as President Nixon was trying to end the Vietnam War, the War on Poverty was also drawing to a close in 1973, the swan song of a vast project to redistribute income that had begun in the 1950s. In March 1973, Nixon publicly abandoned the idea of submitting a revised version to Congress. In 1973, the topic of reform was no longer on the political map. Congress negotiated the conditions for applying SSI in the states. In January 1974, the nation acquired a minimum guaranteed income of $1,680 for a single person living alone and $2,520 for a couple that applied to only the elderly, the vision impaired, and the disabled. The law represented the triumph of the gradual, most conservative approach touted by Wilbur Cohen. Almost thirty years after the invisible War on Poverty started, more than three million deserving poor were benefiting from monetary assistance, a minimal residue of the grand plan developed in postwar America by the poverty community.[42]

Conclusion

THE END OF POVERTY?

In 1963, Swedish economist and public intellectual Gunnar Myrdal published his book *Challenge to Affluence*. His landmark 1944 book, *An American Dilemma*, had already pointed out the gap between apparent abundance and the bitter reality of life for millions of African Americans. Almost twenty years later, his views contradicted the dominant trend by refusing to focus on only the "culture of poverty." Instead, he emphasized the rise of what he was the first to identify as an "underclass of unemployed and, gradually, unemployable persons and families" that was the seemingly inevitable result of structural and technological problems inherent in modern society.[1]

In 1971, eight years after Myrdal's book appeared, the American philosopher John Rawls used the expression "maximin" in *Theory of Justice* to refer to the idea that in order to be egalitarian, a society would have to "maximize the minimum" living conditions that it provides to its citizens. Myrdal and Rawls both saw eliminating poverty as an imperative fundamental necessity in modern, particularly affluent, societies. As historian

Gareth Stedman Jones has suggested, though, this high goal can be traced to the beginnings of Western political modernism and to a belief that concerted intellectual, political, and scientific action could eradicate poverty. This belief was given added impetus by an unbounded postwar faith in the power of technological progress to solve any social problem. *The Experts' War on Poverty* has attempted to show how a community of committed experts attempted to apply Rawls's principle in prosperous America.[2]

When Rawls published his opus, the experts were disheartened. In 1973, the economist Alice Rivlin captured the mood among her peers, explaining that they had been defeated because of their political and scientific "naïveté." Most members of the expert community saw themselves as "physicists" trying "to build a bomb or a bridge." But, as Rivlin pointed out, the War on Poverty presented a far more complex set of problems to solve than did the Manhattan Project and the nuclear bomb. The equally disenchanted economist Robert Lampman, following up on comments by Walter Heller (who also quit the Council of Economic Advisers in its early stages) came to a sobering conclusion about life in Washington, which he claimed "just ruined your family life and everything else." Lampman's discouragement was typical of the feelings of many intellectuals who had been caught up in the political whirlwinds of the period and were left with the vague sense of having contributed to an "uncertain victory," in the historian James Kloppenberg's words. The sullen mood of the early 1970s was exacerbated by nationwide turmoil over the Vietnam War, the Watergate scandal, and the decline of American industry. The failure of income redistribution strategies is only one example of the very mixed record of achievement of other postwar reform initiatives and applied expertise.[3]

Although the idea of grand structural reforms had been abandoned after the 1930s, the debate about the nature and meaning of liberalism in the country persisted well into the 1970s. The concept of the "end of ideology" popularized by liberal intellectuals in the 1950s seemed to suggest that the liberal project had reached a dead end, paving the way for conservatives to replace it with their own set of free market ideals and programs. Although the liberal majority was attempting to retain the "vital center"— the critical voter base that had sustained the New Deal—poverty experts were trying to revitalize liberal reforms in ways that could appeal to both marginalized social groups and middle-class Americans. Nowhere better symbolized this generational swing than the Department of Economics at the University of Wisconsin, which applied the intellectual and political legacy of the labor question to the issue of poverty. In 1969, Lampman continued to express the optimistic view that "the poverty problem can be solved in the near future," adding that "poverty reduction does not require and will not achieve a transformation of society." He concluded by asserting that Americans "should proceed, not with utopian expectations, but with the belief that achievement of this goal, like the achievement of earlier stated health, educational, welfare, and economic goals, will be a worthy achievement in the slow evolution of the good society." The new "Wisconsin idea" was the crowning example of postwar faith in social reform initiatives.[4]

Because this generation of reformers came of age in an era of economic stagnation and the New Deal, they believed that the social contract was still incomplete. Their intellectual discomfort with the status quo drove their commitment to a complete reform of the welfare system. As academics and civil servants, they doubted that every member of society benefited from economic growth and argued that the inherent authenticity of American society meant that it was possible to repair inequalities in the country's social fabric. Indeed, this alliance between technical expertise and ethical idealism, which produced what has sometimes been compared to a religious revival, is among the most intriguing aspects of the postwar environment in the United States. From their offices in federal agencies or on university campuses, poverty experts developed the intellectual and practical tools needed to create and sustain a massive movement for social reform. *The Experts' War on Poverty* challenges the image of an intellectual elite that abandoned the public after the war to protect themselves from the irrationality of the masses. Instead, this book reveals a striking coherence between the goals of the academic elite and youth protest movements in the 1950s and 1960s. Although they failed to find a stable enough common ground to fully achieve their lofty goals, both camps were engaged in a search for real social justice and equality and for deeper authenticity in human and family relationships.[5]

While it has depicted the origins and nature of this idealistic blend of science and activism in the name of eradicating poverty, this book has also exposed the rather haphazard origins of the reform. Experts' attempts to analyze and explain the poverty paradox in the 1950s were often redundant and scattered. Over a period of fifteen years of research and endless meetings and debates, they developed a very complicated, cumbersome catalog of categories and labels for different subgroups while struggling with the empirical and statistical problem of defining and quantifying poverty. Their world was made of numbers, statistics, and charts that provided conflicting and unstable conclusions about society, especially low-income people. The computer age reinforced this trust in numbers and statistical surveys.

The federal government provided a major stabilizing force for the poverty community, which was composed of groups and organizations with shifting boundaries, including the congressional Joint Economic Committee, university research centers, and philanthropic foundations. There was also considerable amateurism and a fair number of shadowy areas in terms of rhetoric and actual practices among researchers during the 1950s. These weaknesses gradually improved, however, eventually enabling consultation and collaboration between the various institutions and individuals who constituted the poverty community. Experts' participation in seminars, task forces, and committees helped them reconcile methodological and ideological differences and professional and institutional rivalries. One source of support for consistency and a common sense of purpose came from dialogue with their British counterparts. Similar reform efforts under way in Britain and other Western countries confirmed that the American fight against poverty was as critically needed as it was in other modern societies.

One of the most significant turning points in the scientific effort to define poverty involved the successful merger of two different scientific approaches. It would be difficult to exaggerate the importance of the encounter between time-honored methods of quantifying working-class and rural family budgets and modern statistical methods for collecting and analyzing large-scale data. The reconciliation of time-honored sociological studies with quantitative methods in turn allowed experts to use hard data to understand, identify, and categorize the segments of the population who could be categorized as "poor." A twenty-year research program made it possible for the reform-minded poverty community to define poverty in a way that established it as directly linked to American prosperity. Poverty came to be seen as relative, massive, and involuntary, a redefinition that allowed the concept of poverty to transcend the idea that it was absolute, circumscribed, and voluntary, an idea that had long undermined social reform initiatives. This newer, relative definition of poverty is reflected in universal solutions to poverty such as tax credits and European-style family allowances. The experts shared the view that a more equitable social contract, backed up by empirical data, would deeply transform society by ensuring equality. They intentionally framed their arguments in universal, color-blind terms to avoid the often violent, racialized characterizations of welfare recipients. This egalitarian approach flowed directly from a more empirically based perspective on actual poor American families and the position of minorities within that broader category. These long-standing and sometimes laborious efforts to quantify poverty and propose evidence-based solutions combined with the objective language of science were important tools in the experts' attempts to win over opponents to welfare reform. One of the many perplexing paradoxes surrounding the poverty community's commitment to reform was that it exacerbated disagreement among the ranks of liberals.[6]

As this book has made clear, and by contrast with the position of much current historical scholarship, the scientific revolution surrounding poverty did not begin after the War on Poverty had begun in 1964. This science did not suddenly appear out of nowhere, but developed in an almost organic process beginning in the 1950s. Once it had acquired a certain amount of visibility, this burgeoning, science-driven understanding of poverty began to appeal to politicians who were looking for progressive policy ideas to support. As this book has also demonstrated, poverty experts were operating against daunting political, scientific, and economic odds as they crafted a new scientific field, a testament to their sustained scientific and political commitment. As French sociologist Christian Topalov has said in discussing late nineteenth-century social movements in France, every reform movement risks remaining "invisible."[7]

For poverty experts, though, the encounter between the scientific and political spheres caused their reformist zeal to take off in new and unexpected directions. Once the political decision to support poverty reform had been made, poverty was recast as a psychological phenomenon, a definitional twist that reflected the prevailing behaviorist among the country's elites. The fact that the experts were ultimately unable to impose their more relativistic perspectives at this critical moment in the poverty narrative left the field open to outsiders who promoted a more ideologically pliable program to help the poor—"Community Action Programs." The rapid failure of the community action approach did not make experts' frantic search for credible alternatives any easier, however. Instead, it unleashed rivalries and conflicts between them. Ideological battles had intruded into the scientific domain, and even a seemingly simple category such as *the poor*, which had not existed before the 1950s, was suddenly the center of a vast public firestorm that endured throughout the 1960s. Higher stakes and increased visibility widened existing professional and institutional divisions among the experts. Economists advocated for a fiscal solution centered on traditional families, while the statisticians and social workers inside the Social Security Administration supported reforming existing welfare programs, complemented by a new system of family allowances.[8]

Later in the presidency of Lyndon Johnson, advocates of a negative income tax gained traction inside the administration, eventually attracting the support of the Office of Economic Opportunity and a number of officials in the Department of Health, Education, and Welfare. However, neither Richard Nixon's Family Assistance Plan nor George McGovern's "demogrant" program, the poverty community's last hurrah, was able to gain political momentum or provide the foundation for a concrete and durable set of solutions. In spite of the adoption of a Supplemental Security Income for specific categories in 1972, social welfare remained a chaotic web of policies that implemented cultural and arguably gender-biased and racialized assumptions about the origins of poverty. As a consequence, antipoverty proposals increasingly faced criticism from conservatives, leaving liberals to defend a system that they themselves knew was fundamentally flawed. The catastrophic image of welfare in the eyes of the middle-class American public continued to worsen throughout the 1970s and 1980s. Although most experts did not subscribe to a view that social pathologies caused a "culture of poverty," this dominant view in the Ronald Reagan era supported the racially biased idea of a chronic underclass that paved the way for the "workfare" strategy promoted by President Bill Clinton and his successors.[9]

The surprisingly circuitous and ultimately disappointing path taken by moves to eradicate poverty in America, and of the science that undergirded the movement, offer excellent evidence that politics rarely incorporates scientific advances. President Lyndon Johnson was later quoted as complaining that he could not understand why Americans made more mistakes fighting poverty than they did reaching the moon. Johnson's remorse does little to explain the erratic decision making that took place during his administration and that further inflamed existing tensions, ultimately thwarting a series of poverty initiatives. While some historians and analysts of the history of the period have argued that there is a causal link between welfare and workfare, this book focuses attention on a major misstep that caused the War on Poverty to take a punitive turn, finally becoming more of a war against the poor. The behaviorist psychological model that supported this cruel twist of fate continues to dominate neoliberal thinking to this day, which increasingly holds the poor responsible for their own social and economic status.[10]

In methodological terms, this book has invited readers to take a sociohistorical perspective toward the recent history of the United States government and its institutions that focuses on civil servants themselves. Governments are composed of flesh-and-blood individuals just like any other organization, and historians run the risk of being bewitched by the spectacles put in place by civil servants who remain in the shadows—with help from the highly structured legal and professional frameworks surrounding them. This institutional show causes experts and civil servants to appear as mere cogs in a technical apparatus whose sole function is to serve the public. This book has attempted to climb down under the decks of the ship of state in order to comprehend the daily experiences and careers—as complex as they are contradictory—of the individuals with the power to influence decisions despite the rigid hierarchical organizations that surround them. Studying second-tier civil servants presents challenges because of the difficulties of unearthing certain aspects of their work in archival sources. But they merit systematic scholarly attention despite these challenges, because their hard work shaped the options that were ultimately available to the administration. Understanding these figures' daily professional lives and interactions offers a richer understanding of the political choices that were ultimately made in the epic—and woefully incomplete—struggle against poverty. As a historian, diving into the belly of the ship of state has helped me understand the real stakes behind these political decisions, as well as the role of failed alternatives. It is my hope that incorporating close personal narratives within a study of the broader scientific, institutional, and human context has enabled me to avoid the two most common pitfalls of traditional political history.

By retracing this grand effort to do battle with poverty in all its political, scientific, and social complexity, I have attempted to explain the current state of the different social welfare systems in the United States and, by extension, in other Western societies. Welfare programs have blind spots in terms of income distribution that are particularly well illustrated by the story of how present-day American welfare policies evolved. Understanding this process contextualizes current discussions of income distribution by showing, in addition to the inevitable oversimplification of social issues in political discourse, the grand designs of postwar social experts that represented—and continue to represent—credible alternatives to the highly unequal status quo. As social worker Alvin Schorr phrased it in 1973, "We are dealing with the distribution of income in the United States, and how it must be altered. It is a difficult, long-term struggle, but that is the struggle." In a country in which over forty million people continue to live under the poverty line first established by Mollie Oshansky, the struggle is very much alive to this day. The poverty paradox is still with us.[11]

Acknowledgments

This book is a translation of a dissertation defended in 2003 at the École des hautes études en sciences sociales in Paris with Jean Heffer and François Weil as my advisers. It was later published by the Editions de l'EHESS in 2008. First and foremost, I want to thank people both at the Editions and at Cornell University Press: on the French side, Agnès Belbezet, Emmanuel Desveaux, Anne Olivier, and Christophe Prochasson; on the American side, Brian Balogh, Michael McGandy, Bethany Wasik, and John Zimmerman. The translation was financed by a five-year grant from the Institut universitaire de France that I obtained from 2008 to 2013. I also benefit from various institutional supports—the French CNRS, the research center Mondes Américains (UMR 8168) and the EHESS. My translator, John Angell, did a wonderful job, even though his task was all the more difficult since I had decided to update some chapters in order to integrate new research. Thanks a lot, John, for working again and again on these pages.

The Center for North-American Studies at the EHESS is my second home, and everybody deserves warm acknowledgments. Over all the years, so many colleagues took time to comment on my work that my intellectual debt is limitless: Yohann Aucante, Nicolas Barreyre, Olivier Bouquet, Véronique Boyer, Eileen Boris, W. Eliott Brownlee, Laurent Césari, Catherine Collomp, Jefferson Cowie, Marianne Debouzy, Andrew Diamond, Axelle Dolino-Brodiez, Caroline Douki, Robin Einhorn, Daniel Geary, Gary Gerstle, Meg Jacobs, Christian Ingrao, Jennifer Klein, Feliciah Kornbluh, Lisa Levenstein, Nelson Lichtenstein, Isaac Martin, Joseph McCartin, Ajay Mehrotra, Molly Michelmore, Philippe Minard, Jennifer Mitellstadt, Alice O'Connor, Thomas Piketty, Alexandre Rios-Bordes, Caroline Rolland-Diamond, Thomas Sugrue, Karen Tani, Cécile Vidal, Jean-Christian Vinel, Mark Wilson, Julian Zelizer, Robert Zimmerman, Olivier Zunz. Outside the academic world, a bunch of friends in Nice, New York, and Paris made my life such a beautiful journey, with coffee, music, and long evenings, to make the world a better place. Thank you all for filling up the blank pages of life.

Ultimately, *The Experts' War on Poverty* is dedicated to my parents, Annick Huret and Antonio Agomeri. My loving sisters and brother helped me in difficult times and are still here to watch the beauty of the days gone by. My wife, Ariane Boissy, made this book possible. If her generosity, wisdom, and patience have bounds, I have not found them. This book was conceived when one of our sons was a young boy, and two were not yet born. Raphaël and Emilien are beautiful teenagers now, and Melvil is a smart young kid. You're the best pages I will ever write.

Notes

Introduction

1. Quote in Robert J. Lampman, Oral History 1981–1985, Oral History Project Interview, Poverty Institutes Series, Department of Economics, UW Madison, 16; Michael Katz, *The Undeserving Poor: From the War on Poverty to the War on Welfare* (New York: Pantheon Books, 1989); Ellen Reese, *Backlash against Welfare Mothers: Past and Present* (Berkeley: University of California Press, 2005); Felicia Kornbluh, *The Battle for Welfare Rights: Politics and Poverty in Modern America* (Philadelphia: University of Pennsylvania Press, 2007); Lisa Levenstein, *A Movement without Marches: African American Women and the Politics of Poverty in Postwar Philadelphia* (Chapel Hill: University of North Carolina Press, 2009); Marisa Chappell, *The War on Welfare: Family, Poverty, and Politics in Modern America* (Philadelphia: University of Pennsylvania Press, 2010).

2. T. Jackson Lears, *Fables of Abundance: A Cultural History of American Advertising* (New York: Basic Books, 1994); Wendy L. Wall, *Inventing the "American Way": The Politics of Consensus from the New Deal to the Civil Rights Movement* (New York: Oxford University Press, 2008).

3. Edward Berkowitz, *America's Welfare State: From Roosevelt to Reagan* (Baltimore: Johns Hopkins University Press, 1991); James Patterson, *America's Struggle against Poverty, 1900–1994* (Cambridge, MA: Harvard University Press, 1994) 99–114; Michael Katz, *In the Shadow of the Poorhouse: A Social History of Welfare in America* (New York: Basic Books, 1996), 259–282; Walter Trattner, *From Poor Law to Welfare State: A History of Social Welfare in America* (New York: Free Press, 1984), 116–162.

4. Joanne Meyerowitz, ed., *Not June Cleaver: Women and Gender in Postwar America, 1945–1960* (Philadelphia: Temple University Press, 2004); Daniel Horowitz, ed., *Anxieties of Affluence: Critiques of American Consumer Culture, 1939–1979* (Amherst: Massachusetts University Press, 2004).

5. Alan Brinkley, *The End of Reform: New Deal Liberalism in Recession and War* (New York: Vintage Books, 1995); Gareth Davies, *From Opportunity to Entitlement: The Transformation and Decline of Great Society Liberalism* (Lawrence: Kansas University Press, 1996); Daniel Geary, *Beyond Civil Rights: The Moynihan Report and Its Legacy* (Philadelphia: University of Pennsylvania Press, 2015).

6. Robert Lieberman, *Shifting the Color Line: Race and the American Welfare State* (Cambridge, MA: Harvard University Press, 1998); Michael Katz and Lorrin Thomas, "The Invention of 'Welfare' in America," *Journal of Policy History* 10 no. 4 (1998): 399–418; Nancy Fraser and Linda Gordon, "Dependency Demystified: Inscriptions of Power in a Keyword of the Welfare State," *Social Policies* 1 (1994): 4–31; Christopher Howard, "The Hidden Side of the American Welfare State," *Political Science Quarterly* 108, no. 3 (1993): 403–436; Jill Quadagno, *The Color of Welfare: How Racism Undermined the War on Poverty* (New York: Oxford University Press, 1994); Daryl Michael Scott, *Contempt and Pity: Social Policy and the Image of the Damaged Black Psyche, 1890–1996* (Chapel Hill: University of North Carolina Press, 1999); Michael Brown, *Race, Money, and the American Welfare State* (Ithaca, NY: Cornell University Press, 1999); Noel A. Cazenave, *Welfare Racism: Playing the Race Card against America's Poor* (New York: Routledge, 2001); Ann Orloff, "Gender in the Welfare State," *Annual Review of Sociology* 22 (1996): 51–78; Mimi Abramovitz, *Regulating the Lives of Women: Social Welfare Policy from Colonial Times to the Present* (Boston: South End Press, 1988); Gwendolyn Mink, *The Wages of Motherhood: Inequality in the Welfare State, 1917–1942* (Ithaca, NY: Cornell University Press, 1995); Linda Gordon, *Pitied but Not Entitled: Single Mothers and the History of Welfare, 1890–1935* (Cambridge, MA: Harvard University Press, 1994).

7. Joseph J. Thorndike, *Their Fair Share: Taxing the Rich in the Age of FDR* (Washington, DC: Urban Institute Press, 2013).

8. Romain Huret and Jean-Christian Vinel, "From the Labor Question to the Piketty Moment: A Journey through the New Deal Order," in Gary Gerstle, Nelson Lichtenstein, and Alice O'Connor, eds., *Beyond the New Deal Order* (College Park: Penn State University Press, forthcoming); Karen M. Tani, "Welfare and Rights before the Movement: Rights as a Language of the State," *Yale Law Journal* 122 (2012): 314–383; Karen M. Tani, *States of Dependency: Welfare, Rights, and American Governance, 1935–1972* (New York: Cambridge University Press, 2016); Glenn Altschuler and Stuart Blumin, *The GI Bill: A New Deal for Veterans* (New York: Oxford University Press, 2009); James T. Sparrow, *Warfare State: World War II Americans and the Age of Big Government* (New York: Oxford University Press, 2011), 252–260.

9. Brian Balogh, "Reorganizing the Organizational Synthesis: Federal-Professional Relations in Modern America," *Studies in American Political Development* 5, no. 1 (1991): 119–172; Brian Balogh, *Chain Reaction: Expert Debate and Public Participation in American Commercial Nuclear Power, 1945–1975* (Cambridge, UK: Cambridge University Press, 1991); Steven Brint, *In an Age of Experts: The Changing Role of Professionals in Politics and Public Life* (Princeton, NJ: Princeton University Press, 1994).

10. For a different perspective, see Davies, *From Opportunity to Entitlement*.

11. Sar Levitan, *The Great Society's Poor Law* (Baltimore: Johns Hopkins University Press, 1969), 49–108 and 309–318; James Sundquist, ed., *On Fighting Poverty: Perspectives from Experience* (New York: Basic Books, 1969); William Ryan, *Blaming the Victim* (New York: Random House, 1976); Frances Fox Piven and Richard Cloward, *Regulating the Poor:*

The Function of Public Welfare (New York: Pantheon Books, 1973); Ira Katznelson, "Was the Great Society a Lost Opportunity?" in Steve Fraser and Gary Gerstle, eds., *The Rise and Fall of the New Deal Order, 1930–1980* (Princeton, NJ: Princeton University Press, 1989), 185–211; Noel A. Cazenave, *Impossible Democracy: The Unlikely Success of the War on Poverty Community Action Programs* (Albany: State University of New York Press, 2007); Annelise Orleck and Lisa Gayle Hazirjian, eds., *The War on Poverty: A New Grassroots History, 1964–1980* (Athens: University of Georgia Press, 2011), 1–28.

12. Brian Steensland, *The Failed Welfare Revolution: America's Struggle over Guaranteed Policy* (Princeton, NJ: Princeton University Press, 2007).

13. Thomas Haskell, ed., *The Authority of Experts: Studies in History and Theory* (Bloomington: Indiana University Press, 1984), ix–xxxix; Steven Brunt, *In an Age of Experts: The Changing Role of Professionals in Politics and Public Life* (Princeton, NJ: Princeton University Press, 1994); Beth Simone Noveck, *The Technologies of Expertise and the Future of Governing* (Cambridge, MA: Harvard University Press, 2015).

14. John C. Teaford, *The Rise of the States: Evolution of American State Government* (Baltimore: Johns Hopkins University Press, 2002); Martha Derthick, *The Influence of Federal Grants: Public Assistance in Massachusetts* (Cambridge, MA: Harvard University Press, 1975); James R. Leiby, "State Welfare Administration in California, 1930–1945," *Southern California Quarterly* 55, no. 3 (1973): 303–318; James Patterson, *The New Deal and the States: Federalism in Transition* (Princeton, NJ: Princeton University Press, 1969); Brian Balogh, *The Associational State: American Governance in the Twentieth Century* (Philadelphia: University of Pennsylvania Press, 2015), 3–22.

15. Alan J. Matusow, *The Unraveling of America: A History of Liberalism in the 1960s* (New York: Harper & Row, 1984); Scott, *Contempt and Pity*; Ruth Feldstein, *Motherhood in Black and White: Race and Sex in American Liberalism, 1930–1965* (Ithaca, NY: Cornell University Press, 2009); Robert Self, *All in the Family: The Realignment of American Democracy since the 1960s* (New York: Hill & Wang, 2012).

16. Paul Pierson, "Increasing Returns, Path Dependence, and the Study of Politics," *American Political Science Review* 94 (June 2000): 251–267; Daniel P. Carpenter, "The Political Foundations of Bureaucratic Autonomy," *Studies in American Political Development* 15, no. 1 (2001): 113–122; Daniel Carpenter, *The Forging of Bureaucratic Autonomy: Reputations, Networks, and Policy Innovation in Executive Agencies, 1862–1928* (Princeton, NJ: Princeton University Press, 2001).

17. Theda Skocpol, ed., *Social Security in the United States: Future Possibilities in Historical Perspective* (Princeton, NJ: Princeton University Press, 1995); Edwin Amenta, *Bold Relief: Institutional Politics and the Origins of Modern American Social Policy* (Princeton, NJ: Princeton University Press, 1998); Martha Derthick, *Policymaking for Social Security* (Washington, DC: Brookings Institution, 1979); Brian Balogh, "Securing Support: The Emergence of the Social Security Board as a Political Actor, 1935–1939," in Ellis Hawley and Donald T. Critchlow, eds., *Federal Social Policy: The Historical Dimension* (University Park: Pennsylvania State University Press, 1998); Jerry Cates, *Insuring Inequality: Administrative Leadership in Social Security, 1935–1954* (Ann Arbor: Michigan University Press, 1983); Edward Berkowitz, *Mr. Social Security: The Life of Wilbur J. Cohen* (Lawrence: University Press of Kansas, 1995); Edward Berkowitz, *Robert Ball and the Politics of Social Security* (Madison: University of Wisconsin Press, 2005).

18. Alice O'Connor, *Poverty Knowledge: Social Science, Social Policy, and the Poor in Twentieth-Century U.S. History* (Princeton, NJ: Princeton University Press, 2001); because the word *nebula* does not have the same meaning in French and English, I have chosen to use the word *community* to describe the "nebula" of poverty experts. Christian Topalov, ed., *Laboratoires du nouveau siècle: La Nébuleuse réformatrice et ses réseaux en France, 1880–1914*

(Paris: Editions de l'EHESS, 1999); for an American perspective on communities of researchers, see Michael Lacey and Mary Furner, eds., *The State and Social Investigation in Britain and the United States* (Cambridge, MA: Woodrow Wilson Center Press, 1993); Mary Furner and Barry Supple, eds., *The State and Economic Knowledge: The American and British Experience* (Cambridge: Cambridge University Press, 1990).

19. Felicia Kornbluh, *The Battle for Welfare Rights: Politics and Poverty in Modern America* (Philadelphia: University of Pennsylvania Press, 2007); Chappell, *The War on Welfare*. For the ways in which public debates concerning expertise tend to undermine trust, see Balogh, *Chain Reaction*.

1. The Poverty Paradox

1. U.S. Congress, Joint Economic Committee, *Low-Income Families and Economic Stability; Materials on the Problem of Low Income Families Assembled by the Staff of the Subcommittee on Low-Income Families* (Washington, DC: U.S. Government Printing Office, 1950), 475; Dorothy S. Brady and Rose D. Friedman, "Studies in Income and Wealth," Conference on Research in Income and Wealth, National Bureau of Economic Research, NBER Book Series Studies on Income and Wealth, 1947, 247–265; Richard A. Easterlin, "Dorothy Stahl Brady, 1903–1977," *Journal of Economic History* 38, no. 1 (1978): 301–303; Michael Katz, *In the Shadow of the Poorhouse: A Social History of Welfare in America* (New York: Basic Books, 1996), 185–212; Alice O'Connor, *Poverty Knowledge: Social Science, Social Policy, and the Poor in Twentieth-Century U.S. History* (Princeton, NJ: Princeton University Press, 2001), 99–123; Kathleen G. Donohue, *Freedom from Want: American Liberalism and the Idea of the Consumer* (Baltimore: Johns Hopkins University Press, 2003), 244–275.

2. Olivier Zunz, *Why the American Century?* (Chicago: University of Chicago Press, 1999); Lizabeth Cohen, *A Consumer's Republic: The Politics of Mass Consumption in Postwar America* (New York: W. W. Norton, 2003), 345–397; Wendy L. Wall, *Inventing the "American Way": The Politics of Consensus from the New Deal to the Civil Rights Movement* (New York: Oxford University Press, 2008), 163–200; Meg Jacobs, *Pocketbook Politics: Economic Citizenship in Twentieth-Century America* (Princeton, NJ: Princeton University Press, 2005), 221–261; Ted Ownby, *American Dreams in Mississippi: Consumers, Poverty, and Culture, 1830–1998* (Chapel Hill: University of North Carolina Press, 1999), 130–148.

3. The Social Security Administration underwent numerous changes. It began in 1936 as an independent agency (Social Security Board) then was a subcabinet agency (Federal Security Agency) until 1946, when it became the Social Security Administration.

4. Although the name of the research unit of the Social Security Administration has changed over the years from the Bureau of Research and Statistics (1935 to 1948) to the Office of Research (between 1948 and 1949), the Division of Research (from 1949 to 1957), the Division of Program Research (from 1957 to 1963), the Division of Research and Statistics (from 1963 to 1965), and the Office of Research and Statistics (until 1972), I use the name Bureau of Research and Statistics throughout the book; Memo from Ida Merriam to Isidore Falk, May 14, 1946, File Fears concerning new social programs, Box 6, Ida Merriam Papers (hereafter IMP); Peter Corning, *The Evolution of Medicare . . . from Idea to Law* (Washington, DC: Social Security Administration, 1969).

5. For more on Ida Merriam's formative years, see Ida Merriam Oral History, Women in Federal Government Oral History Project, November 20, 22, 23, 1983, Schlesinger Library, Radcliffe College, 1984 (hereafter IMOH); "In Memory of Ida Merriam," *Social Security Bulletin* 60, no. 1 (1997): 62; "In Memory of Ida Merriam," *Social Insurance Update* 1, no. 2 (1996): 9–10; "Merriam, Ida Craven," in Jacques Cattel, ed., *American Men and Women of Science* (New York: R. R. Bowker, 1973), 1678; "Ida Merriam Dies at 92," *Washington Post,*

April 9, 1997; Paul Boyer, *Urban Masses and Moral Order, 1880–1920* (Cambridge: Cambridge University Press, 1978); Zunz, *Why the American Century?*, 27–30.

6. Anthony Wright, *R. H. Tawney* (Manchester: Manchester University Press, 1987); Ellen Fitzpatrick, *Endless Crusade: Women Social Scientists and Progressive Reform* (New York: Oxford University Press, 1990); Joanne L. Goodwin, *Gender and the Politics of Welfare Reform: Mothers' Pensions in Chicago, 1911–1929* (Chicago: Chicago University Press, 1997), 133–135; Barry Karl, *Charles Merriam and the Study of Politics* (Chicago: Chicago University Press 1974).

7. Donald T. Critchlow, *The Brookings Institution, 1916–1952: Expertise and Public Interest in a Democratic Society* (De Kalb: Northern Illinois University Press 1985); Robyn Muncy, *Creating a Female Dominion in American Reform (1890–1935)* (New York: Columbia University Press, 1991); Margaret Rossiter, *Women Scientists in America: Before Affirmative Action, 1940–1972* (Baltimore: Johns Hopkins University Press, 1991), 277–303; Evelyn L. Forget, "American Women and the Economics Profession in the Twentieth Century," *Oeconomica* 1, no. 1 (2011): 19–30.

8. Edwin R. A. Seligman, ed., *Encyclopaedia of the Social Sciences* (New York: Macmillan, 1930); Zunz, *Why the American Century?*, 27, 34; Ajay K. Mehrotra, *Making the Modern American Fiscal State: Law, Politics, and the Rise of Progressive Taxation, 1877–1929* (Cambridge: Cambridge University Press, 2013), 98–99.

9. IMOH, 20.

10. Gary Gerstle, "The Protean Character of American Liberalism," *Journal of American History* 99, no. 4 (1994): 1043–1073.

11. Mark Smith, *Social Science in the Crucible: The American Debate over Objectivity and Purpose, 1918–1941* (Durham: Duke University Press, 1991).

12. Charles McKinley and Robert Frase, *Launching Social Security: A Capture and Record Account, 1935–1937* (Madison: University of Wisconsin Press, 1970), 458–472; Martha Derthick, *Policymaking for Social Security* (Washington, DC: Brookings Institution 1979), 15–23; IMOH, 45; Daniel Hirshfield, *The Lost Reform: The Campaign for Compulsory Health Insurance in the United States from 1932 to 1943* (Cambridge, MA: Harvard University Press 1970), 42–70.

13. Ida Merriam, "The Alleged Communists Characters of the National Health Act: Lessons from American History," Folder Fears on New Social Programs, Box 6, IMP.

14. Edward Berkowitz, *Mr. Social Security: The Life of Wilbur J. Cohen* (Lawrence: Kansas University Press, 1995), 11.

15. Herman Miller, *Rich Man, Poor Man* (New York: Thomas Y. Cravell, 1964), 9–10. Herman Miller's itinerary was reconstructed from the few biographical details in a note in the archives of Wilbur Cohen, Folder 7, Administrative Files 1961–1968, Presidential Award for Civilian Service, 1963–1968, Box 110, Wilbur J. Cohen Papers, State Historical Society of Wisconsin (hereafter WJCP); "Washington Area—Obituaries of Note," *Washington Post*, July 29, 2015.

16. Shelton Duncan and William Shelton, *Revolution in the United States: 1926–1976* (Washington, DC: U.S. Department of Commerce, 1978); Margo Anderson, *The American Census: A Social History* (New Haven, CT: Yale University Press, 1988); Paul Schor, *Classer et compter: Histoire des recensements américains* (Paris: Editions de l'EHESS, 2009).

17. Herman Miller, *Income Distribution in the United States* (Washington, DC: U.S. Government Printing Office, 1955), 17.

18. Ibid., 17; Philip Hauser, "Some Aspects of Methodological Research in the 1950 Census," *Public Opinion Quarterly* 14, no. 1 (1950): 5–13.

19. Herman Miller, "An Appraisal of the 1950 Census Income Data," *Journal of the American Statistical Association* 48, no. 261 (1953): 34.

20. Martin David, "Welfare, Income, and Budget Needs," *Review of Economics and Statistics* 16, no. 3 (1959): 393–399; James Cicarelli and Julianne Cicarelli, "Selma F. Goldsmith (1912–1962)," in *Distinguished Women Economist* (Westport, CT: Greenwood, 2003), 80–83.

21. Ibid., 194.

22. Herman Miller, "Factors Related to Recent Changes in Income Distribution in the United States," *Review of Economics and Statistics* 33, no. 3 (1951): 214–218 and "Changes in Income Distribution in the United States," *Journal of the American Statistical Association* 46, no. 256 (1951): 438–441; Horst Mendershausen, *Changes in Income Distribution during the Great Depression* (New York: National Bureau of Economic Research, 1946).

23. Ibid., 217.

24. James Leiby, *Carroll Wright and Labor Reform: The Origin of Labor Statistics* (Cambridge, MA: Harvard University Press, 1960); Lawrence Glickman, *A Living Wage: American Workers and the Making of Consumer Society* (Ithaca, NY: Cornell University Press, 1997); Richard Kirkendall, *Social Scientists and Farm Politics in the Age of Roosevelt* (Columbia: University of Missouri Press, 1966).

25. Joseph P. Goldberg and William T. Moye, *The First Hundred Years of the Bureau of Labor Statistics* (Washington, DC: U.S. Government Printing Office, 1985), 178–212; "Ewan Clague, 90; U.S. Labor Official," *New York Times*, April 15, 1987.

26. Ewan Clague, "Fact Finding and Thinking as Tools of Social Policy Making," National Conference of Social Work, Atlantic City, May 14, 1951, Folder Speeches, Box 15, Ewan Clague Papers, 1919–1978 (hereafter ECP).

27. Dorothy Brady, Ed., *Family Income and Expenditures*, Part 2, U.S. Department of Agriculture, Miscellaneous Publication, no. 396 (Washington, DC: U.S. Government Printing Office, 1940); Helen Lamale, "Changes in Concepts of Income Adequacy over the Last Century," *American Economic Review* 48, no. 2 (1958): 291–299; Carlie Zimmerman, "Ernest Engel's Law of Expenditures for Food," *Quarterly Journal of Economics* 47, no. 1 (1932): 76–92.

28. Dorothy Brady and Lester Kellog, "The City Worker's Family Budget," *Monthly Labor Review* 66, no. 2 (1948): 125–144.

29. Helen Lamale and Margaret Stotz, "The Interim City Worker's Family Budget," *Monthly Labor Review* 83, no. 8 (1960): 785–808.

30. Helen Pundt, *American Home Economics Association* (Washington, DC: American Home Economics Association, 1980); Sarah Stage and Virginia Vincenti, eds., *Rethinking Home Economics: Women and the History of a Profession* (Philadelphia: Temple University Press, 1997); Carolyn Goldstein, *Creating Consumers: Home Economists in Twentieth-Century America* (Chapel Hill: University of North Carolina Press, 2012).

31. Hazel Stiebeling and Miriam Birdseye, *Adequate Diets for Families with Limited Incomes*, U.S. Department of Agriculture, Miscellaneous Publication no. 113 (Washington, DC: U.S. Government Printing Office, 1931); Alfred E. Harper, "Contributions of Women Scientists in the U.S. Development of Recommended Dietary Allowances," *American Society for Nutritional Sciences*, 133 (2003): 3698–3702.

32. Stiebeling and Birdseye, *Adequate Diets for Families with Limited Incomes*; Hazel Stiebeling, Report on Nutrition Information, December 9, 1949, Folder Nutrition, Box 75, Record of the Office of the Secretary of Agriculture, General Correspondence 1906–1975, RG 16; Faith Clark, *Background Statement on Derivation of Cost of Nutrition Economy Diet Proposed for Pilot Food Stamp Plan* (Washington, DC: U.S. Government Printing Office, 1961); Bureau of Human Nutrition and Home Economics, *Helping Families Plan Food Budgets*, U.S. Department of Agriculture, Publication no. 662 (Washington, DC: U.S. Government Printing Office, 1948); *Food Consumption and Dietary Levels of Households in the*

United States: Some Highlights from the Households Food Consumption Survey (Washington, DC: U.S. Government Printing Office, 1957); Goldstein, *Creating Consumers*, 248–249.

33. Eloise Coifer, Evelyn Grossman, and Faith Clark, *Family Food Plans and Food Costs for Nutritionists and Other Leaders Who Develop or Use Food Plans*, Home Economics Research Report, no. 20, Consumer and Food Economics Research Division, Agricultural Research Service, U.S. Department of Agriculture (Washington, DC: U.S. Government Printing Office, 1962).

34. Blanche Bernstein, *The Research Needs of SSA: A Review of Current Research and Statistics and of the Research Needs of SSA*, Fall 1960, Box 19, Folder The Research Needs of SSA, Division of Program Research, General Correspondence, Record Group 47 Social Security Administration Series (hereafter RG 47); Edward Berkowitz, *Robert Ball and the Politics of Social Security* (Madison: Wisconsin University Press, 2001).

35. IMOH, 67; Ida Merriam and Alfred Skolnik, *Social Welfare Expenditures under Public Programs in the United States*, Department of Health, Education and Welfare, SSA, Office of Research and Statistics, Research Report no. 25 (Washington, DC: U.S. Government Printing Office, 1966).

36. McKinley and Frase, *Launching Social Security*, 407–425; *A Research Program for the Social Security Administration: Report of the Advisory Group to the Commissioner of Social Security*, Department of Health, Education and Welfare, Social Security Administration, August 1961 (Washington, DC: U.S. Government Printing Office, 1961).

37. Major Work Projects for Fiscal 1963, Folder DRS Work Plans, Box 2, IMP; Economic Status of the Aged Person, December 1957, Folder Health of the Aged, Box 15, IMP; Peter Corning, *The Evolution of Medicare . . . from Idea to Law*, US Department of Health, Education and Welfare, Social Security Administration, Office of Research and Statistics, Research Report no. 29, 1969, 45–56.

38. Income Needs of the Aged, Folder Cost of Health Insurance, Box 14, IMP; Lenore Bixby, *The Aged Population of the United States*, Research Report no. 7, Social Security Administration (Washington, DC: U.S. Government Printing, 1962).

39. Memo from the CEA to Advisory Board on Economic Growth and Stability, March 19, 1954, Folder Task Force on Low Income, Box 20, IMP; Memo from Ida Merriam to Robert Ball, Subject: Studies of Poverty among Families with Children, October 3, 1962, Folder SSA Research Program 1949–1960, Box 2, IMP; Major Work Projects for Fiscal 1963, Folder DRS Work Plans, Box 2, IMP.

40. Folder Advisory Group on Welfare Expenditure Series, Box 4, SSA, Division of Program Research, General Correspondence, RG 47; Ellen Schrecker, *Many Are The Crimes: McCarthyism in America* (Boston: Little, Brown, 1998).

41. Selma Goldsmith, "Change in the Size Distribution of Income," *American Economic Review* 47, no. 2 (1957): 506.

2. The Poverty Culture

1. Daryl Scott, *Contempt and Pity: Social Policy and the Damaged Black Psyche* (Chapel Hill: University of North Carolina Press, 1997); Ruth Feldstein, *Motherhood in Black and White: Race and Sex in American Liberalism, 1930–1965* (Ithaca, NY: Cornell University Press, 2000); Marisa Chappell, *The War on Welfare: Family, Poverty, and Politics in Modern America* (Philadelphia: University of Pennsylvania Press, 2009).

2. Ellen Herman, *The Romance of American Psychology: Political Culture in the Age of Experts* (Berkeley: University of California Press, 1995); Alice O'Connor, *Poverty Knowledge: Social Science, Social Policy, and the Poor in Twentieth-Century U.S. History* (Princeton, NJ: Princeton University Press, 2001); Elizabeth Hinton, *From the War on Poverty to*

the War on Crime (Cambridge, MA: Harvard University Press, 2016); for a conservative approach, see William A. Kelso, *Poverty and the Underclass: Changing Perceptions of the Poor in America* (New York: New York University Press, 1994).

3. Paul Ylvisaker's Commencement Address to Swarthmore High School, 06/04/1956, Folder Swarthmore [Correspondence and Syllabi], Box 3, Paul Ylvisaker Papers (hereafter PYP), Harvard University.

4. Letter from Paul Ylvisaker to Imogene Treichel, November 16, 1975, Folder General Correspondence, Box 12, PYP; Paul Ylvisaker, "The Church in Public Affairs," October 13, 1964, Paper Presented to the Conference on the Church and the City, General Convention of the Episcopal Church, Folder Speeches, Box 19, PYP. The sources for Ylvisaker's background here are the Paul Ylvisaker Oral History, May 16, 1972, Ford Foundation Archives. A posthumous collection of articles provided additional information: Virginia Esposito, ed., *Conscience and Community: The Legacy of Paul Ylvisaker* (New York: Peter Lang, 1999); Olivier Zunz, *Philanthropy in America: A History* (Princeton, NJ: Princeton University Press, 2012), 211–213.

5. Paul Ylvisaker's Commencement Address, 6; Paul Ylvisaker Oral Interview with Walter Phillips, 11/04/1977, Folder General Biographical, Box 1, PYP; Robert Caro, *The Power Broker: Robert Moses and the Fall of New York* (New York: Knopf, 1974).

6. John Bauman, *Public Housing, Race, and Renewal: Urban Planning in Philadelphia, 1920–1974* (Philadelphia: Temple University Press, 1987); Thomas J. Sugrue, *The Origins of the Urban Crisis: Race and Inequality in Postwar Detroit* (Princeton, NJ: Princeton University Press, 1996), 3–14; Lisa Levenstein, *A Movement without Marches: African American Women and the Politics of Poverty in Postwar Philadelphia* (Chapel Hill: University of North Carolina Press, 2009); Paul Ylvisaker, "Metropolitan Government: For What?" Paper Presented to the Conference on Metropolitan Problems, Berkeley, CA, July 24, 1958, Folder Speeches, Box 17, PYP.

7. Paul Ylvisaker, "The Brave New Urban World," August 21, 1961, Paper Presented to the World Traffic Engineering Conference, Washington, DC, Folder Speeches, Box 19, PYP.

8. Levenstein, *A Movement without Marches*, 81–83.

9. Paul Ylvisaker, "Planning in a Period of Change," Speech before the American Institute of Planners, New York, October 27, 1958, Folder Speeches, Box 17, PYP; Paul Ylvisaker Oral History, 26.

10. U.S. Congress, *National Science Foundation: Hearings before a Subcommittee on Interstate and Foreign Commerce*, 81st Congress, 1st session (Washington, DC: U.S. Government Printing Office, 1949), 16.

11. Daniel Kleinman, *Politics on the Endless Frontier: Postwar Research Policy in the United States* (Durham, NC: Duke University Press, 1995); Robert Maddox, "The Politics of World War Two Science: Senator Harley M. Kilgore and the Legislative Origins of the National Science Foundation," *West Virginia History* 41 (1979): 20–39; Otto Larsen, *Milestones and Millstones: Social Sciences at the National Science Foundation, 1945–1991* (New Brunswick, NJ: Transaction, 1992); U.S. Congress, *National Science Foundation*, 16; Public Law 507–81st Congress, Section 7(b); Mark Solovey, *Shaky Foundations: The Politics-Patronage-Social Nexus in Cold War America* (New Brunswick, NJ: Rutgers University Press, 2013).

12. Mark Chesler, Joseph Sander, and Debra Kalmuss, *Social Science in Court: Mobilizing Experts in the School Desegregation Cases* (Madison: University of Wisconsin Press), 3–26; Zunz, *Philanthropy in America*, 189–200.

13. Chesler, Sander, and Kalmuss, *Social Science in Court*, 3–26; John Lankford, *Congress and the Foundations in the Twentieth Century* (River Falls: Wisconsin State University, 1964); Select Committee to Investigate Foundations, *Final Report of the Select Committee to Investigate Foundations and Other Organizations*, 82nd Cong., 2nd session, House Report

no. 2514 (Washington, DC: U.S. Government Printing Office, 1951), 3497–3499; E. E. Cox, "Investigation of Certain Educational and Philanthropic Foundations," Congressional Record, 82d Cong., House, 1st session, August 1, 1951, pt. 14, Appendix, A4833-A4834 (Washington, DC: U.S. Government Printing Office, 1951); William Fulton, *Let's Look at Our Foundations* (New York: Guardians of American Education, 1952), 1.

14. U.S. Congress, *Tax-Exempt Foundations*, Hearings before the Special Committee to Investigate Tax-Exempt Foundations and Comparable Organizations, House, 83rd Cong., 2nd session (Washington, DC: Government Printing Office, 1954).

15. Robert Bremner, *American Philanthropy* (Chicago: Chicago University Press, 1988), 165–169; Ford Foundation, Annual Report, 1955, 33; Research program on the Behavioral Sciences and the Law, #002117, October 29, 1952, Ford Foundation Archives (hereafter FFA).

16. Bernard Berelson Oral History, Oral History Collection, FFA; Bernard Berelson, "Five Year Report on Program V," 9, Folder 4, 08/05/1956, FFA.

17. Memorandum on the Comparative Value of the Encyclopedia of the Social Sciences, #002686, p. 21, November 15, 1954, FFA.

18. Guy Alchon, "Mary Van Kleeck and Social-Economic Planning," *Journal of Policy History* 3, no. 1(1991): 17–23; David Hammack and Stanton Wheeler, *Social Science in the Making: Essays on the Russell Sage Foundation, 1907–1972* (New York: Russell Sage Foundation, 1994), 81–94; Herman, *The Romance of American Psychology*, 126–130.

19. James Gilbert, *A Cycle of Outrage: America's Reaction to the Juvenile Delinquent in the 1950s* (New York: Oxford University Press, 1986).

20. Richard Magat, "In Search of the Ford Foundation," in Ellen Condliffe Lagemann, ed., *Philanthropic Foundations: New Scholarship, New Possibilities* (Bloomington: Indiana University Press, 1999), 296–318; Untitled page of biographical information on H. Rowan Gaither, Assistant to the President, Folder 28, Box 3, FFA; Rowan Gaither, ed., *Report of the Study for the Ford Foundation on Policy and Program*, Detroit, Ford Foundation, 1949, 3.

21. Paul Ylvisaker, "The Deserted City," *Journal of the American Institute of Planners* 25, no. 1 (1959): 16–26; Ylvisaker, "The Deserted City"; Martin Anderson, *The Federal Bulldozer: A Critical Analysis of Urban Renewal, 1949–1962* (Cambridge, MA: MIT Press, 1962).

22. Gregory Kaynor, "The Ford Foundation's War on Poverty: Private Philanthropy and Race Relations in New York City, 1948–1968," in Lagemann, *Philanthropic Foundation*, 195–228; Paul Ylvisaker, "Community Action: A Response to Some Unfinished Business," Address to the Citizen's Conference Community Planning, Indianapolis, Indiana, 01/11/1963, Folder Speeches, Box 19, PYP.

23. Memorandum from Paul Ylvisaker to Henry Heald, "Status of the 'Gray Areas': Great Cities School Improvement Programs," 01/04/1961, Folder Gray Areas Program, Box 5, PYP; Paul Ylvisaker Oral Interview, 1977, 36; Memorandum from Ylvisaker to Head, "Status and Future of the Great Cities–Gray Areas Program," October 24, 1961, Folder Gray Areas Program, Box 5, PYP; Martha Davis, *Brutal Need: Lawyers and the Welfare Rights Movement, 1960–1973* (New Haven, CT: Yale University Press, 1993), 26–28; Noel A. Cazenave, *Impossible Democracy: The Unlikely Success of the War on Poverty Community Action Programs* (Albany: State University of New York, 2007), 19–31.

24. Norman Dodd, *Report Prepared for the Special Committee of the House of Representatives*, Folder 34, Box 3, FFA; Richard Cloward and Lloyd Ohlin, *Delinquency and Opportunity: A Theory of Delinquent Gangs* (Glencoe, IL: Free Press, 1960).

25. Allan Matusow, *The Unraveling of America. A History of Liberalism in the 1960s* (New York: Harper Torchbooks, 1984), 107–108.

26. Robert Geiger, *Research and Relevant Knowledge: American Research Universities since World War Two* (New York: Oxford University Press, 1993), 53–55; Jean M. Converse,

Survey Research in the United States: Roots and Emergence, 1890–1960 (Berkeley: University of California Press, 1987)

27. Preliminary Summary of Major Topics Discussed at the Faculty Seminar in Income Maintenance 1956–1957, Folder 8, Box 70, Wilbur J. Cohen Papers.

28. The Impact of Income Maintenance Programs on the Achievement Motive of the Individual, 11/09/1956, Folder 8—Faculty Seminar on Income Maintenance Programs 1956–1957, Box 70, WJCP; David McClelland, *The Achievement Motive* (New York: Appleton-Century-Crofts, 1953).

29. Discussion of Morgan Thomas' Propositions of Poverty, Faculty Seminar on Income Maintenance Program, Thirteenth Meeting, December 12, 1956, Folder 8, Box 70, WJCP; Discussion of Charles Metzner, Faculty Seminar on Income Maintenance, Tenth Meeting, November 21, 1956, Folder 8, Box 70, WJCP; Edward Berkowitz's biography, *Mr. Social Security: The Life of Wilbur J. Cohen* (Lawrence: University Press of Kansas, 1995).

30. Cohen, *Mr. Social Security*, 96.

31. Ibid., 108.

32. Ibid, 108; Discussion of Twenty Fourth Meeting, 04/03/1957, Folder 8, Box 70, WJCP; Henry Brazer, Wilbur Cohen, Martin David, and James Morgan, *Income and Welfare in the United States* (New York: McGraw Hill, 1962); Letter from Eleanor Snyder to Wilbur Cohen, 05/01/1958, Folder 2, Box 59, WJCP.

33. Brazer, Cohen, David, and Morgan, *Income and Welfare*, 190.

34. Ibid., 190; Berkowitz, *Mr. Social Security*, 103.

35. Robert Lampman, "Income and Welfare in the United States: A Review Article," *Review of Economics and Statistics* 45, no. 3 (1963): 314–317.

36. Oscar Lewis, *Five Families: Mexican Case Studies in the Culture of Poverty* (New York: Basic Books, 1959); O'Connor, *Poverty Knowledge*, 114–120; Susan Rigdon, *The Culture Facade: Art, Science, and Politics in the Work of Oscar Lewis* (Urbana: University of Illinois Press, 1988).

3. The New Wisconsin Idea

1. Merle Curti, "A New Golden Age for Social Studies at Wisconsin?" unpublished speech, 1950, cited in Mark Solovey, "Shattered Dreams and Unfulfilled Promises: The Wisconsin Social Systems Research Institute and Interdisciplinary Social Science Research," 1945–1965 (master's thesis, Department of History, University of Madison–Wisconsin, 1990), 16; Charles McCarthy, *The Wisconsin Idea* (New York: Macmillan, 1912); Thomas McCraw, *Prophets of Regulation: Charles Francis Adams, Louis Brandeis, James Landis, Alfred Kahn* (Cambridge, MA: Harvard University Press, 1984); Clarence Wunderlin, *Visions of a New Industrial Order: Social Science and Labor Theory in America's Progressive Era* (New York: Columbia University Press, 1992), 113–129; David Thelen, *The New Citizenship: The Origins of Progressivism in Wisconsin, 1885–1900* (Columbia: University of Missouri Press, 1972); Merle Curti and Vernon Cartensen, *The University of Wisconsin: A History, 1848–1925* (Madison: University of Wisconsin Press, 1949); E. David Cronon, "Merle Curti: An Appraisal and Bibliography of His Writings." *Wisconsin Magazine of History* 54, no. 2 (1970–1971): 119–135.

2. Robert Lampman, ed., *Economists at Wisconsin, 1892–1992* (Madison: University of Wisconsin Press, 1993); Jean-Christian Vinel, *Employee: A Political History* (Philadelphia: University of Pennsylvania Press, 2014); Cronon, "Merle Curti"; Alice Kessler-Harris, *In Pursuit of Equity: Women, Men, and the Quest for Economic Citizenship in Twentieth-Century America* (Princeton, NJ: Princeton University Press, 2001), 81–84.

3. Nelson Lichtenstein, *Walter Reuther: The Most Dangerous Man in Detroit* (New York: Basic Books, 1995), 283.

4. For Robert Lampman's biography, see Robert Lampman Oral History 1981–1985, Oral History Project Interview, Poverty Institute Series, Department of Economics, University of Wisconsin Archives (hereafter RLOH); Peter Passell, "Robert Lampman, 76, Economist Who Helped in War on Poverty," *New York Times*, March 8, 1997; Frank C. Genovese, "In Memoriam: Robert Lampman, 1920–1997," *American Journal of Economics and Sociology* 57, no. 1 (1998): 115–118; Robert Cohen, *When the Old Left Was Young: Student Radicals and America's First Mass Student Movement, 1929–1941* (New York: Oxford University Press, 1993); Elizabeth Brandeis Oral History, June 26, 1974, University of Wisconsin–Madison Oral History Project, 28; Lampman, *Economists at Wisconsin*, 235.

5. Glenn Altschuler and Stuart Blumin, *The GI Bill: A New Deal for Veterans* (New York: Oxford University Press, 2009); Robert Lampman, *Collective Bargaining of West Coast Laborers, 1885–1947* (PhD diss., Department of Economics, University of Madison–Wisconsin, 1950).

6. Robert Lampman, Dean Worcester, "Income, Ability, and Size of Family in the United States," *Journal of Political Economy* 58, no. 5 (1950): 436–442; Carol Carson, "The History of the United States National Income and Product Accounts: The Development of an Analytical Tool," *Review of Income and Wealth* 21 (1975): 153–181; Guy Alchon, *The Invisible Hand of Planning: Capitalism, Social Science, and the State in the 1920s* (Princeton, NJ: Princeton University Press, 1985); Michael Bernstein, *A Perilous Progress: Economists and Public Purpose in Twentieth-Century America* (Princeton, NJ: Princeton University Press, 2001), 78–80.

7. Simon Kuznets, *Studies in Income and Wealth* (New York: National Bureau of Economic Research, 1950).

8. In December 1954, Kuznets gave a paper at the annual convention of the association in Detroit that was published the following year under the title *Economic Growth and Income Inequality*; Simon Kuznets, *Shares of Upper Income Groups in Income and Savings* (New York: National Bureau of Economic Research, 1953); Simon Kuznets, "Economic Growth and Economic Inequality," *American Economic Review* 45, no. 1 (1950): 1–28; Thomas Piketty, *Capital in the Twenty-First Century* (Cambridge, MA: Harvard University Press, 2014).

9. Robert Lampman, "Recent Changes in Income Inequality Reconsidered," *American Economic Review* 44, no. 3 (1954): 251–268; Joseph Pechman, "Distribution of Income before and after Federal Income Tax, 1941 and 1947," *Studies in Income and Wealth*, vol. 13 (New York, National Bureau of Economic Research, 1952).

10. Robert Lampman, *Change in the Share of Wealth Held by Top Wealth-Holders, 1922–1956* (New York: National Bureau of Economic Research, 1960).

11. David E. Cronon and John W. Jenkins, *University of Wisconsin: Renewal to Revolution, 1945–1971* (Madison: University of Wisconsin Press, 1999); data from Fred Harrington, William Young, and Robert Taylor, "The University of Wisconsin and the Ford Foundation, 1951–1965: A Study of the Impact of Changing Resources on the Functions and Objectives of Higher Education," April 16, 1964, Box 33, Schedule IX, 91, 100, Table F, University of Wisconsin Archives (hereafter UWA).

12. The Research Council of the Graduate Division of the Social Sciences to the Graduate Division of the Social Sciences, *Progress Report regarding Centralized Social Science Research Facilities on This Campus*, April 16, 1949, Box 145, UWA; "Report of the Special Committee on the Situation of Social Science Research to the President," Folder Ad Hoc Committee's Scope of Work, Box 1, UWA.

13. Fred Harvey Harrington, *The University and the State* (Madison: University of Wisconsin Press, 1962); Cronon and Jenkins, *The University of Wisconsin*, 163–224; Robert Geiger, "Science, Universities, and National Defense: 1945–70," *Osiris* 7 (1992): 26–48; see also Rebecca Lowen, *Creating the Cold War University: The Transformation of Stanford* (Berkeley: University of California Press, 1997).

14. Bernstein, *A Perilous Progress*; Guy Orcutt, "From Engineering to Microsimulation: An Autobiographical Reflection," *Journal of Economic Behavior and Organization* 14 (1990): 5–27.

15. Guy Orcutt, "A New Regressive Analyzer," *Journal of the Royal Statistical Society*, series A, CXI (1948): 16–45.

16. Guy Orcutt, "A New Type of Socio-Economic System," *Review of Economics and Statistics* 39, no. 2 (1957): 116–123; in 1961, with Martin Greenberger, John Korbel, and Alice Rivlin, he co-published the results of his studies begun at Harvard and continued at Wisconsin: *Microanalysis of Socio-Economic Systems: A Simulation Study* (New York: 1961).

17. RLOH, 35; quantitative data excerpted from Solovey, "Shattered Dreams and Unfulfilled Promises," 16.

18. Robert Lampman, "Recent Thought on Egalitarianism," *Quarterly Journal of Economics* 71, no. 2 (1957): 258.

19. Ibid., 266.

20. Eugene Smolensky, "Lorenz Curve," in Douglas Greenwald, *Encyclopedia of Economics* (New York: McGraw Hill, 1982): 246–254; Robert Lampman, "The Effectiveness of Some Institutions in Changing the Distribution of Income," *American Economic Review* 47, no. 2 (1957): 519–528.

21. *Interdepartmental Committee on Low Incomes*, New York, State of New York, 1958.

22. Eleanor Snyder, *Public Assistance Recipients in New York State: A Study of the Causes of Dependency during a Period of High-Level Employment*, State of New York, Interdepartmental Committee on Low Incomes, October 1958; *Characteristics of the Population, New York State, 1956–1957*, State of New York, Interdepartmental Committee on Low Incomes, October 1958; Eleanor Snyder, "Low-Income in Urban Areas," *American Economic Review* 50, no. 2 (1960): 250.

23. Lampman, The Effectiveness of Some Institutions in Changing the Distribution of Income," 526.

24. Robert J. Lampman, "Population Change and Poverty Reduction, 1947–1975," in Leo Fishman, ed., *Poverty amid Affluence* (New Haven, CT: Yale University Press, 1966), 18–42; Albert N. Votaw, "The Hillbillies Invade Chicago," *Harper's*, February 1958, 64–67.

25. Wunderlin, *Visions of a New Industrial Order*, 128–129.

26. Gabriel Kolko, "The American 'Income Revolution,'" *Dissent* 4, no. 1 (1957): 35–55; Conference on Economic Progress, *Consumption: Key to Full Prosperity*, Washington, DC, May 1957, 4 and 30–33.

27. David A. Reisman, *Galbraith and Market Capitalism* (New York: New York University Press, 1980).

28. Stephen P. Dunn, *The Economics of John Kenneth Galbraith: Introduction, Persuasion, and Rehabilitation* (Cambridge: Cambridge University Press, 2010), 146; Howard Brick, *Transcending Capitalism: Visions of a New Society in Modern American Thought* (Ithaca, NY: Cornell University Press, 2006); Gareth Davies, *From Opportunity to Entitlement: The Transformation and Decline of Great Society Liberalism* (Lawrence: University Press of Kansas, 1996), 28–29; Kaaryn Gustafson, *Cheating Welfare: Public Assistance and the Criminalization of Poverty* (New York: New York University Press, 2011).

29. Galbraith, *Affluent Society*, 325–326; ibid., 329.

30. Lampman, "Recent Thought on Egalitarianism."

31. Paul Douglas, *In the Fullness of Time: The Memoirs of Paul Douglas* (Boston: Houghton Mifflin, 1971); Roger Biles, *Crusading Liberal: Paul H. Douglas of Illinois* (DeKalb: Northern Illinois University Press, 2002); Robert Lampman, *The Low Income Population and Economic Growth*, Study Paper no. 12, Joint Economic Committee, U.S. Congress (Washington, DC: U.S. Government Printing Office, 1959), 1.

32. Lampman, *The Low Income Population and Economic Growth*, 2.

33. U.S. Congress, *Making Ends Meet on Less Than $2,000 Year: A Communication to the Joint Committee on the Economic Report from the Conference Group on Low Income Families of Nine National Voluntary Organizations Convened by the National Social Welfare Assembly* (Washington, DC: U.S. Government Printing Office, 1951); U.S. Congress, *Joint Committee on the Economic Report, Low-Income Families: Hearings before the Subcommittee on Low-Income Families of the Joint Committee on the Economic Report*, Eighty-Fourth Congress, 1st session, pursuant to sec. 5 (a) of Public Law 304, 79th Congress (Washington, DC: U.S. Government Printing Office, 1955); U.S. Congress, *Joint Committee on the Economic Report*; U.S. Congress, *Joint Committee on the Economic Report*, 40–41; Council of Economic Advisers, *Annual Report to the President* (Washington, DC: U.S. Government Printing Office, 1955) 16.

34. RLOH, 166.

35. Lampman, *The Low Income Population and Economic Growth*, 4.

36. Ibid., 4, 28.

37. Selma Goldsmith, "Change in the Size Distribution of Income," *American Economic Review* 47, 2 (1957): 506.

4. Beyond the Affluent Society

1. Stephen P. Dunn, *The Economics of John Kenneth Galbraith: Introduction, Persuasion, and Rehabilitation* (Cambridge: Cambridge University Press, 2010), 146; Howard Brick, *Transcending Capitalism: Visions of a New Society in Modern America Thought* (Ithaca, NY: Cornell University Press, 2006); Gareth Davies, *From Opportunity to Entitlement: The Transformation and Decline of Great Society Liberalism* (Lawrence: University Press of Kansas, 1996), 28–29; Kaaryn Gustafson, *Cheating Welfare: Public Assistance and the Criminalization of Poverty* (New York: New York University Press, 2011).

2. Alvin Schorr, "The Family Cycle and Income Development," *Social Security Bulletin*, February 1966, 14–25.

3. Quotation in Linda Gordon, *Pitied but Not Entitled: Single Mothers and the History of Welfare* (Cambridge, MA: Harvard University Press, 1994), 221; "Frank J. Bruno (1874–1955): Social Work Educator, Administrator, and Author," *Social Welfare History Project*, http://socialwelfare.library.vcu.edu/people/bruno-frank-j/.

4. For the biography of Alvin Schorr, I've used his autobiography, *Passion and Policy: A Social Worker's Career* (Cleveland, OH: David Press, 1997), his personal papers at the Social Welfare History Archives of the University of Minnesota, and correspondence to supplement information.

5. Virginia Robinson, *A Changing Psychology in Social Work* (Chapel Hill: University of North Carolina Press, 1930); John Ehrenreich, *The Altruistic Imagination: A History of Social Work and Social Policy in the United States* (Ithaca, NY: Cornell University Press, 1985), 102–103; James Leiby, *A History of Social Welfare and Social Work in the United States* (New York: Columbia University Press, 1978); Karen M. Tani, *States of Dependency: Welfare, Rights, and American Governance, 1935–1972* (New York: Cambridge University Press, 2016), 83–87.

6. Guy Alchon, "Mary Van Kleeck and Social-Economic Planning," *Journal of Policy History*, 3, no. 1 (1991): 1–23; quotation in Tani, *States of Dependency*, 225.

7. Alvin Schorr, "Applying Short-Contact Skills to Interviewing Selectees," *Social Service Review* 19, no. 1 (1945) : 11–17 and "A Three-County Approach to Casework Service" *Family Service Highlights*, July 1955, Box 3, Articles and Speeches, ASP.

8. Schorr, *Passion and Policy*, 49; Gordon, *Pitied but Not Entitled*, 15–35; Theda Skocpol, *Protecting Soldiers and Mothers: The Political Origins of Social Policy in the United States* (Cambridge, MA: Harvard University Press, 1992), 535–536.

9. Gilbert Steiner, *Social Insecurity: The Politics of Welfare* (Chicago: Rand McNally, 1969), 71–73; Lisa Levenstein, *A Movement without Marches: African American Women and the Politics of Poverty in Postwar Philadelphia* (Chapel Hill: University of North Carolina Press, 2009), 52–56; Tani, *States of Dependency*, 224–227.

10. Blanche Coll, *Safety Net: Welfare and Social Security, 1929–1979* (New Brunswick, NJ: Rutgers University Press, 1995) 176–204; Alvin Schorr, "Problems in the ADC Program," *Social Work*, vol. 6, no. 1 1960, 6–18.

11. Schorr, *Passion and Policy*, 49–55; Levenstein, *A Movement without Marches*, 194–199.

12. Coll, *Safety Net*, 200; Alvin Schorr, *Filial Responsibility in the United States* (Washington, DC: Social Security Administration, U.S. Government Printing Office, 1960); Schorr, *Passion and Policy*, 54–55.

13. Edgar May, *The Wasted Americans: Cost on Welfare Dilemma* (New York: Harper and Row, 1964); Joseph Ritz, *The Despised Poor: Newburgh's War on Welfare* (Boston: Beacon Press, 1966); quoted in Steiner, *Social Insecurity*, 64; Ray Moseley, "Detroit Welfare Empire," *Atlantic Monthly*, April 1960, 43–46; Taryn Lindhorst and Leslie Leighninger, "'Ending Welfare as We Know It' in 1960: Louisiana's Suitable Home Law," *Social Service Review* 77, no. 4 (2003): 564–584; Edward D. Berkowitz, *America's Welfare State: From Roosevelt to Reagan* (Baltimore: Johns Hopkins University Press, 1991), 100–107; Gustafson, *Cheating Welfare*, 17–22; Anders Walker, "Legislating Virtue: How Segregationists Disguised Racial Discrimination as Moral Reform Following Brown v. Board of Education," *Duke Law Journal* 47 (1997): 399–424.

14. Joseph McDowell Mitchell, untitled address, ca. 1961, Box 1, Elizabeth Wickenden Papers, State Historical Society of Wisconsin (hereafter EWP); Lisa Levenstein, "From Innocent Children to Unwanted Migrants and Unwed Moms: Two Chapters in the Public Discourse on Welfare in the United States, 1960–1961," *Journal of Women's History* 11, no. 4 (2000): 11–24.

15. An Address by the City Manager of the City of Newburgh, Folder Attack on Public Welfare, Box 1, EWP; Meg Greenfield, "The 'Welfare Chiselers' of Newburgh, N.Y.," *Reporter*, August 17, 1961, 37.

16. A. H. Raskin, "Newburgh's Lessons for the Nation," *New York Times Magazine*, December 17, 1961, 16–24; Fletcher Knebel, "Welfare: Has It Become a Scandal?" *Look*, November 7, 1961, 3–4; editorial, *Wall Street Journal*, July 18, 1961, 1.

17. Norman Lourie, *Will the Newburgh Plan Work in Your City?* pamphlet published by the National Association of Social Workers, undated, Folder 15 Attack on Public Welfare, Box 1, EWP.

18. Wilbur Cohen and Robert Ball, "The Public Welfare Amendments of 1962," *Public Welfare* 20 (1962): 16–34.

19. Herman Miller, *Rich Man, Poor Man* (New York: Thomas Y. Cravell, 1964): 37–55; Edwin Seligman and Alvin Johnson, eds., *Encyclopedia of Social Sciences* (New York: Macmillan, 1930), 166.

20. Ida Merriam, *"Are We Spending Enough for Social Welfare?"* paper presented at the National Conference of Social Welfare, San Francisco, May 25, 1954, Folder Ida Merriam, Box 16, SSA, Division of Program Research, General Correspondence, RG 47.

21. Ida Merriam, "Social Welfare Opportunities and Necessities on Disarmament," *Social Security Bulletin* (1963): 10–14; Letter of Ida Merriam to Alvin Schorr, *Future Work Plans for Family Life Studies*, 18/11/1958, Folder Family Life, SSA, Division of Program Research, General Correspondence, RG 28.

22. Quotation in Herman Miller, *Income Distribution in the United States* (Washington, DC: U.S. Government Printing Office, 1955), 8.

23. Paul Ylvisaker, "Community Action: A Response to Some Unfinished Business," Address to the Citizen's Conference Community Planning, Indianapolis, Indiana, 01/11/1963, PYP.

Paul Ylvisaker, "What Is New in American Philanthropy," paper presented to the Eleventh Conference of the National Conference Philanthropy, October 19–21, 1966, PYP.

24. Daniel Rodgers, *Atlantic Crossings: Social Policy in a Progressive Age* (Cambridge, MA: Harvard University Press, 1998); Daniel Scroop and Andrew Heath, eds., *Transatlantic Social Politics, 1800–Present* (New York: Palgrave Macmillan, 2014); to retrace the transatlantic exchanges, I have consulted, in addition to the personal papers of poverty experts already cited, the personal papers of Richard Titmuss, held at the London School of Economics.

25. Among frequently cited books are David Thomson, *Equality* (1949), as well as work by the French thinker Bertrand de Jouvenel, translated into English in the late 1940s and published as Bertrand de Jouvenel, *Ethics of Redistribution* (Cambridge, Cambridge University Press, 1953); Richard Tawney, *Equality* (London: G. Allen & Unwin, 1931); Paul Homan, "Socialist Thought in Great Britain," *American Economic Review* 47, no. 7 (1958): 350–362.

26. Quoted in Monica Charlot, *Poverty and Inequality in Great-Britain, 1942–1990* (Paris: PUF, 2000), 71.

27. Ralf Dahrendorf, *The London School of Economics: A History, 1895–1995* (New York: Oxford University Press, 1995); David Reisman, *Welfare and Society* (London: Palgrave, 2001): 23.

28. B. S. Rowntree and G. R. Lavers, *Poverty and the Welfare State: A Third Survey of York Dealing with Economic Questions*, London: Longmans Green, 1951; Peter Townsend, "The Meaning of Poverty," *British Journal of Sociology* 13, no. 3 (1962): 210–227; Victor Fuchs, "Toward a Theory of Poverty," in Task Force on Economic Growth and Opportunity, *The Concept of Poverty* (Washington, DC: Chamber of Commerce of the United States, 1965), 66–86.

29. Schorr, *Passion and Policy*, 61,

30. Jean-Paul Revauger, "La pensée sociale de Titmuss," in Jacques Carré and Jean-Paul Revauger, *Ecrire la pauvreté: Les enquêtes sociales britanniques aux XIXème et XXème siècles* (Paris: PUF, 1995), 246–226; Letter from Wilbur Cohen to Richard Titmuss, April 28, 1959, Wilbur Cohen Correspondence, 56–60, Folder 4, Box 67, WJCP; Letter from Richard Titmuss to Wilbur Cohen, 05/07/1959, Folder Michigan, Box 67, WJCP.

31. Richard Titmuss, *Social Policy: An Introduction* (London: Allen & Unwin, 1974), 50; Richard Titmuss, *The Gift Relationship: From Human Blood to Social Policy* (London: Penguin Books, 1970), 270–277. Thanks are expressed to Ida Merriam in the introduction for her theoretical contribution. See also Philippe Fontaine, "Blood, Politics, and Social Science: Richard Titmuss and the Institute of Economic Affairs, 1957–1973," *Isis* 93, no. 3 (2002): 401–434; Richard Titmuss, "Equality Britain and the U.S.A.," Box 1/49, Folder USA, Richard Titmuss Papers (hereafter RTP).

32. Christian Topalov, *Naissance du chômeur, 1880–1920* (Paris: Albin Michel, 1994); Robert Lampman, "Income Distribution and Social Change: A Critical Study in British Statistics," *American Economic Review* 53, no. 5 (1963): 114–116; Richard Titmuss, *Income Distribution and Social Change: A Study in Criticism* (London: G. Allen & Unwin, 1962).

33. Lampman, "Income Distribution and Social Change."

34. Richard Titmuss, "Poverty in the 1960s," box 3/444, Folder Ida Merriam, RTP.

35. Richard Titmuss, "Some Problems in the Application of Sociological Knowledge to Social Welfare Research" unpublished lecture, undated, TP 3/370, RTP.

36. Dwight McDonald, "The Invisible Poor," *New Yorker*, January 19, 1963, 130–139; Homer Bigart, "Kentucky Miners: A Grim Winter," *New York Times*, October 20, 21, 1963, 21 and Michael Harrington, "Close-Up on Poverty," *Look*, August 25, 1964, 66–72; Michael Harrington, *The Other America: Poverty in the United States* (New York: Macmillan, 1962); Linda M. Keefe, "Dwight Macdonald and Poverty Discourse, 1960–1965: The Art and Power of a Seminal Book Review," *Poverty and Public Policy* 2, no. 2 (2010): 147–188; Daniel Horowitz, "From the Affluent Society to the Poverty of Affluence, 1960–1962," in *The*

Anxieties of Affluence: Critiques of American Consumer Culture, 1939–1979 (Amherst: University of Massachusetts Press, 2004), 129–161.

37. "Invisible Poor," *Newsweek*, March 19, 1962, 108; David Abrahamson, *Magazine-Made America: The Cultural Transformation of the Postwar Periodical* (Cresskill, NY: Hampton Press, 1996); Maurice Isserman, *The Other American: The Life of Michael Harrington* (New York: Public Affairs, 2000); Ella Howard, *Homeless: Poverty and Place in Urban America* (Philadelphia: University of Pennsylvania Press, 2013), 88.

38. Gregory D. Sumner, *Dwight Macdonald and the Politics Circle: The Challenge of Cosmopolitan Democracy* (Ithaca, NY: Cornell University Press, 1996); Michael Wreszin, *A Rebel in Defense of Tradition* (New York: Basic Books, 1995).

5. An Economist at War

1. "Kennedy Asks Better Foodstuffs for Needy," *Evening Star*, 20/04/1960, Folder '60 Campaign by State, Box 69, John Fitzgerald Kennedy Library (hereafter JFK Library); Remarks of Senator John F. Kennedy, April 25, 1960, Folder Public Speech and Statements, Pre-presidential '60 Campaign, Box 69, JFK Library.

2. Elizabeth Hinton, *From the War on Poverty to the War on Crime: The Making of Mass Incarceration* (Cambridge, MA: Harvard University Press, 2016), 30–34; Sar A. Levitan, *Federal Aid to Depressed Areas* (Baltimore: Johns Hopkins University Press, 1964); Daniel Knapp, *Scouting the War on Poverty: Social Reform in the Kennedy Administration* (Lexington, MA: Heath Lexington Books, 1971); James Sundquist, *Politics and Policy: The Eisenhower, Kennedy, and Johnson Years* (Washington, DC: Brookings Institution Press, 1968); Wilbur J. Cohen and Robert M. Ball, "Public Welfare Amendments of 1962 and Proposals for Health Insurance for the Aged," *Social Security Bulletin* 3 (1962), 3–22.

3. Michael Bernstein, *A Perilous Progress: Economists and Public Purpose in Twentieth-Century America* (Princeton, NJ: Princeton University Press, 2004); Irving Bernstein, *Promises Kept: JFK's New Frontier* (New York: Oxford University Press, 1991).

4. "Heller's Personal Memorandum for the Record," December 23, 1960, Folder Appointment of Heller 1960–1964 and undated, Box 5, Walter Heller Papers (hereafter WH Papers), JFK Library. Biographical information about Walter Heller is based on information in the Walter Heller Papers at the John Kennedy Library. The author also drew on a eulogy by James Tobin, "Walter W. Heller (08/27/1915–06/15/1987)," *Proceedings of the American Philosophical Society*, vol. 135, no. 1 (March 1991): 100–107.

5. Walter Heller, *State Income Tax Administration* (PhD diss., University of Wisconsin, 1941); Randolph Paul, *Taxation in the United States* (Boston: Little Brown, 1954); Bartholomew Sparrow, *From the Outside In: World War II and the American State* (Princeton, NJ: Princeton University Press, 1996), 97–160; Mark Leff, *The Limits of Symbolic Reform: The New Deal and Taxation, 1933–1939* (Cambridge: Cambridge University Press, 1984); Carolyn Jones, "Mass-Based Income Taxation: Creating a Taxpaying Culture, 1940–1952," in Elliot Brownlee, ed., *Funding the Modern American State, 1941–1995: The Rise and Fall of the Era of Easy Finance* (Cambridge: Cambridge University Press, 1996), 107–147; Elliot Brownlee, *Federal Taxation in America: A Short History* (Cambridge, MA: Woodrow Wilson Center Press, 1996), 96–98; Romain D. Huret, *American Tax Resisters* (Cambridge: Harvard University Press, 2014).

6. Julian Zelizer, *Taxing America: Wilbur D. Mills, Congress, and the State, 1945–1975* (Cambridge: Cambridge University Press, 1999), 85.

7. U.S. Congress, Subcommittee of the Committee on Ways and Means, *Internal Revenue Investigation: Hearings, February 3–March 1953* (Washington, DC: U.S. Government Printing Office, 1953); Zelizer, *Taxing America*, 93.

8. James Tobin, *The New Economics: One Decade Older* (Princeton, NJ: Princeton University Press, 1974), 4–6.

9. Oral History with Walter Heller, Kermit Gordon, James Tobin, Gardner Ackley and Paul Samuelson (hereafter CEA Oral History) JFK Library, 72–73; Author interview with Harold Weisbrod, May 26, 2000; Burton Weisbrod, "Education and Investment in Human Capital," *Journal of Political Economy* 70, no. 5 (1962): 106–123.

10. Heller used the term *fine-tuning*, which was subsequently strongly criticized. See Milton Friedman and Walter Heller, *Monetary vs. Fiscal Policy* (New York: W. W. Norton, 1969), 34; CEA Oral History, 316–322; author interview with W. Lee Hansen, March 23, 2000; published in 1947 under the direction of the Harvard economist, *The New Economics* represented a Keynesian-inspired approach; in July 1962, the journalist James Pugash quoted the title in an article for *Newsweek* before it came into widespread public use.

11. Council of Economic Advisers, *Annual Economic Report to the President* (Washington, DC: U.S. Government Printing Office, 1962); James Tobin, "Growth about Taxation," *New Republic*, July 25, 1960, 13–18.

12. Arthur Okun, *The Political Economy of Prosperity* (Washington, DC: Brookings Institution, 1969), 132–145; Tobin, *The New Economics*, 31; Oral History Interview with Arthur Okun, March 20, 1969, Lyndon Baines Johnson Library (hereafter LBJ Library), 15. CEA History, II-32; Tobin, *The New Economics*, 23–24.

13. RLOH 1981–1985, Poverty Institute Series, UW Madison, 39.

14. RLOH, June 26, 1983, LBJ Library, 2; regarding Lampman's years on the CEA, the author has also drawn on written accounts of interviews conducted in 1983 and 1985: "Notes from an Interview by Barbara Newell with Lampman concerning His 1959–1964 Efforts to Convince the White House to Begin a War on Poverty," June 16, 1965, State Historical Society of Wisconsin Collection, University of Madison; "Notes from an Interview," 1–2.

15. Robert Lampman, "Approaches to the Reduction of Poverty," *American Economic Review* 55, no. 1/2 (1965): 523.

16. Robert Lampman, ed., *Economists at Wisconsin, 1892–1992* (Madison: University of Wisconsin Press, 1992), 118–121; Brian Steensland, *The Failed Welfare Revolution. America's Struggle over Guaranteed Income Policy* (Princeton, NJ: Princeton University Press, 2008), 36–38.

17. Robert Lampman, "Approaches to the Reduction of Poverty," lecture delivered at the Seventy-Seventh Annual Meeting of the American Economic Association, Chicago, December 30, 1964, Folder Poverty—CEA, Box 20, IMP; Milton Friedman, *Capitalism and Freedom* (Chicago: University of Chicago Press, 1962); Angus Burgin, *The Great Persuasion: Reinventing Free Markets since the Depression* (Cambridge, MA: Harvard University Press, 2012), 181.

18. Herman P. Miller, "The American Poor: The Tools They Need," *The Nation*, January 26, 1963, 65–68.

19. Robert Lampman, "In the Midst of Plenty," *The New Leader*, December 24, 1962, 20–21; Lampman, "In the Midst of Plenty," 21; Gregory Summer, *Dwight McDonald and the Politics Circle: The Challenge of Cosmopolitan Democracy* (Ithaca, NY: Cornell University Press, 1996).

20. Oscar Ornati, "Definition of Poverty," in Seminar on Poverty in Plenty, Gaston Hall, Georgetown University, January 23, 1964, stenographic transcript, 49–66.

21. Gabriel Kolko, "The American Income Revolution," *Dissent* 4, no. 1 (1957): 35–55.

22. Allen Matusow, *The Unraveling of America: A History of Liberalism in the 1960s* (New York: harper Torchbooks, 1984), 54–56; Bernstein, *A Perilous Progress*, 138–139; Letter from Rashi Fein to Jo Ann Lampman, 3/12/1997, Institute for Research on Poverty Archives (hereafter IRPA); Douglas Martin, "Rashi Fein, Economist Who Urged Medicare, Dies at 88," *New York Times*, September 13, 2014.

23. Robert Lampman, "Notes on Changes in the Distribution of Wealth and Income: From 1953 through 1961–1962," Box 37, WH Papers, JFK Library; the author wishes to thank Elizabeth Evanson, director of the Institute for Poverty Research, for having given him a copy of the report bearing Walter Heller's editorial markings and comments. The document was given by Robert Lampman in the late 1980s; Robert Lampman, Memorandum for the President—Progress and Poverty, 05/01/1963, Box 37, WH Papers, JFK Library.

24. Memo from Hackett to Heller, 1/12/1963, WH Papers, Box 37, JFK Library; RLOH 1983, 5; RLOH 1983, 7; based on the Labor Department's opposition, particularly by Jack Conway: RLOH 1983, 23; RLOH 1983, 12; Lampman, "Approaches to the Reduction of Poverty"; Michael L. Gillette, *Launching the War on Poverty: An Oral History* (New York: Oxford University Press, 2010), 2–11.

25. Memo to Cohen from Eugene Sullivan, 12/6/1963, Folder 10—Poverty 1963–1968: Background Material and Studies, Box 124, (WJCP); Carl Brauer, "Kennedy, Johnson, and the War on Poverty," *Journal of American History* 69, no.1 (1982): 112; RLOH 1983, 8; created by Kennedy, the term *Irish Mafia* describes the president's close advisers, most of whom were of Irish ancestry and worked for him for many years.

26. Mark Stern, *Calculating Visions: Kennedy, Johnson, and Civil Rights* (New Brunswick, NJ: Rutgers University Press, 1992); William P. Jones, *The March on Washington: Jobs, Freedom, and the Forgotten History of Civil Rights* (New York: W. W. Norton; 2013).

27. Charles Schultze Oral History, March 28, 1969, LBJ Library; Memo from Lampman to Heller, 10/06/1963, Box 37, WH Papers, JFK Library; Note from an interview, 3; Memo from Walter Heller to the Secretary of Agriculture, 11/05/1963, Box 37, WH Papers, 5.

28. Quoted in Brauer, "Kennedy, Johnson, and the War on Poverty," 111.

29. Walter Heller, "Confidential Notes on Meeting with the President," October 21, 1963, Folder 18/10/1963–31/10/1963, Box 13, WH Papers, JFK Library; Memo to Theodore Sorensen, undated, Files Poverty Eastern Kentucky, Box 37, Theodore Sorensen Papers (hereafter TSP); Homer Bigart, "Kentucky Miners: A Grim Winter," *New York Times*, October 20, 1963.

30. RLOH 1983, 14.

31. Oral History with Joseph Pechman, March 19, 1969, LBJ Library and Walter Heller, "Notes on Meeting with President Johnson, 7:40 p.m. November, 23, 1963," Folder 16/11/1963–30/11/1963, Box 13, JFK Library; Nicholas Lemann, *The Promised Land: The Great Black Migration and How It Changed America* (New York: Knopf, 1991), 143; Heller, "Notes on Meeting with President Johnson," 2.

32. Memo from the chairman of the CEA to Ida Merriam, Subject Legislative Program for "Widening Participation in Prosperity—An Attack on Poverty," November 14, 1963, Folder Poverty CEA, Box 20; Memorandum of CEA for Ida Merriam, Conference Progress and Poverty, November 26, 1963, IMP; Memo from Ida Merriam to Bill Capron and Burt Weisbrod, 12/04/ 1963, Folder Poverty—Council of Economic Advisers, Box 20, Ida Merriam Papers and Letter from the Council of Economic Advisers to Ida Merriam, December 26, 1964, Folder Poverty—CEA, Box 20, IMP; Memo from Hackett to Heller, 12/01/1963, Box 37, WH Papers.

33. *Poverty and Urban Policy*, Brandeis University Conference, JFK Library, 1973, 141; Edward Berkowitz, *Mr. Social Security: The Life of Wilbur J. Cohen* (Lawrence: University Press of Kansas, 1995), 196; Gillette, *Launching the War on Poverty*, 10–20.

34. Council of Economic Advisers, *Economic Report of the President Transmitted to the Congress January 1964 Together with the Annual Report of the Council of Economic Advisers* (Washington, DC: U.S. Government Printing Office, 1964), 16–38; Robert Lampman, "The 30th Anniversary of the War on Poverty: Economists and the Making of Antipoverty Policy Then and Now," Fifteenth Annual Research Conference of the Association for Public

Policy Analysis and Management, Washington, DC, October 1993; Council of Economic Advisers, *Economic Report*, 57–58.

35. Walter Rostow, *The Diffusion of Power: An Essay in Recent History* (New York: Mc-Millan, 1972), 305; *Poverty and Urban Policy*, Brandeis University Conference, John Fitzgerald Kennedy Library, Boston, 1973, 162; Robert Dallek, *Flawed Giant: Lyndon Johnson and His Times* (New York: Oxford University Press, 1998), 75.

36. CEA Staff Memorandum, Program for a Concerted Assault on Poverty, October 29, 1963, Folder 9, Box 193, WJCP.

37. Ibid.

38. RLOH, 10; CEA Staff Memorandum, Program for a Concerted Assault on Poverty; Memorandum from CEA for Sorensen, December 20, 1963, Folder 6, Box 125, WJCP.

39. Alice O'Connor, *Poverty Knowledge: Social Science, Social Policy, and the Poor in Twentieth-Century U.S. History* (Princeton, NJ: Princeton University Press, 2001), 152–158. Margaret Weir, *Politics and Jobs: The Boundaries of Employment Policy in the United States* (Princeton, NJ: Princeton University Press, 1992), 53–56; Annelise Orleck and Lisa Gayle Hazirjian, eds., *The War on Poverty: A New Grassroots History, 1964–1980* (Athens: University of Georgia Press, 2011), 1–28.

6. A Pyrrhic Victory

1. Michael Harrington, "Close-Up on Poverty," *Look*, August 25, 1964; Lizabeth Cohen, *A Consumers' Republic: The Politics of Mass Consumption in Postwar America* (New York: Vintage Books, 2004), 113–115; "Poverty, U. S. A.," *Newsweek*, Feb. 17, 1964.

2. Sar A. Levitan, "The Community Action Program: A Strategy to Fight Poverty," *Annals of the American Academy of Political and Social Science* 385 (1969): 63–75; Alice O'Connor, *Poverty Knowledge: Social Science, Social Policy, and the Poor in Twentieth-Century U.S. History* (Princeton, NJ: Princeton University Press, 2001), 168–170; Daniel Patrick Moynihan, *Maximum Feasible Misunderstanding: Community Action in the War on Poverty* (New York: Free Press, 1969); Noel A. Cazenave, *Impossible Democracy: The Unlikely Success of the War on Poverty Community Action Programs* (Albany: State University of New York Press, 2007); Annelise Orleck and Lisa Gayle Hazirjian, eds., *The War on Poverty: A New Grassroots History, 1964–1980* (Athens: University of Georgia Press, 2011), 1–28.

3. Paul R. Hengeller, *In His Steps: Lyndon Johnson and the Kennedy Mystique* (Chicago: Ivan R. Dee, 1991); Robert Dallek, *Flawed Giant: Lyndon Johnson and His Times* (New York: Oxford University Press, 1998), 74–76 and Anthony Lewis, "Shriver Moves into Front Rank," *New York Times*, March 15, 1964, 1; RLOH, 34–35; Sargent Shriver Oral History, August 20, 1980, LBJ Library, 6; Elizabeth Cobbs Hoffman, *All You Need Is Love: The Peace Corps and the Spirit of the 1960s* (Cambridge, MA: Harvard University Press, 2000).

4. Michael Latham, *Modernization as Ideology: American Social Science and "Nation Building" in the Kennedy Era* (Chapel Hill: University of North Carolina, 2001).

5. Information about Adam Yarmolinsky's career was found in the Adam Yarmolinsky Oral History by Paige Mulhollan, July 13, 1970, LBJ Library, Austin, TX (hereafter AYOH) and the Adam Yarmolinsky Papers (hereafter AYP) in the collections of the JFK Library; Deborah Shapley, *Promise and Power: The Life and Time of Robert McNamara* (Boston: Little, Brown, 1999).

6. AYOH, 13; *Poverty and Urban Policy*, Brandeis Conference, JFK Library, 1973, 342; Eva Bertram, *The Workfare State: Public Assistance Politics from the New Deal to the New Democrats* (Philadelphia: University of Pennsylvania Press, 2015), 34–36.

7. Memo from David Hackett to Walter Heller, 12/01/1963, Box 37, WH Papers, JFK Library, and *Poverty and Urban Policy*, 86–88; Franck Mankiewicz Oral History (hereafter

FMOH), April 4, 1969, LBJ Library; Michael L. Gillette, *Launching the War on Poverty: An Oral History* (New York: Oxford University Press, 2010), 50.

8. Mobilization to End Poverty, undated, Legislative Background of the Economic Opportunity Act, Box 1, LBJ Library; *Poverty and Urban Policy*, 173.

9. This Office of the Budget employee was a University of Chicago graduate who was highly knowledgeable about urban experiments in fighting delinquency. See *Poverty and Urban Policy*, 61a–62. For more on Saul Alinsky, see "Chicago Influences on the War on Poverty,"; Legislative Background of the Economic Opportunity Act, Box 1, LBJ Library; Joseph Califano, *The Triumph and Tragedy of Lyndon Johnson: The White House Years* (New York: Simon & Schuster, 1991), 123; Memo to task force members, 02/05/1964, Folder 6, Box 125, WJCP. The task force records were not preserved at the Johnson Presidential Library; the author has had access to only the final report and was forced to extrapolate using other sources. The author has also used Adam Yarmolinsky's narrative, "The Beginnings of OEO," in James Sunquist, ed., *On Fighting Poverty* (New York: Basic Books, 1969), 34–51.

10. Edgar May, *The Wasted Americans: Cost on Welfare Dilemma* (New York: Harper & Row, 1964); Gillette, *Launching the War on Poverty*; Michael B. Katz, *The Undeserving Poor: America's Confrontation with Poverty* (New York: Oxford University Press, 2013), 102–155.

11. Daniel Geary, *Beyond Civil Rights: The Moynihan Report and Its Legacy* (Philadelphia: University of Pennsylvania Press, 2015), 28–30.

12. AYOH, 8; RLOH, 28, 21.

13. Thomas Hughes, *Rescuing Prometheus* (New York: Pantheon Books, 1998), 176–185; President's Task Force on Manpower Conservation, *One-Third of A Nation: A Report on Young Men Found Unqualified for Military Service* (Washington, DC: Government Printing Office, 1964).

14. *Poverty and Urban Policy*, 175, 227.

15. Ibid., 150; Kevin Boyle, *The UAW and the Heyday of American Liberalism, 1945–1968* (Ithaca, NY: Cornell University Press, 1995), 41–43; 140–144; Dallek, *Flawed Giant*; *Poverty and Urban Policy*, 97; Geary, *Beyond Civil Rights*, 21–23.

16. Norbert Schlei Oral History, May 15, 1980, LBJ Library, 17; Note from Harold Horowitz to task force members, 02/11/1964, Folder OEA, Box 4A38, Harold Horowitz Papers (hereafter HH Papers), LBJ Library; Notes from Harold Horowitz to task force members, February 21, 1964, Folder OEA, Box 4A38, HH Papers; quotation in Geary, *Beyond Civil Rights*, 30; Gillette, *Launching the War on Poverty*, 82.

17. Draft A, Bill to mobilize the human and financial resources of the nation to combat poverty in the United States, February 22, 1964, Box A38A, HH Papers; Christopher Weeks, *Job Corps: Dollars and Dropouts* (Boston: Little Brown, 1976), 76; AYOH, II, 8; Dallek, *Flawed Giant*, 75.

18. Cazenave, *Impossible Democracy*; William S. Clayson, *Freedom Is Not Enough: The War on Poverty and the Civil Rights Movement in Texas* (Austin: University of Texas Press, 2010), 13–38; Geary, *Beyond Civil Rights*, 42–78.

19. Geary, *Beyond Civil Rights*, 31.

20. Notes from interview of Robert Lampman by Barbara Newell, June 16, 1965, Madison, Wisconsin, State Historical Society of Wisconsin, 5; RLOH 1983, 18, 42–43; Gillette, *Launching the War on Poverty*, 31–80.

21. Quoted in Edward Berkowitz, *Mr. Social Security: The Life of Wilbur J. Cohen* (Lawrence: University Press of Kansas, 1995), 201; Memo from Robert Ball to Wilbur Cohen, Proposed Approach to Poverty Problem, December 12, 1963, Folder Poverty—CEA, Box 20, IMP.

22. As was the case with the meeting minutes and notes from the task force meetings in February 1964, the presidential library preserved only the final report, *Outside 1964 Task Force on Income Maintenance*, November 1964, LBJ Library. For information on the internal workings of the committee, the author has used other sources, particularly the personal papers of Wilbur Cohen, Elizabeth Wickenden (EWP), and Alvin Schorr (ASP); Alice Kesseler-Harris, *In Pursuit of Equity: Women, Men, and the Quest for Economic Citizenship in Twentieth-Century America* (Princeton, NJ: Princeton University Press, 2001), 273–274.

23. Dallek, *Flawed Giant*, 189; Memo from John Corson, July 18, 1964, Folder Task Force on Income Maintenance, July 1964, LBJ Library; Memo to members of the task force on income maintenance, August 28, 1964, Folder 8 Task Force Commission: Income Maintenance, August 17–31, 1964, Box 188, WJCP.

24. Memo to chairman John Corson by Michael March, August 26, 1964, Subject: Redraft of the opening section of the report, Folder 8 Task Force Commission Income maintenance, August 17–31; New Draft by Corson and March, "Toward Greater Security and Opportunity for the Individual," Folder 2 Task Force on Income Maintenance Sept-25-28, 1964, Box 189, WJCP, 64; Memo from Elizabeth Wickenden to Ball, 10/01/1964, Confidential Notes on Task Force on Income Maintenance, Folder 23 Task Force on Income Maintenance, Box 2, EWP.

25. Memo from Elizabeth Wickenden to Ball, 10/01/1964, Confidential Notes on Task Force on Income Maintenance, 3, Folder 23 Task Force on Income Maintenance, Box 2, EWP; Memorandum for Miss Wickenden from Michael S. March, October 15, 1964, Folder 3 Task Force on Income Maintenance, Box 189, WJCP; Letter from Miss Wickenden to Michael S. March, October 16, 1964, Folder 3 Task Force on Income Maintenance, Box 189, WJCP.

26. Memo from Ida Merriam to members of the Income Maintenance Task Force, August 31, 1964,

27. Robert Lampman, "Approaches to the Reduction of Poverty," lecture delivered at the Seventy-Seventh Annual Meeting of the American Economic Association, Chicago, December 30, 1964, Folder Poverty—CEA, Box 20, IMP; Robert Lampman, "Prognosis for Poverty," paper prepared for delivery at the convention of the National Tax Association, Pittsburgh, September 15, 1964, Folder 2 Income Maintenance, Box 189, WJCP; Christopher Howard, *The Hidden Welfare State: Tax Expenditures and Social Policy in the United States* (Princeton, NJ: Princeton University Press, 1999).

28. Lampman, "Prognosis for Poverty," 10, 11; "Use of Income Tax System to Provide Financial Assistance to Poverty-Stricken Families with Dependent Children," October 13, 1964, Folder 3, TFC IM, Box 189, October 15–16, 1964, WJCP.

29. Memo from Ida Merriam to Wilbur Cohen, September 30, 1964, Folder 3 Task Force on Income Maintenance—October 15–16, 1964, Box 189, WJCP.

30. Ibid., 8

31. Memo from Elizabeth Wickenden to Ball, 10/01/1964, Confidential Notes on Task Force on Income Maintenance, Folder 23 Task Force on Income Maintenance, Box 2, EWP, 2/3; Elizabeth Wickenden Oral History 1986–82, Folder 3, Box 16, EWP, 20.

32. President's Task Force on Income Maintenance, 1, Box 2, EWP ; Toward Greater Security and Opportunity for Americans, Final Draft of the Income Task Force, November 14, 1964, Folder 5, Task Force on Income Maintenance, October 1–13, 1964, Box 189, WJCP.

33. Herman Miller, *Major Elements of a Research Program for the Study of Poverty, Institute of Government and Public Affairs*, UCLA, Institute of Government and Public Affairs, 1964, 4, 5.

34. *Poverty and Urban Policy*, 147.

35. Julian Zelizer, *The Fierce Urgency of Now: Lyndon Johnson, Congress, and the Battle for the Great Society* (New York: Penguin Press, 2015).

7. Uncertainty of Numbers, Certainty of Decisions

1. Irving Kristol, "The Lower Fifth," *The New Leader*, February 17, 1964, 9–10; Michael Harrington, "A Glib Fallacy," *The New Leader*, March 30, 1964, 18–20; Michael Harrington, *The Other America*: Poverty in the United States (New York: Macmillan, 1962; Brian Balogh, *Chain Reaction: Expert Debate and Public Participation in American Commercial Nuclear Power, 1945–1975* (New York: Cambridge University Press, 1991); Charles Murray, *Losing Ground: American Social Policy* (New York: Basic Books, 1984), 63–68, 270–271.

2. Balogh, *Chain Reaction*.

3. Robert Hershey, "Q. & A.: Mollie Orshansky—The Hand That Shaped America's Poverty Line as the Realistic Index," *New York Times*, August 4, 1989, A11; Sewell Chan, "Mollie Orshansky, Statistician, Dies at 91," *New York Times*, April 17, 2007; Deborah Stone, "Making the Poor Count," *The American Prospect* 17 (1994): 78–89; Linda Gordon, *Pitied but Not Entitled: Single Mothers and the History of Welfare* (Cambridge, MA: Harvard University Press, 1994), 88–98.

4. Ennis Blake, Corinne LeBovit, Mary Ann Moss, and Mollie Orshansky, "Food Consumption and Dietary Levels of Rural Families in the North Central Region, 1952," *Agricultural Information Bulletin*, no. 157 (Washington, DC, U.S. Department of Agriculture, 1957); Food Consumption and Dietary Levels of Households in the United States: Some Highlights from the Households Food Consumption Survey, Agricultural Research Service, U.S. Department of Agriculture, Spring 1955, ARS 62-6 (Washington, DC: U.S. Government Printing Office, 1957); Mollie Orshansky, Facts About Financial Resources of the Aged, Research and Statistics, December 19, 1960, Note no 30, US Department of Health, Education and Welfare, IMP.

5. Mollie Orshansky, "Children of the Poor," *Social Security Bulletin* 26, no. 7 (1963): 5; Oscar Lewis, *The Children of Sanchez: Autobiography of a Mexican Village* (New York: Random House, 1961); Orshansky, "Children of the Poor," 13.

6. Mollie Orshansky, "Who's Who among the Poor: A Demographic View on Poverty," *Social Security Bulletin* 28, no. 7 (1965): 8; Eloise Cofer, Evelyn Grossman, and Faith Clark, *Family Food Plans and Food Costs for Nutritionists and Other Leaders Who Develop or Use Food Plans*, Home Economics Research Report no. 20, Washington, DC, Consumer and Food Economic Research Division, Agricultural Research Service, U.S. Department of Agriculture, November 1962 (Washington, DC: U.S. Government Printing Office, 1962).

7. Mollie Orshansky, "Counting the Poor: Another Look at the Poverty Profile," *Social Security Bulletin* 28, no. 1 (1965): 8.

8. Stone, "Making the Poor Count," 83.

9. *Annual Report of the Council of Economic Advisers*, January (Washington, DC, U.S. Government Printing Office, 1964), 2.

10. Herman Miller, *Major Elements of a Research Program for the Study of Poverty*, Institute of Government and Public Affairs (Los Angeles: UCLA, 1964), 10; U.S. Congress, *Hearings before the Subcommittee on the War on Poverty Programs*, House Committee on Education and Labor, 88th Congress, 2nd session, April 1964 (Washington, DC: U.S. Government Printing Office, 1964), 166.

11. Rose Friedman, *Poverty: Definition and Perspective* (Washington, DC: American Enterprise Institute, 1965); Milton Friedman and Rose Friedman, *Two Lucky People* (Chicago: University of Chicago Press, 1998), 58; Bruce Weber, "Rose Friedman, Economist and Collaborator, Dies at 98," *New York Times*, August 18, 2009; Angus Burgin, *The Great Persuasion: Reinventing Free Markets since the Depression* (Cambridge, MA: Harvard University Press, 2015), 153; Kim Philipps-Fein, *Invisible Hands: The Making of the Conservative Movement from the New Deal to Reagan* (New York: W. W. Norton, 2009).

12. Friedman, *Poverty*, 32.

13. Ibid., 41.

14. Rick Perlstein, *Before the Storm: Barry Goldwater and the Unmaking of the American Consensus* (New York: Hill & Wang, 2001).

15. Memo from Ida Merriam to Robert Ball, Subject: The Poor: Number and Characteristics, 09/04/1964, 1064, Folder 1, Box 125, WJCP; Orshansky, "Counting the Poor," 2.

16. Orshansky, "Counting the Poor," 22.

17. Memo from Mollie Orshansky to Herman Miller, May 27, 1964, Division of Research and Statistics, Social Security Administration, IMP; Orshansky, "Counting the Poor," 7.

18. The term *rural* corresponds to the statistical category *farm*, which refers to the rural but not exclusively active agricultural population.

19. *Economic Report of the President Transmitted to the Congress* (Washington, DC, U.S. Government Printing Office, 1965), 65; Letter from Leon Gilgoff to OEO Senior Staff, 05/10/1965, roll no. 6, OEO microfilm, LBJ Library; Memo from Lenore Epstein to Gertrude Weiss, Folder Poverty Line, Box 8, IMP; Summary of Meeting of Ad Hoc Advisory Group, 05/04/1965, Folder Poverty Line, Box 16, IMP.

20. Elizabeth Hinton, *From the War on Poverty to the War on Crime* (Cambridge, MA: Harvard University Press, 2016), 50–54; Daniel Geary, *Beyond Civil Rights: The Moynihan Report and Its Legacy* (Philadelphia: University of Pennsylvania Press, 2015), 13–41.

21. James Patterson, *America's Struggle against Poverty* (Cambridge, MA: Harvard University Press, 1994), 143–146; Brian Steensland, *The Failed Welfare Revolution: America's Struggle over Guaranteed Income Policy* (Princeton, NJ: Princeton University Press, 2008), 48–54.

22. Memo from Joseph Kershaw to Senior Staff, through Lisle Carter to Delegated Agency Heads, 10/1/1965, OEO Microfilm, roll no. 1, LBJ Library.

23. Memo from Robert Levine to Robert Schultze, 07/09/ 1965, OEO Microfilm, roll no. 2, LBJ Library; Alvin Schorr, "Against a Negative Income Tax," *The Public Interest*, 2 (1966): 24–32.

24. Major Work Projects for Fiscal 1963, Folder DRS Work Plans, Box 2, IMP; Alvin Schorr, *Social Security and Social Services in France*, Department of Health, Education and Welfare, Division of Research and Statistics, Research Report no. 7 (Washington, DC: U.S. Government Printing Office, 1964); Alvin Schorr, *Poor Kids* (New York: Basic Books, 1966).

25. Edward Berkowitz, *Mr. Social Security: The Life of Wilbur J. Cohen* (Lawrence: Kansas University Press, 1995), 116; Alvin Schorr, *Passion and Policy: A Social Worker's Career* (Cleveland: David Press, 1997), 26; James Tobin, "The Case for an Income Guarantee," *The Public Interest* 4 (1966): 31–44; Memo from Sargent Shriver to Charles Schultze, October 20, 1965, Folder Anti-poverty Plan 1965, Box 7, Alvin Schorr Papers (hereafter ASP); Gareth Davies, *From Opportunity to Entitlement: The Transformation and Decline of Great Society Liberalism* (Lawrence: University Press of Kansas, 1996), 75–99; Robert Dallek, *Flawed Giant: Lyndon Johnson and His Times* (New York: Oxford University Press, 1998), 222–228.

26. Memo from Sargent Shriver to the President, October 20, 1965, 4, 9, Folder Anti-Poverty Plan Box 7, ASP.

27. RLOH 1981–1985 Oral History Project Interview, Poverty Institutes Series, Department of Economics, University of Wisconsin Madison Archives, 38; Wilbur Cohen Oral History, December 8, 1968, LBJ Library, 12.

28. RLOH 1981–1985, 41; Memo from Robert Levine to Joseph Kershaw, 5, Folder Anti-Poverty Plan Box 7, ASP.

29. Berkowitz, *Mr. Social Security*, 251.

30. Alice Rivlin, *Systematic Thinking for Social Action* (Washington, DC: Brookings Institution, 1971), 24–25; Sidney Fine, *Violence in the Model City: The Cavanagh Administration, Race Relations, and the Detroit Riot of 1967* (Ann Arbor: Michigan State University

Press, 1989); Davies, *From Opportunity to Entitlement*, 179–180; Steensland, *The Failed Welfare Revolution*, 71–72.

31. Terence Kelly and Leslie Singer, "The Gary Income Maintenance Experiment: Plans and Progress," *American Economic Review* 61 (May 1971): 56–67; Lee Bawden, "Income Maintenance and the Rural Poor: An Experimental Approach," *American Journal of Agricultural Economics* 52, no. 6 (1970): 45–57.

32. Outline of a Program to Provide a Basic Income Guarantee, May 31, 1968, Folder 11 Basic Income Guarantee 1968, Box 131, WJCP.

33. RLOH 1981–1985, 29; Memo from the chairman of the Council of Economic Advisers to Joseph Califano, 01/08/ 1968, Folder Guaranteed Minimum Income Commission, Box 19, Files of Joseph Califano, LBJ Library.

8. A Doomed Alternative

1. David Farber, *Chicago 68* (Chicago: University of Chicago Press, 1988); Daniel Geary, *Beyond Civil Rights: The Moynihan Report and Its Legacy* (Philadelphia: University of Pennsylvania Press, 2015), 79–109; Martha Davis, *Brutal Need: Lawyers and the Welfare Rights Movement, 1960–1973* (New Haven, CT: Yale University Press, 1993).

2. Robert Lampman, *Nixon's Family Assistance Plan*, Discussion Paper no. 57 (Madison, WI: Institute for Research on Poverty, 1969), 6.

3. Gerald McKnight, *The Last Crusade: Martin Luther King, Jr., the FBI, and the Poor People's Campaign* (Boulder, CO: Westview, 1998); Romain Huret, "Les experts sociaux face à la société civile aux États-Unis: La Campagne des pauvres et le ministère de la Santé, de l'Éducation et du Welfare (avril-juin 1968)," *Revue d'histoire moderne et contemporaine* 51, no. 2 (2004): 118–140; Felicia Kornbluh, *The Battle for Welfare Rights: Politics and Poverty in Modern America* (Philadelphia: University of Pennsylvania Press, 2007), 51–54; Undated letter from Mary Switzer to Ralph David Abernathy and Mrs. Johnnie Tillman, Folder Poor People Campaign DHEW, Social and Rehabilitative Services, Box 15, ASP; the source of these statistics is a study by the NAACP and lawyer Marian Wright. See Dona Cooper and Charles Cooper, *The Dual Agenda: The African-American Struggle for Civil and Economic Equality* (New York: Columbia University Press, 2000), 168. See also Frances Fox Piven and Richard Cloward, *Regulating the Poor: The Function of Public Welfare* (New York: Pantheon Books, 1973), 190–196.

4. Undated letter from Mary Switzer to Ralph David Abernathy and Mrs. Johnnie Tillman, Folder Poor People Campaign DHEW, Social and Rehabilitative Services, Box 15, ASP; quotation in Amy Nathan Wright, "Civil Rights Unfinished Business": Poverty, Race, and the 1968 Poor People's Campaign" (PhD diss., University of Texas, Austin, 2007), 212.

5. Blanche Coll, *Welfare and Social Security: Welfare and Social Security, 1929–1979* (New Brunswick: Rutgers University Press, 1995), 243–246; Memo from Mary Switzer to all SRS Employees, May 10, 1968, Folder Poor People's Campaign, Box 12, HEW Papers, LBJ Library; Alvin Schorr, *Passion and Policy: A Social Worker's Career* (Cleveland, OH: David Press, 1997), 78; Federal Employees for Democratic Society Campaign, May 23, 1968, Folder DHEW Employees, Box 15, ASP.

6. Memorandum from Mary E. Switzer, Subject: Courteous Treatment of Clientele, Folder Poor People Campaign DHE Responses (3), Box 15, ASP; Lisa Levenstein, *A Movement without Marches: African American Women and the Politics of Poverty in Postwar Philadelphia* (Chapel Hill: University of North Carolina Press, 2001), 196–199.

7. Edward Berkowitz, *Mr. Social Security: The Life of Wilbur J. Cohen* (Lawrence: Kansas University Press, 1995); "Questions and Answers about the New Anti-welfare Law," NOW, Official Publications of the National Welfare Rights Organization, February 2, 1968,

WJCP; Gareth Davies, *From Opportunity to Entitlement: The Transformation and Decline of Great Society Liberalism* (Lawrence: University Press of Kansas, 1996), 157–161; Jennifer Mitelstadt, *From Welfare to Workfare: The Unintended Consequences of Liberal Reform, 1945–1965* (Chapel Hill: University of North Carolina Press, 2005), 157.

8. Memo from Alvin Schorr to Wilbur J. Cohen, A Small Glossary, Folder Poor People Campaign, May 28, 1968, WJCP. Italicized expressions are underlined in the original text.

9. Schorr, *Passion and Policy*, 79.

10. Memorandum from Alvin Schorr to Secretary Cohen, Subject: Poor People's Campaign, June 15, 1968, Folder 3 Administrative Files 1961–1968: Poor People's March, 1968, Box 110, WJCP; Statement of Rev. Ralph David Abernathy on Goals of Poor People's Campaign, Draft Responses to Poor People's Demands, June 7, 1968, Folder Poor People Campaign: DHEW Responses (2), Box 15, ASP; Memo from Alvin Schorr to Secretary, June 15, 1968, Box 110, WJCP.

11. Michael Katz, *The Undeserving Poor: From the War on Poverty to the War on Welfare* (New York: Pantheon Books, 1989); Marisa Chappell, *The War on Welfare: Family, Poverty, and Politics in Modern America* (Philadelphia: University of Pennsylvania Press, 2010); quotation at 295; Edward R. Schmitt, *President of the Other America: Robert Kennedy and the Politics of Poverty* (Amherst: University of Massachusetts Press, 2010), 220–230.

12. "Transcript of Nixon's Address to Nation Outlining Proposals for Welfare Reform," *New York Times*, August 9, 1969, 10; Kornbluh, *The Battle for Welfare Rights*, 145–146; Kenneth Bowler, *The Nixon Guaranteed Income Proposal: Substance and Proposal in Policy Change* (Cambridge. MA: Ballinger, 1974), 39.

13. Daniel Patrick Moynihan, *Miles to Go: A Personal History of Social Policy* (Cambridge, MA: Harvard University Press, 1996); Robert Katzmann, ed., *Daniel Patrick Moynihan: The Intellectual in Public Life* (Washington, DC: Woodrow Wilson Center Press, 1998); Dean Kotlowski, *Nixon's Civil Rights: Politics, Principle, and Policy* (Cambridge, MA: Harvard University Press, 2001), 12; Alice O'Connor, *Poverty Knowledge: Social Science, Social Policy, and the Poor in Twentieth-Century U.S. History* (Princeton, NJ: Princeton University Press, 2001).

14. Nick Kotz and Mary Lynn Kotz, *A Passion for Equality: George Wiley and the Movement* (New York: W. W. Norton, 1977); Larry Jackson and William Johnson, *Protest by the Poor* (Lexington, MA: Lexington Books, 1974).

15. Marisa Chappell, *The War on Welfare: Family, Poverty, and Politics in Modern America* (Philadelphia: University of Pennsylvania Press, 2010); "Protests Disrupt Welfare Centers," *New York Times*, August 30, 1968, 31; quotation in Kornbluh, *The Battle for Welfare Rights*, 139; Chappell, *The War on Welfare*, 71; Vincent Burke and Vee Burke, *Nixon's Good Deed: Welfare* (New York: Columbia University Press, 1974), 53; Richard Nathan, *Report of a President-Elect's Transitional Task Force on Public Welfare*, December 28 (Washington, DC, U.S. Government Printing Office, 1968); Brian Steensland, *The Failed Welfare Revolution: America's Struggle over Guaranteed Income* (Princeton, NJ: Princeton University Press, 2008), 110–112.

16. Burke and Burke, *Nixon's Good Deed*, 55.

17. Address to the Nation on Domestic Programs, August 8, 1969, Public Papers of Richard Nixon, 1969, 637–638. See also Chappell, *The War on Welfare*, 75–78.

18. Cited in Burke and Burke, *Nixon's Good Deed*, 123; Alvin Schorr, editorial, *Social Work 35*, no. 1 (1969): 1.

19. Regarding the creation of the IRP, see File R. A. Levine, March 9, 1965, Memorandum of conversation at the University of Wisconsin, Folder Genesis, Institute of Research on Poverty Archives.

20. Walter Williams, *The Struggle for a Negative Income Tax* (Washington, DC: Institute for Governmental Research, 1972). For a theoretical view on incentives, see Larry

Orr, Robinson Hollister, and Myron Lefcowitz, *Income Maintenance: Interdisciplinary Approaches to Research* (Chicago: IRP Monograph Series, 1971); Harold Watts, "Graduated Work Incentives: An Experiment in Negative Taxation," *American Economic Review* 59 (1969): 463–472; Letter from David Kershaw to John Wilson, July 1, 1970, Folder New Jersey NIT Experiment, Box 9, UWA.

21. Approximately five thousand dollars for a four-member family.

22. Julian Zelizer, *Taxing America: Wilbur D. Mills, Congress, and the State, 1945–1975* (Cambridge, UK: Cambridge University Press, 1999); Fred Cock, "When You Just Give Money to the Poor," *New York Times*, May 3, 1970, 10; OEO, Preliminary Results of the New Jersey Graduated Work Incentive Experiment, February 18, 1970, OEO microfilm, roll no. 6, LBJ Library; Harold Watts, Adjusted and Extended Preliminary Results from the Urban Graduated Work Incentive Experiment, Discussion Papers, 06/10/1970 (Madison, WI: Institute for Research on Poverty, 1970).

23. U.S. Congress, Committee on Ways and Means, *The Family Assistance Act of 1970*, 91st Congress, 2nd session, 1970 (Washington, DC, U.S. Government Printing Office, 1970), 404–405; Steensland, *The Failed Welfare Revolution*, 160–174.

24. Daniel Patrick Moynihan, *The Politics of Guaranteed Income: The Nixon Administration and the Family Assistance Plan* (New York: Random House, 1973), 469; quote in Timothy J. Sampson, *Welfare: A Handbook for Friend and Foe* (New York: United Church Press, 1972), 152; U.S. Congress, Rules Committee, *The Family Assistance Act of 1970: Hearings on HR 16311*, 91st Congress, 2nd session (Washington, DC, U.S. Government Printing Office, 1970), 1048; Jill Quadagno, *The Color of Welfare: How Racism Undermined the War on Poverty* (New York: Oxford University Press, 1994).

25. Kornbluh, *The Battle for Welfare Rights*, 153.

26. Chappell, *The War on Welfare*, 89–92; Moynihan, *The Politics of Guaranteed Income*, 462–463.

27. Quadagno, *The Color of Welfare*.

28. U.S. Congress, *Social Security Amendments of 1971*, Hearings before the Senate Finance Committee, 91st Congress, 1st session (Washington, DC: U.S. Government Printing Office, 1971), 48; U.S. Congress, *Social Security Amendments of 1971*, 5; U.S. Congress, *Social Security Amendments of 1971*, 187.

29. Quoted in Chappell, *The War on Welfare*, 105.

30. Bruce Miroff, *The Liberals' Moment: The McGovern Insurgency and the Identity Crisis of the Democratic Party* (Lawrence: University Press of Kansas, 2007); Robert P. Watson, ed., *George McGovern: A Political Life, a Political Legacy* (Pierre: South Dakota State Historical Society Press, 2004).

31. Quoted in Moynihan, *The Politics of Guaranteed Income*, 26.

32. McGovern's quotation in Bowler, *The Nixon Guaranteed Income Proposal*, 16; Schorr, *Passion and Policy*, 131.

33. Memo from Alvin Schorr to George McGovern, August 8, 1972, Folder 2 McGovern Presidential Campaign 1969–1972, Box 222, WJCP; author interview with Robert Levine. Regarding the violence of the two camps' strategies, the author preferred to speak off record; Schorr, *Passion and Policy*.

34. Memo from Alvin Schorr to Senator George McGovern, undated, Folder McGovern Income Redistribution, Box 14, ASP; Alvin Schorr and Nancy Amidei, Two Income Maintenance Strategies, undated, Folder McGovern Income Redistribution, Box 14, ASP.

35. Memo from Alvin Schorr to George McGovern; Memo from Alvin Schorr to Senator George McGovern, 5, Folder 2 McGovern Presidential Campaign 1969–1972, Box 222, WJCP.

36. Schorr, *Passion and Policy*, 132; James Tobin, Joseph Pechman and Peter Mieszkowski: "Is a Negative Income Tax Practical?" *Yale Law Journal*, vol. 77 (1967): 16–26.

37. Outline for Jesse Jackson and Dave Wallace by Alvin Schorr, undated, Folder McGovern Income Redistribution, Box 14, ASP; quoted in Jack Valenti, *A Very Human President* (New York: W. W. Norton, 1975), 386.

38. Letter from Cohen to Douglas Brown, July 31, 1972, Folder Correspondence, WJCP; Steensland, *The Failed Welfare Revolution*, 175–176.

39. Schorr, *Passion and Policy*, 132–133; Letter from Wilbur Cohen to Douglas Brown, August 31, 1972, Folder Correspondence, WJCP; cited in Burke and Burke, *Nixon's Good Deed*, 151; Bruce J. Schulman, *The Seventies: The Great Shift in American Culture, Society, and Politics* (New York, Da Capo Press, 2001); Jefferson Cowie, *Stayin' Alive: The 1970s and the Last Days of the Working Class* (New York: The New Press, 2010), 94–102.

40. Alvin Schorr, *Welfare Reform Failure and Remedies* (Westport, CT: Praeger, 2000), 111; Edward D. Berkowitz and Larry DeWitt, *The Other Welfare: Supplemental Security Income and U.S. Social Policy* (Ithaca, NY: Cornell University Press, 2013), 14–29.

41. Memo from Carol Khosrovi to OEO Staff, 02/1970, OEO microfilm, roll no. 6, LBJ Library; the Office of Management and Budget (OMB) replaced the Office of the Budget in 1970.

42. David Kershaw, "A Negative Income Tax Experiment," *Scientific American* 46, no. 227 (1972): 19–24; Richard Nathan, *The Plot That Failed: Nixon and the Administrative Presidency* (New York: Wiley & Sons, 1978), 190–192.

Conclusion. The End of Poverty?

1. Gunnar Myrdal, *Challenge to Affluence* (London: Victor Gollancz, 1963); Örjan Appelqvist and Stellan Anderson, eds., *The Essential Gunnar Myrdal* (New York: Free Press, 2005), ix–xvii; Walter Jackson, *Gunnar Myrdal and the America's Conscience: Social Engineering and Racial Liberalism, 1938–1987* (Chapel Hill: University of North Carolina Press, 1990).

2. John Rawls, *A Theory of Justice* (Oxford: Oxford University Press, 1971); Philippe Van Parijs and Jean Ladriere, eds., *Fondements d'une théorie de la justice: Essais critiques sur la philosophie politique de John Rawls* (Louvain, Belgium: Editions de l'Institut européen de philosophie, 1984); Gareth Stedman Jones, *An End to Poverty? A Historical Debate* (New York: Columbia University Press, 2008).

3. James Kloppenberg, *Uncertain Victory: Social Democracy and Progressivism in European and American Thought, 1870–1920* (New York: Oxford University Press, 1986); Daniel Bell, *The End of Ideology* (Glencoe, IL: Free Press, 1960). Regarding Bell, see Howard Brick, *Daniel Bell and the Decline of Intellectual Radicalism* (Madison: University of Wisconsin Press, 1986).

4. Quoted in Robert J. Lampman, "Steps to Remove Poverty from America," prepared for delivery at the Wisconsin Symposium, January 13, 1969, Institute of Research on Poverty Archives, Madison, 5.

5. Hugh Heclo, "The Sixties' False Dawn: Awakenings, Movements, and Postmodern Policy-Making," in Brian Balogh, ed., *Integrating the Sixties: The Origins, Structures, and Legitimacy of Public Policy in a Turbulent Decade* (University Park: Pennsylvania State University Press, 1996): 34–63; Doug Rossinow, *The Politics of Authenticity: Liberalism, Christianity, and the New Left in America* (New York: Columbia University Press, 1998); Daniel Geary, *Beyond Civil Rights: The Moynihan Report and Its Legacy* (Philadelphia: University of Pennsylvania Press, 2015).

6. Christian Topalov, *Naissance du chômeur, 1880–1920* (Paris: Albin Michel, 1994).

7. Henry Aaron, *Politics and the Professors: The Great Society in Perspective* (Washington, DC: Brookings Institution, 1978); Robert Haveman, *Poverty Policy and Poverty*

Research: The Great Society and the Social Sciences (Madison: University of Wisconsin Press 1987); Alice O'Connor, *Poverty Knowledge: Social Science, Social Policy, and the Poor in Twentieth-Century U.S. History* (Princeton, NJ: Princeton University Press 2001); Christian Topalov, ed., *Laboratoires du nouveau siècle: La nébuleuse réformatrice et ses réseaux en France 1880–1914* (Paris: Editions de l'EHESS, 1999), 464.

8. Felicia Kornbluh, *The Battle for Welfare Rights: Politics and Poverty in Modern America* (Philadelphia: University of Pennsylvania Press, 2007); Brian Balogh, *Chain Reaction: Expert Debate and Public Participation in American Commercial Nuclear Power, 1945–1975* (Cambridge: Cambridge University Press, 1991).

9. Edward Berkowitz and Larry DeWitt, *The Other Welfare: Supplemental Security Income and U.S. Social Policy* (Ithaca, NY: Cornell University Press, 2013); Michael Katz, ed., *The "Underclass" Debate: Views from History* (Princeton, NJ: Princeton University Press, 1993), 3–23; Lisa Levenstein, *African American Women and the Politics of Poverty in Postwar Philadelphia* (Chapel Hill: University of North Carolina, 2009), 23–24.

10. David Ellwood, "Welfare Reform as I Knew It," *American Prospect*, May–June 1996, 22; Doris Kearns, *Lyndon Johnson and the American Dream* (New York: Harper & Row, 1976): 291; Jennifer Mittelstadt, *From Welfare to Workfare: The Unintended Consequences of Welfare Reform, 1945–1965* (Chapel Hill: University of North Carolina Press, 2005); Elizabeth Hinton, *From the War on Poverty to the War on Crime: The Making of Mass Incarceration in America* (Cambridge, MA: Harvard University Press, 2016); Michael B. Katz, *The Undeserving Poor: America's Enduring Confrontation with Poverty* (New York: Oxford University Press, 2013).

11. Thomas Piketty, *Capital in the Twenty-First Century* (Cambridge, MA: Harvard University Press, 2014); Matthew Desmond, *Evicted: Poverty and Profit in an American City* (New York: Penguin House, 2016); Nancy Isenberg, *White Trash: The 400-Year Untold History of Class in America* (New York: Viking, 2016).

BIBLIOGRAPHY

Archival Collections

Adam Yarmolinsky Papers, John Fitzgerald Kennedy Presidential Library, Dorchester, MA.

Alice Rivlin Papers, Library of Congress, Washington, DC.

Alvin Schorr Papers, Elmer Andersen Library, Minnesota State Historical Society, St. Paul, MN.

Bernard Boutin Papers, Lyndon Baines Johnson Presidential Library, Austin, TX.

Bertrand Harding Papers, Lyndon Baines Johnson Presidential Library, Austin, TX.

Deirdre Henderson Papers, John Fitzgerald Library, Dorchester, MA.

Elizabeth Wickenden Papers, State Historical Society of Wisconsin, Madison, WI.

Ida Craven Merriam Papers, Special Collections and University Archives, George Washington University, Washington, DC.

Institute for Research in Poverty, Administrative Files 1966–1969, Madison, WI.

National Science Foundation, National Archives, College Park, MD.

Paul Ylvisaker Papers, University Archives, Harvard University, Cambridge, MA.

Record Group 47, Social Security Administration, National Archives, College Park, MD.

Record Group 257, Bureau of Labor and Statistics, National Archives, College Park, MD.

Record Group 281, Department Health, Education, and Welfare, National Archives, College Park, MD.

Record Group 381, Office of Economic Opportunity, National Archives, College Park, MD.

Richard Titmuss Papers, London School of Economics, London, Great Britain.
Theodore Sorensen Papers, John Fitzgerald Kennedy Library, Dorchester, MA.
University of Wisconsin Archives, Madison, WI.
Walter Heller Papers, John Fitzgerald Library, Dorchester, MA.
Wilbur Cohen Papers, State Historical Society of Wisconsin, Madison, WI.

Bibliography

Aaron, Henry. *Politics and the Professors: The Great Society in Perspective.* Washington, DC: Brookings Institution, 1978.

Abrahamson, David. *Magazine-Made America: The Cultural Transformation of the Postwar Periodical.* Cresskill, NY: Hampton Press, 1996.

Abramovitz, Mimi. *Regulating the Lives of Women: Social Welfare Policy from Colonial Times to the Present.* Boston: South End Press, 1988.

Alchon, Guy. "Mary Van Kleeck and Social-Economic Planning." *Journal of Policy History* 3, no. 1 (1991): 17–23.

Amenta, Edwin. *Bold Relief: Institutional Politics and the Origins of Modern American Social Policy.* Princeton, NJ: Princeton University Press, 1998.

Anderson, Margo. *The American Census: A Social History.* New Haven, CT: Yale University Press, 1988.

Appelqvist, Örjan, and Stellan Anderson, eds. *The Essential Gunnar Myrdal.* New York: Free Press, 2005.

Balogh, Brian. *The Associational State: American Governance in the Twentieth Century.* Philadelphia: University of Pennsylvania Press, 2015.

Balogh, Brian. *Chain Reaction. Expert Debate and Public Participation in American Commercial Nuclear Power, 1945–1975.* Cambridge: Cambridge University Press, 1991.

Balogh, Brian, ed. *Integrating the Sixties: The Origins, Structures, and Legitimacy of Public Policy in a Turbulent Decade.* University Park: Pennsylvania State University Press, 1996.

Balogh, Brian. "Reorganizing the Organizational Synthesis: Federal-Professional Relations in Modern America." *Studies in American Political Development,* 5, no. 1 (1991): 119–172.

Bauman, John. *Public Housing, Race, and Renewal: Urban Planning in Philadelphia, 1920–1974.* Philadelphia: Temple University Press, 1987.

Berkowitz, Edward. *America's Welfare State: From Roosevelt to Reagan.* Baltimore: Johns Hopkins University Press, 1991.

Berkowitz, Edward. *Mr. Social Security: The Life of Wilbur J. Cohen.* Lawrence, KA: University Press of Kansas, 1995.

Berkowitz, Edward. *Robert Ball and the Politics of Social Security.* Madison: University of Wisconsin Press, 2005.

Berkowitz, Edward, and Larry DeWitt. *The Other Welfare: Supplemental Security Income and U.S. Social Policy.* Ithaca, NY: Cornell University Press, 2013.

Bernstein, Irving. *Promises Kept: JFK's New Frontier.* New York: Oxford University Press, 1991.

Bernstein, Michael. *A Perilous Progress: Economists and Public Purpose in Twentieth-Century America*. Princeton, NJ: Princeton University Press, 2004.

Bowler, Kenneth. *The Nixon Guaranteed Income Proposal: Substance and Proposal in Policy Change*. Cambridge, MA: Ballinger, 1974.

Bremner, Robert. *American Philanthropy*. Chicago: Chicago University Press, 1988.

Brick, Howard. *Daniel Bell and the Decline of Intellectual Radicalism*. Madison: University of Wisconsin Press, 1986.

Brick, Howard. *Transcending Capitalism: Visions of a New Society in Modern America Thought*. Ithaca, NY: Cornell University Press, 2006.

Brinkley, Alan. *The End of Reform: New Deal Liberalism in Recession and War*. New York: Vintage Books, 1995.

Brint, Steven. *In an Age of Experts: The Changing Role of Professionals in Politics and Public Life*. Princeton, NJ: Princeton University Press, 1994.

Brown, Michael. *Race, Money, and the American Welfare State*. Ithaca, NY: Cornell University Press, 1999.

Brownlee, Elliot. *Federal Taxation in America: A Short History*. Cambridge, MA: Woodrow Wilson Center Press, 1996.

Brownlee, Elliot, ed. *Funding the Modern American State, 1941–1995: The Rise and Fall of the Era of Easy Finance*. Cambridge: Cambridge University Press, 1996.

Burgin, Angus. *The Great Persuasion: Reinventing Free Markets since the Depression*. Cambridge, MA: Harvard University Press, 2012.

Carpenter, Daniel. *The Forging of Bureaucratic Autonomy: Reputations, Networks, and Policy Innovation in Executive Agencies, 1862–1928*. Princeton, NJ: Princeton University Press, 2001.

Carpenter, Daniel P. "The Political Foundations of Bureaucratic Autonomy." *Studies in American Political Development* 15, no. 1 (2001): 113–122.

Cates, Jerry. *Insuring Inequality: Administrative Leadership in Social Security, 1935–1954*. Ann Arbor: Michigan University Press, 1983.

Cazenave, Noel A. *Impossible Democracy: The Unlikely Success of the War on Poverty Community Action Programs*. Albany: State University of New York Press, 2007.

Cazenave, Noel A. *Welfare Racism: Playing the Race Card against America's Poor*. New York: Routledge, 2001.

Chappell, Marisa. *The War on Welfare: Family, Poverty, and Politics in Modern America*. Philadelphia: University of Pennsylvania Press, 2010.

Chesler, Mark, Joseph Sander, and Debra Kalmuss. *Social Science in Court: Mobilizing Experts in the School Desegregation Cases*. Madison: University of Wisconsin Press, 1988.

Cohen, Lizabeth. *A Consumer's Republic: The Politics of Mass Consumption in Postwar America*. New York: W. W. Norton, 2003.

Coll, Blanche. *Safety Net: Welfare and Social Security, 1929–1979*. New Brunswick, NJ: Rutgers University Press, 1995.

Cooper, Dona, and Charles Cooper. *The Dual Agenda: The African-American Struggle for Civil and Economic Equality*. New York: Columbia University Press, 2000.

Cowie, Jefferson. *Stayin' Alive. The 1970s and the Last Days of the Working Class*. New York: The New Press, 2010.

Critchlow, Donald T. *The Brookings Institution, 1916–1952: Expertise and Public Interest in a Democratic Society*. De Kalb: Northern Illinois University Press, 1985.

Dallek, Robert. *Flawed Giant: Lyndon Johnson and His Times*. New York: Oxford University Press, 1998.

Dauber, Michele Landis. *The Sympathetic State: Disaster Relief and the Origins of the American Welfare State*. Chicago: University of Chicago Press, 2012.

Davies, Gareth. *From Opportunity to Entitlement: The Transformation and Decline of Great Society Liberalism*. Lawrence: Kansas University Press, 1996.

Davis, Martha. *Brutal Need: Lawyers and the Welfare Rights Movement, 1960–1973*. New Haven, CT: Yale University Press, 1993.

Derthick, Martha. *The Influence of Federal Grants: Public Assistance in Massachusetts*. Cambridge, MA: Harvard University Press, 1975.

Derthick, Martha. *Policymaking for Social Security*. Washington, DC: Brookings Institution, 1979.

Desmond, Matthew. *Evicted: Poverty and Profit in an American City*. New York: Penguin House, 2016.

Donohue, Kathleen G. *Freedom from Want: American Liberalism and the Idea of the Consumer*. Baltimore: Johns Hopkins University Press, 2003.

Duncan, Shelton, and William Shelton. *Revolution in the United States: 1926–1976*. Washington, DC: U.S. Department of Commerce, 1978.

Dunn, Stephen P. *The Economics of John Kenneth Galbraith: Introduction, Persuasion, and Rehabilitation*. Cambridge: Cambridge University Press, 2010.

Ehrenreich, John. *The Altruistic Imagination: A History of Social Work and Social Policy in the United States*. Ithaca, NY: Cornell University Press, 1985.

Farber, David. *Chicago 68*. Chicago: University of Chicago Press, 1988.

Feldstein, Ruth. *Motherhood in Black and White: Race and Sex in American Liberalism, 1930–1965*. Ithaca, NY: Cornell University Press, 2009.

Fine, Sidney. *Violence in the Model City: The Cavanagh Administration, Race Relations, and the Detroit Riot of 1967*. Ann Arbor: Michigan State University Press, 1989.

Fitzpatrick, Ellen. *Endless Crusade: Women Social Scientists and Progressive Reform*. New York: Oxford University Press, 1990.

Fox, Cybelle. *Three Worlds of Relief: Race, Immigration, and the American Welfare State from the Progressive Era to the New Deal*. Princeton, NJ: Princeton University Press, 2012.

Fraser, Nancy, and Linda Gordon. "Dependency Demystified: Inscriptions of Power in a Keyword of the Welfare State." *Social Policies* 1 (1994): 309–336.

Furner, Mary, and Barry Supple, eds. *The State and Economic Knowledge: The American and British Experience*. Cambridge: Cambridge University Press, 1990.

Geary, Daniel. *Beyond Civil Rights: The Moynihan Report and Its Legacy*. Philadelphia: University of Pennsylvania Press, 2015.

Gerstle, Gary. "The Protean Character of American Liberalism." *Journal of American History* 99, no. 4 (1994): 1043–1073.

Gilbert, James. *A Cycle of Outrage: America's Reaction to the Juvenile Delinquent in the 1950s*. New York: Oxford University Press, 1986.

Gillette, Michael L. *Launching the War on Poverty: An Oral History*. New York: Oxford University Press, 2010.

Glickman, Lawrence. *A Living Wage: American Workers and the Making of Consumer Society*. Ithaca, NY: Cornell University Press, 1997.

Goldstein, Carolyn. *Creating Consumers: Home Economists in Twentieth-Century America*. Chapel Hill: University of North Carolina Press, 2012.

Goodwin, Joanne L. *Gender and the Politics of Welfare Reform: Mothers' Pensions in Chicago, 1911–1929*. Chicago: Chicago University Press, 1997.

Gordon, Linda. *Pitied but Not Entitled: Single Mothers and the History of Welfare, 1890–1935*. Cambridge, MA: Harvard University Press, 1994.

Gustafson, Kaaryn. *Cheating Welfare: Public Assistance and the Criminalization of Poverty*. New York: New York University Press, 2011.

Haskell, Thomas, ed. *The Authority of Experts: Studies in History and Theory*. Bloomington: Indiana University Press, 1984.

Haveman, Robert. *Poverty Policy and Poverty Research: The Great Society and the Social Sciences*. Madison: University of Wisconsin Press, 1987.

Hawley, Ellis, and Donald T. Critchlow, eds. *Federal Social Policy: The Historical Dimension*. University Park: Pennsylvania State University Press, 1998.

Hengeller, Paul R. *In His Steps: Lyndon Johnson and the Kennedy Mystique*. Chicago: Ivan R. Dee, 1991.

Herman, Ellen. *The Romance of American Psychology: Political Culture in the Age of Experts*. Berkeley: University of California Press, 1995.

Hinton, Elizabeth. *From the War on Poverty to the War on Crime*. Cambridge, MA: Harvard University Press, 2016.

Hirshfield, Daniel. *The Lost Reform: The Campaign for Compulsory Health Insurance in the United States from 1932 to 1943*. Cambridge, MA: Harvard University Press, 1970.

Hoffman, Elizabeth Cobbs. *All You Need Is Love: The Peace Corps and the Spirit of the 1960s*. Cambridge, MA: Harvard University Press, 2000.

Horowitz, Daniel, ed. *Anxieties of Affluence: Critiques of American Consumer Culture, 1939–1979*. Amherst: University of Massachusetts Press, 2004.

Howard, Christopher. "The Hidden Side of the American Welfare State." *Political Science Quarterly* 108, no. 3 (1993): 403–436.

Howard, Christopher. *The Hidden Welfare State: Tax Expenditures and Social Policy in the United States*. Princeton, NJ: Princeton University Press, 1999.

Howard, Ella. *Homeless: Poverty and Place in Urban America*. Philadelphia: University of Pennsylvania Press, 2013.

Hughes, Thomas. *Rescuing Prometheus*. New York: Pantheon Books, 1998.

Huret, Romain. "Les experts sociaux face à la société civile aux États-Unis: La Campagne des pauvres et le ministère de la Santé, de l'Éducation et du Welfare (avril–juin 1968)." *Revue d'histoire moderne et contemporaine* 51, no. 3 (2004): 118–140.

Huret, Romain D. *American Tax Resisters*. Cambridge, MA: Harvard University Press, 2014.

Isenberg, Nancy. *White Trash: The 400-Year Untold History of Class in America*. New York: Viking, 2016.

Isserman, Maurice. *The Other American: The Life of Michael Harrington*. New York: Public Affairs, 2000.

Jackson, Walter. *Gunnar Myrdal and the America's Conscience: Social Engineering and Racial Liberalism, 1938–1987*. Chapel Hill: University of North Carolina Press, 1990.

Jacobs, Meg. *Pocketbook Politics: Economic Citizenship in Twentieth-Century America*. Princeton, NJ: Princeton University Press, 2005.

Jensen, Laura. *Patriots, Settlers, and the Origins of American Social Policy*. Cambridge, MA: Harvard University Press, 2003.

Jones, Gareth Stedman. *An End to Poverty? A Historical Debate*. New York: Columbia University Press, 2008.

Jones, William P. *The March on Washington: Jobs, Freedom, and the Forgotten History of Civil Rights*. New York: W. W. Norton, 2013.

Karl, Barry. *Charles Merriam and the Study of Politics*. Chicago: University of Chicago Press, 1974.

Katz, Michael. *In the Shadow of the Poorhouse: A Social History of Welfare in America*. New York: Basic Books, 1996.

Katz, Michael, ed. *The "Underclass" Debate: Views from History*. Princeton, NJ: Princeton University Press, 1993.

Katz, Michael. *The Undeserving Poor: From the War on Poverty to the War on Welfare*. New York: Pantheon Books, 1989.

Katz, Michael, and Lorrin Thomas. "The Invention of 'Welfare' in America." *Journal of Policy History* 10, no. 4 (1998): 399–418.

Katz, Michael B. *The Undeserving Poor: America's Confrontation with Poverty*. New York: Oxford University Press, 2013.

Katzmann, Robert, ed. *Daniel Patrick Moynihan: The Intellectual in Public Life*. Washington, DC: Woodrow Wilson Center Press, 1998.

Katznelson, Ira. *Fear Itself: The New Deal and the Origins of Our Time*. New York: Liveright, 2014.

Keefe, Linda M. "Dwight Macdonald and Poverty Discourse, 1960–1965: The Art and Power of a Seminal Book Review." *Poverty and Public Policy* 2, no. 2 (2010): 147–188.

Kelso, William A. *Poverty and the Underclass: Changing Perceptions of the Poor in America*. New York: New York University Press, 1994.

Kesseler-Harris, Alice. *In Pursuit of Equity: Women, Men, and the Quest for Economic Citizenship in Twentieth-Century America*. Princeton, NJ: Princeton University Press, 2001.

Kirkendall, Richard. *Social Scientists and Farm Politics in the Age of Roosevelt*. Columbia: University of Missouri Press, 1966.

Kleinman, Daniel. *Politics on the Endless Frontier: Postwar Research Policy in the United States*. Durham, NC: Duke University Press, 1995.

Kloppenberg, James. *Uncertain Victory: Social Democracy and Progressivism in European and American Thought, 1870–1920*. New York: Oxford University Press, 1986.

Knapp, Daniel. *Scouting the War on Poverty: Social Reform in the Kennedy Administration*. Lexington, MA: Heath Lexington Books, 1971.

Kornbluh, Felicia. *The Battle for Welfare Rights: Politics and Poverty in Modern America*. Philadelphia: University of Pennsylvania Press, 2007.

Kotlowski, Dean. *Nixon's Civil Rights: Politics, Principle, and Policy*. Cambridge, MA: Harvard University Press, 2001.

Lacey, Michael, and Mary Furner, eds. *The State and Social Investigation in Britain and the United States*. Cambridge, MA: Woodrow Wilson Center Press, 1993.

Larsen, Otto. *Milestones and Millstones: Social Sciences at the National Science Foundation, 1945–1991*. New Brunswick, NJ: Transaction Publishers, 1992.

Latham, Michael. *Modernization as Ideology: American Social Science and "Nation Building" in the Kennedy Era*. Chapel Hill: University of North Carolina, 2001.

Lears, T. Jackson. *Fables of Abundance: A Cultural History of American Advertising*. New York: Basic Books, 1994.

Lee, Sophia Z. *The Workplace Constitution from the New Deal to the New Right*. New York: Cambridge University Press, 2014.

Leff, Mark. *The Limits of Symbolic Reform: The New Deal and Taxation, 1933–1939*. Cambridge: Cambridge University Press, 1984.

Leiby, James R. *Carroll Wright and Labor Reform: The Origin of Labor Statistics*. Cambridge, MA: Harvard University Press, 1960.

Leiby, James R. *A History of Social Welfare and Social Work in the United States*. New York: Columbia University Press, 1978.

Leiby, James R. "State Welfare Administration in California, 1930–1945." *Southern California Quarterly* 55, no. 3 (1973): 303–3018.

Levenstein, Lisa. "From Innocent Children to Unwanted Migrants and Unwed Moms: Two Chapters in the Public Discourse on Welfare in the United States, 1960–1961." *Journal of Women's History* 11, no. 4 (2000): 11–24.

Levenstein, Lisa. *A Movement without Marches: African American Women and the Politics of Poverty in Postwar Philadelphia*. Chapel Hill: University of North Carolina Press, 2009.

Levitan, Sar. *The Great Society's Poor Law*. Baltimore: Johns Hopkins University Press, 1969.

Levitan, Sar A. *Federal Aid to Depressed Areas*. Baltimore: Johns Hopkins University Press, 1964.

Lieberman, Robert. *Shifting the Color Line: Race and the American Welfare State*. Cambridge, MA: Harvard University Press, 1998.

Lindhorst, Taryn, and Leslie Leighninger. "'Ending Welfare as We Know It' in 1960: Louisiana's Suitable Home Law." *Social Service Review* 77, no. 4 (2003): 564–584.

Maddox, Robert. "The Politics of World War Two Science: Senator Harley M. Kilgore and the Legislative Origins of the National Science Foundation." *West Virginia History* 41 (1979): 20–39.

Matusow, Alan J. *The Unraveling of America: A History of Liberalism in the 1960s*. New York: Harper & Row, 1984.

McKinley, Charles, and Robert Frase. *Launching Social Security: A Capture and Record Account, 1935–1937*. Madison: University of Wisconsin Press, 1970.

McKnight, Gerald. *The Last Crusade: Martin Luther King, Jr., the FBI, and the Poor People's Campaign*. Boulder, CO: Westview, 1998.

Meyerowitz, Joanne, ed. *Not June Cleaver: Women and Gender in Postwar America, 1945–1960*. Philadelphia: Temple University Press, 2004.

Mink, Gwendolyn. *The Wages of Motherhood: Inequality in the Welfare State, 1917–1942*. Ithaca, NY: Cornell University Press, 1995.

Miroff, Bruce. *The Liberals' Moment: The McGovern Insurgency and the Identity Crisis of the Democratic Party*. Lawrence: University Press of Kansas, 2007.

Mittelstadt, Jennifer. *From Welfare to Workfare: The Unintended Consequences of Liberal Reform, 1945–1965*. Chapel Hill: University of North Carolina Press, 2005.

Muncy, Robyn. *Creating a Female Dominion in American Reform (1890–1935)*. New York: Columbia University Press, 1991.

Murch, Donna. *Living for the City: Migration, Education, and the Rise of the Black Panther Party in Oakland, California*. Chapel Hill: University of North Carolina Press, 2010.

Murray, Charles. *Losing Ground: American Social Policy*. New York: Basic Books, 1984.

Nathan, Richard. *The Plot That Failed: Nixon and the Administrative Presidency*. New York: Wiley & Sons, 1978.

Noveck, Beth Simone. *Smart Citizens, Smarter State: The Technologies of Expertise and the Future of Governing*. Cambridge, MA: Harvard University Press, 2015.

O'Connor, Alice. *Poverty Knowledge: Social Science, Social Policy, and the Poor in Twentieth-Century U.S. History*. Princeton, NJ: Princeton University Press, 2001.

O'Connor, John. "U.S. Social Welfare Policy: The Reagan Record and Legacy." *Journal of Social Policy* 27, no. 1 (1998): 37–61.

Orleck, Annelise, and Lisa Gayle Hazirjian, eds. *The War on Poverty: A New Grassroots History, 1964–1980*. Athens: University of Georgia Press, 2011.

Orloff, Ann. "Gender in the Welfare State." *Annual Review of Sociology* 22 (1996): 51–78.

Ownby, Ted. *American Dreams in Mississippi: Consumers, Poverty, and Culture, 1830–1998*. Chapel Hill: University of North Carolina Press, 1999.

Patterson, James. *America's Struggle against Poverty, 1900–1994*. Cambridge, MA: Harvard University Press, 1994.

Patterson, James. *The New Deal and the States: Federalism in Transition*. Princeton, NJ: Princeton University Press, 1969.

Perlstein, Rick. *Before the Storm: Barry Goldwater and the Unmaking of the American Consensus*. New York: Hill & Wang, 2001.

Philipps-Fein, Kim. *Invisible Hands: The Making of the Conservative Movement from the New Deal to Reagan*. New York: W. W. Norton, 2009.

Pierson, Paul. "Increasing Returns, Path Dependence, and the Study of Politics." *American Political Science Review* 94 (June 2000): 251–267.

Piketty, Thomas. *Capital in the Twenty-First Century*. Cambridge, MA: Harvard University Press, 2014.

Porter, Theodore. *Trust in Numbers: The Pursuit of Objectivity in Science and Public Life*. Princeton, NJ: Princeton University Press, 1995.

Quadagno, Jill. *The Color of Welfare: How Racism Undermined the War on Poverty*. New York: Oxford University Press, 1994.

Reese, Ellen. *Backlash against Welfare Mothers: Past and Present*. Berkeley: University of California Press, 2005.

Rodgers, Daniel. *Atlantic Crossings: Social Policy in a Progressive Age.* Cambridge, MA: Harvard University Press, 1998.

Rossiter, Margaret. *Women Scientists in America: Before Affirmative Action, 1940–1972.* Baltimore: Johns Hopkins University Press, 1991.

Schmitt, Edward R. *President of the Other America: Robert Kennedy and the Politics of Poverty.* Amherst: University of Massachusetts Press, 2010.

Schor, Paul. *Classer et compter: Histoire des recensements américains.* Paris: Editions de l'EHESS, 2009.

Schrecker, Ellen. *Many Are the Crimes: McCarthyism in America.* Boston: Little, Brown, 1998.

Schulman, Bruce J. *The Seventies: The Great Shift in American Culture, Society, and Politics.* New York: Da Capo Press, 2001.

Scott, Daryl. *Contempt and Pity: Social Policy and the Image of the Damaged Black Psyche.* Chapel Hill: University of North Carolina Press, 1997.

Scroop, Daniel, and Andrew Heath, eds. *Transatlantic Social Politics, 1800–Present.* New York: Palgrave Macmillan, 2014.

Self, Robert. *All in the Family: The Realignment of American Democracy since the 1960s.* New York: Hill & Wang, 2012.

Shapley, Deborah. *Promise and Power: The Life and Time of Robert McNamara.* Boston: Little, Brown, 1999.

Skocpol, Theda. *Protecting Soldiers and Mothers: The Political Origins of Social Policy in the United States.* Cambridge, MA: Harvard University Press, 1992.

Skocpol, Theda, ed. *Social Security in the United States: Future Possibilities in Historical Perspective.* Princeton, NJ: Princeton University Press, 1995.

Smith, Jason Scott. *Building New Deal Liberalism: The Political Economy of Public Works, 1933–1956.* New York: Cambridge University Press, 2009.

Smith, Mark. *Social Science in the Crucible: The American Debate over Objectivity and Purpose, 1918–1941.* Durham, NC: Duke University Press, 1991.

Solovey, Mark. *Shaky Foundations: The Politics-Patronage-Social Nexus in Cold War America.* New Brunswick, NJ: Rutgers University Press, 2013.

Sparrow, Bartholomew. *From the Outside In: World War II and the American State.* Princeton, NJ: Princeton University Press, 1996.

Stage, Sarah, and Virginia Vincenti, eds. *Rethinking Home Economics: Women and the History of a Profession.* Philadelphia: Temple University Press, 1997.

Steensland, Brian. *The Failed Welfare Revolution: America's Struggle over Guaranteed Policy.* Princeton, NJ: Princeton University Press, 2007.

Steiner, Gilbert. *Social Insecurity: The Politics of Welfare.* Chicago: Rand McNally, 1969.

Stern, Mark. *Calculating Visions: Kennedy, Johnson, and Civil Rights.* New Brunswick, NJ: Rutgers University Press, 1992.

Sugrue, Thomas J. *The Origins of the Urban Crisis: Race and Inequality in Postwar Detroit.* Princeton, NJ: Princeton University Press, 1996.

Sumner, Gregory D. *Dwight Macdonald and the Politics Circle: The Challenge of Cosmopolitan Democracy.* Ithaca, NY: Cornell University Press, 1996.

Sundquist, James, ed. *On Fighting Poverty: Perspectives from Experience.* New York: Basic Books, 1969.

Sundquist, James. *Politics and Policy: The Eisenhower, Kennedy, and Johnson Years.* Washington, DC: Brookings Institution Press, 1968.

Tani, Karen M. *States of Dependency: Welfare, Rights, and American Governance, 1935–1972.* New York: Cambridge University Press, 2016.

Tani, Karen M. "Welfare and Rights before the Movement: Rights as a Language of the State." *Yale Law Journal* 122 (2012): 314–383.

Teaford, John C. *The Rise of the States: Evolution of American State Government.* Baltimore: Johns Hopkins University Press, 2002.

Topalov, Christian, ed., *Laboratoires du nouveau siècle: La Nébuleuse réformatrice et ses réseaux en France, 1880–1914.* Paris: Editions de l'EHESS, 1999.

Topalov, Christian. *Naissance du chômeur, 1880–1920.* Paris: Albin Michel, 1994.

Trattner, Walter. *From Poor Law to Welfare State: A History of Social Welfare in America.* New York: Free Press, 1984.

Wall, Wendy L. *Inventing the "American Way": The Politics of Consensus from the New Deal to the Civil Rights Movement.* New York: Oxford University Press, 2008.

Watson, Robert P., ed. *George McGovern: A Political Life, a Political Legacy.* Pierre: South Dakota State Historical Society Press, 2004.

Weir, Margaret. *Politics and Jobs: The Boundaries of Employment Policy in the United States.* Princeton, NJ: Princeton University Press, 1992.

Wreszin, Michael. *A Rebel in Defense of Tradition.* New York: Basic Books, 1995.

Wright, Anthony. *R. H. Tawney.* Manchester, NH: Manchester University Press, 1987.

Zelizer, Julian. *The Fierce Urgency of Now: Lyndon Johnson, Congress, and the Battle for the Great Society.* New York: Penguin Press, 2015.

Zelizer, Julian. *Taxing America: Wilbur D. Mills, Congress, and the State, 1945–1975.* Cambridge: Cambridge University Press, 1999.

Zunz, Olivier. *Why the American Century?* Chicago: University of Chicago Press, 1999.

INDEX

CPSIA information can be obtained
at www.ICGtesting.com
Printed in the USA
LVHW04*1704151018
593660LV00004B/84/P